Charles Clarke

Practice and procedure in the Legislative Assembly of the Province of Ontario

Charles Clarke

Practice and procedure in the Legislative Assembly of the Province of Ontario

ISBN/EAN: 9783337717407

Printed in Europe, USA, Canada, Australia, Japan

Cover: Foto ©ninafisch / pixelio.de

More available books at **www.hansebooks.com**

PRACTICE AND PROCEDURE

IN THE

LEGISLATIVE ASSEMBLY

OF THE

PROVINCE OF ONTARIO.

BY
CHARLES CLARKE,
Clerk of the Legislative Assembly of Ontario.

SECOND EDITION, 1898.

Toronto:
WARWICK BRO'S & RUTTER, PRINTERS.
1898.

TABLE OF CONTENTS.

🙦 🙦 🙦

	PAGE.
1. The Legislative Assembly of Ontario	7
2. The Address	13
3. Etiquette of the House	14
4. Order of Procedure	17
5. Petitions	18
6. Motions	21
7. Questions	24
8. Debate	25
9. Amendments	29
10. Divisions	33
11. Committees	35
12. Public Bills	39
13. Private Bills	47
14. Adjournments	54
15. Mr. Speaker	57
16. Powers and Privileges of Legislative Assembly	57
17. Payment of Members	60
18. Ontario Cabinet	64
19. Postage	81
20. Library	84
21. Table of Precedence	87
22. Decisions of Mr. Speaker and Index thereto	91
23. Rules, Orders and Forms of Proceeding, Legislative Assembly	131
24. Index to Rules, etc.	149
25. Lists of Members of Legislature from Confederation	157
26. Meetings of Legislatures	170
27. General Elections, Ontario	171
28. Members of Ontario Cabinets	172
29. Lieutenant-Governors of Ontario	176
30. Premiers and Speakers of Ontario	177
31. British North America Act	183
32. Act relating to Boundaries of Ontario	219
33. Index to Decisions of Mr. Speaker	221
34. General Index to Member's Manual	227

PREFACE.

The experience of more than a quarter of a century of legislation, with a single Chamber, has fairly tested the system inaugurated upon this Continent on a large scale when the Province of Ontario adopted it in 1867. It has developed a Parliamentary Practice which, while fashioned upon that of the British Isles, and adhering as closely to it as circumstances have permitted, has, from the fact that there is no second Chamber in Ontario, made some slight departures from the great constitutional original upon which it was based.

To give an intelligent outline of the Procedure of the Legislative Assembly of Ontario, as it exists to-day, has been the aim of the compiler of this little work. He makes no claim to originality in conception or execution of it, and frankly admits how deeply he has been indebted to the British Parliamentary authorities from whom he has freely quoted. This reference to British Practice has been rendered necessary by Rule 113 of the Ontario Legislature, which expressly declares that "in all unprovided cases, the Rules, Usages and Forms of the United Kingdom of Great Britain and Ireland, as in force at the time, shall be followed."

He has not sought to make a big book, but to produce a short compendium of Parliamentary Law which shall be of ready use to those for whom it is prepared, and facilitate any reference which may be necessary to more voluminous authorities.

A few abbreviations have been used to which the following is the key : "B. H. of C." signifies "British House of Commons"; the numerous references to MAY are to the most recent edition of the well-known "Parliamentary Practice"; the Rules referred to are those of the Legislative Assembly of Ontario; and the Speaker's Decisions are those of Speakers of the Ontario Assembly collected in this work.

TORONTO, 1898.

The Member's Manual.

THE LEGISLATIVE ASSEMBLY OF ONTARIO.

In the Parliament of Canada, on 2nd August, 1866, concurrence was asked in the Fifth of the Confederation Resolutions, when Hon. J. H. Cameron, the representative for the County of Peel, moved, in amendment to the proposition for a Single Chamber in this Province, that "the Legislature of Upper Canada should be composed of two Chambers to be called the Legislative Council and the Legislative Assembly." His motion found a seconder in the Hon. Alexander Morris, soon to be Lieutenant-Governor of Manitoba, and subsequently a prominent member of the Legislative Assembly of Ontario. After a discussion of an interesting if not exciting character, a division was taken, and it was found that but thirteen members favoured a double chamber for Upper Canada, while no less than eighty-six recorded themselves against it. Of the thirteen composing the minority, it is fair to state the fact, nine represented Upper Canadian constituencies. The large majority against the amendment comprised the leading men of the two great parties, who for the time had called a truce and voted as conviction dictated. Conspicuous amongst the supporters of a single chamber were five men destined to take an important part in the deliberations of the first Legislature of Ontario. Hon. John Sandfield Macdonald, Matthew Crooks Cameron, John Carling and Edmund Burke Wood, afterwards members of the first Ontario Cabinet, rose with Archibald McKellar, the coming leader of the first Ontario Opposition, to give their votes against the amendment. It was not a question upon which there was a partizan difference of opinion. A common desire to minimize the necessary cost of a local government evidently influenced the majority of Upper Canadian representatives. That was the declared intention of George Brown, of Matthew C. Cameron, and of John S. Macdonald. Said Mr. Brown, during the Confederation Debate: "Undoubtedly the mode in which the local government shall be constructed will very much affect the cost of the whole scheme; but if we adopt (as I earnestly hope we shall) simple and inexpensive machinery for local purposes, I am quite satisfied that there will be a reduction to the people of Canada in the amount they now contribute." Said Mr. M. C. Cameron: "If we are really to have a Local Legislature, we want it to be as inexpensive in its character as possible,—we want to construct it, as much as possible, with a view to economy, in order that the public burdens may be lessened to the lowest practical point." And said Hon. J. S. Macdonald, in Feb., 1871, then looking back over three years' experience of the new condition of things : "I am sincerely attached to a single chamber, for it has been proved that it can manage satisfactorily the affairs of two millions of people without a second chamber, consisting of members appointed for life, and who, once elected, do not care for anybody."

Not less hopeful of the new order of things was the House itself when it unanimously addressed Lieutenant-Governor Stisted, in reply to the first Speech from the Throne to the Legislative Assembly of Ontario, and said that for years past it had been the aim and effort of Upper Canada to secure a more direct and unlimited control over her own local affairs than was attainable in legislative alliance with another province, and that, while sensible of the many advantages which had accrued to both sections of Canada from the Union of 1841, the people of Western Canada had, nevertheless, desired a wider and more elastic governmental system which should afford larger opportunities for their own particular growth and experience. They added that this object had been attained, and that while the provision for the future government of the Province was, in one particular, exceptional, for it conferred upon them the exclusive privilege of framing laws, in relation to matters within their jurisdiction, unaided and unchecked by the supervisory control of another Chamber, it remained for them to justify, by their wisdom, moderation and forethought, the confidence so freely reposed in them by the Imperial Government.

In every succeeding Legislature the one chamber has proved itself to be even a greater success than was anticipated when it was first proposed. It cheapens the cost of legislation ; facilitates the passage of needed laws ; removes the delay which, under the double system, checks the completion if not the introduction of measures embodying salutary reforms; is quickly responsive to the touch of public opinion; and gives opportunity for prompt correction of legislative errors should such find entrance to the statute book. With a single chamber, Ontario has, in annual sessions of about two months' duration, provided necessary changes in the laws governing more than two millions of people, possessing large centres of urban population and hundreds of rural municipalities in all stages of growth. She has been able to keep pace with the numerous wants of a territory enormous in extent and varying in character from the unbroken wilderness to the cultivated settlement of an older country. She has fostered education, administered justice, protected property, developed enterprise, stimulated agricultural progress, dispensed charity, aided the unfortunate, and effected legislation dealing with private interests to an extent which can only be thoroughly appreciated after an inspection of her statute books. These things have been done smoothly, promptly, thoroughly, and with little or no necessity for appeal to the courts against any Act beyond her powers. The members of the Single Chamber, conscious of the fact that their legislation was practically final, and therefore impressed with a full sense of their responsibilities, have deliberately considered every disputable point, and given ample consideration to any measure submitted to them. In short, for over thirty years the system has been on its trial, and has so justified the prediction of its promoters that it commands the respect and warm support of all classes in the community. Its success is no party victory. It was the outcome of a general desire for a common-sense reform, and, as has been shown, was the product of the best minds of Upper Canada. The result of their wise co-operation has already made its influences felt beyond Ontario. Of the Provinces entering Confederation, Ontario alone adopted the Single Chamber. To-day a Single Chamber exists in New Brunswick, Manitoba, British Columbia, Prince Edward Island, and the Northwest Territories. And it is safe to predict that, before many years have passed away, each Province of the Dominion will be governed by a Legislative Assembly, and that the Legislative Councils existent now will have been thrown aside as complicated, expensive and needless portions of legislative machinery.

By the British North America Act of 1867, the Province of Ontario was divided into eighty-two Electoral Districts, with a like number of representatives, but the opening of new terri-
<small>Representation in 1867.</small> tory since that date, and the growth of population in various sections, from time to time made necessary an increase in the representation. As illustrative of the developing requirements of the Province, it may be noted that
<small>Representation in 1898.</small> while in 1867 the number of members was eighty-two, it was increased to eighty-eight in 1880, ninety-one in 1891, and ninety-four in 1894, with ninety-three constituencies, at which number it now stands.

By Chap. 9, Sec. 3, R. S. O. 1897, it is provided that "no qualification in real estate shall be required of a candidate for a seat in the Legislative Assembly," nor is other require-
<small>Property qualification unnecessary.</small> ment prescribed as to qualification. There are, however various classes who are declared ineligible for election as Members of the Legislature of Ontario. Amongst these
<small>Classes ineligible.</small> are Senators, Members of the House of Commons, and persons holding office at the nomination of the Crown. Here again there are exceptions. Officers in the Army and Navy and Militia Officers (other than Officers on the Staff of
<small>Exceptions.</small> the Militia receiving permanent salaries), Justices of the Peace, Coroners, or Notaries Public are eligible for election. No person who is surety for a Sheriff, Registrar, County Attorney, Clerk or Bailiff of a Division Court, or other Public
<small>Sureties not eligible.</small> Officer, shall sit or vote in the Legislative Assembly. He may be elected to that position, but must take and complete such action as may be requisite to relieve him from any thereafter accruing liability in respect of his suretyship, before he can legally occupy a seat in the Chamber. (See chap. 12, R. S. O. 1897.)

The Legislative Assembly is called together, for the despatch of business, through a Proclamation from the Lieutenant-Governor, which is published in the *Ontario Gazette*. By a change
<small>Calling of Legislature.</small> in the law, made in 42 Vict., it is unnecessary to issue a formal proclamation for the assembling of the Legislature when it is not intended that the meeting shall be for the despatch of business. No fixed rule now exists as to the length of time to

elapse between the issue of the proclamation and the meeting of the House, but in practice the interval is always sufficient to enable every Member to be apprised of the fact that a summons has been made. The call must be so made that twelve months shall not intervene between the last sitting in one Session and the first sitting in the next. The Clerk communicates by letter with each member, announcing to him the fact that a meeting of the Legislature has been called.

Time between sessions.

A Member elect, before taking his seat, makes an affidavit as to certain expenditures incurred in connection with his election, takes the oath of allegiance, as prescribed by sec. 128 of the B. N. A. Act, and signs the roll. (See sec. 18, chap. 12, R.S.O. 1897.

Preliminaries in taking seat.

OPENING OF LEGISLATIVE ASSEMBLY AND ELECTION OF SPEAKER.

His Honor the Lieutenant-Governor, attended by his suite, proceeds to the Chamber of the Legislative Assembly on the day of the opening of the new Legislature, and, ascertaining that a Speaker has not been elected, directs it to be announced by the Provincial Secretary that he will not declare the cause for calling a meeting of the Legislature until a choice has been made. He retires, and the appointment of a Speaker is proceeded with. The Clerk, sitting at the head of the Table in the Chamber, receives nominations for the position. If not more than one is made, the election of the nominee is declared. If more than one name is submitted, the first nomination is first put to the vote. As the selection is generally from the ranks of the predominating party, it is seldom that more than one name is offered. In the nine Legislatures which have been convened in Ontario, each Speaker has been called to his position without active opposition.

Selection of Speaker.

The newly-elected Speaker is conducted to the Chair by his mover and seconder, and, standing on the upper step, in conformity with an ancient custom, briefly expresses his thanks for the honor conferred upon him. The Speaker takes his seat and the Mace is laid upon the table. After congratulatory addresses have been made, the House is for a brief period adjourned or until the following day.

Mr. Speaker returns thanks.

On the day following the election of Mr. Speaker, or in accordance with recent practice, at a fixed hour on the same day, His Honor returns to the House, when Mr. Speaker addresses him, informing him of his appointment and claiming the undoubted rights and privileges of the House. His Honor, through a brief formal address delivered by the Provincial Secretary, assures the Assembly that its constitutional privileges will be recognized, and then proceeds to open the Session with the reading of the Speech from the Throne. This Speech, prepared in Council, is regarded as an outline of the policy of the Government, and of the most important legislation to be introduced during the Session. Immediately after the delivery of his Speech, the Lieutenant-Governor retires, and the Speaker then takes the Chair and informs the House of the receipt, by the Clerk, of Reports from the Judges, and of other matters, if any, pertaining to the Elections, etc.

<small>Mr. Speaker accepted.</small>

<small>Speech from the Throne.</small>

A Bill, *pro forma*, is now introduced, as an assertion of the rights of the House to proceed with legislation before consideration of the Speech, and the Address in reply thereto, and the Speaker announces that, "to prevent mistakes," he has secured a copy of the Speech delivered by His Honor. The Speech is ordered to be taken into consideration on some named future day, and the House adjourns.

<small>Bill introduced "pro forma."</small>

A similar routine is gone through at the opening of every succeeding Session of a Parliament, with the exception of the proceedings at the election of a Speaker.

PROROGATION.

Ordinarily, when the business of the Session is completed, His Honor proceeds with his suite to the Chamber of the Assembly, and taking his seat on the Throne, listens to the reading, by the Clerk Assistant, of the Titles of Bills passed during the Session. The Clerk, when the reading of the titles is completed, turns to His Honor, who signifies his assent, by a slight inclination of the head, and the Clerk then proclaims that "In Her Majesty's name, His Honor the Lieutenant-Governor doth assent to these Bills."

<small>Prorogation.</small>

<small>Royal assent.</small>

The Supply Bill is not included in the Bills thus assented to, but, after the Royal Assent to other Bills, is presented by Mr. Speaker, in a formal speech, expressive of "unfeigned devotion to Her Majesty's person and Government," when His Honor signifies his acceptance, and the Clerk announces that "His Honor the Lieutenant-Governor doth thank Her Majesty's dutiful and loyal subjects, accept their benevolence, and assent to this Bill in Her Majesty's name." His Honor then reads a Speech usually congratulating Mr. Speaker and Gentlemen of the Legislative Assembly upon the close of their labors, and the House is thereupon prorogued by the Provincial Secretary making announcement that "It is His Honor's will and pleasure that this Legislative Assembly be prorogued, and this Legislative Assembly is accordingly prorogued."

Supply Bill.

Prorogation.

THE ADDRESS.

In the early days of the Ontario Parliament, it was necessary to propose an Address in reply to the Speech from the Throne, which was, in all essential particulars, a mere echo of the Speech itself. In the Session of 1891, a new departure was made, when the Address moved in acknowledgement of the Speech of His Honor the Lieutenant-Governor was worded in the most simple possible form, and thanked him for the gracious Speech which he had addressed to the Assembly. This change found favor with both Ministerialists and the members of the Opposition, and has been continued to the present date. A proposed amendment to the Address now takes the form of an addition thereto, and as such amendments can be moved indefinitely, the Opposition is not in any manner precluded from the constitutional expression of opinion which the abandoned form was deemed to specially favor.

It may be observed that the prolonged and adjourned discussion of the Address does not preclude the transaction of the ordinary business of the House. Bills may be introduced, motions made, and Committees struck, and in the British House of Commons debate on consideration of the Address has been postponed from day to day whilst a motion of censure of the Government has been under consideration.

ETIQUETTE OF HOUSE.

Obeisance to Chair. Members uncover and make a bow to Mr. Speaker when entering, leaving, or crossing the floor of the House, and, although permitted to wear a head covering when seated, uncover when rising to address the Chair or to vote. In case of sickness or bodily infirmity, a member is permitted by general acquiescence, to retain his seat when addressing the House.

Message from Lieutenant-Governor. When a Message is received from the Lieutenant-Governor, "signed by his own hand," the members stand uncovered while the Speaker reads it.

Entrance of Lieutenant Governor. Upon the Lieutenant-Governor or his representative entering the House, at the Opening or Prorogation of the Legislature, the members remain standing until he requests them to be seated.

Adjournment. When the House adjourns, the Members are directed by Rule 3 to retain their seats until the Speaker has left the Chair.

Order after a Division. Members retain their seats after the "Yeas" and "Nays" have been taken, and until the result of a Division is announced by the Speaker.

Member speaking and the Chair. When a member is speaking, no other ought to pass between him and the Chair; but, if absolutely compelled to do so, must so carry himself as not to obstruct the view of the one by the other.

Not to pass between Speaker and Mace. When the Speaker is in the Chair, no member may pass between him and the mace.

Position of Mace. The mace is placed upon and across the table when the Speaker is in the Chair, but below it when the House is in Committee.

Removal of strangers. At the request of five members, the galleries and floor of the House may, at any time during a sitting, be cleared of strangers.

Who shall speak. If two or more members rise at the same time to speak, the Speaker designates the one who first caught his eye as entitled to then address the House.

Use of proper names. In debate, no member shall speak of another by his proper name, but designate him by the title of the official position which he may occupy, or the constituency which he represents.

"Mr. Chairman." In the British House of Commons, it is customary to address the Chairman of Committee by his proper name, but, in the Legislative Assembly of Ontario, he is addressed as "Mr. Chairman."

Selection of Seats. The Legislative Chamber is furnished with desks and seats. Those on the right of the Speaker—half of the total number—are reserved for the supporters of the Government, while those on his left are filled by the members of the Opposition and such Ministerial followers as cannot find room on what is known as the Government side. The Members of the Government are seated near to the Speaker's right, and the leaders of the Opposition occupy the seats nearest to his left. The selection of seats is made by members, through the Clerk, before the opening of a new Parliament, but, as a matter of courtesy, members of the preceding Parliament are permitted to retain their former seats, if they desire to do so.

First business of Session. Although no important business is entered upon at the beginning of the Session, until the Government is formally assured of the confidence of a majority of the House, by the passage of the Address in reply to the Speech from the Throne, it is usual to introduce a Bill, *pro forma*, for the purpose of asserting the right of the House to legislate without direction from the Crown. In the Journal of the B. H. C., 22nd March, 1603, it is ordered, "That the first day of every sitting in every Parliament, some one Bill, and no more, receive a first reading for form sake."

Disrespectful allusions forbidden. Any member speaking disrespectfully of the Sovereign, a member of the Royal Family, the Governor-General, or Lieutenant-Governor, or using offensive words against any other member, will be at once called to order.

Reading speeches. While members may make free use of notes during the delivery of a speech, they must not read the speech itself, and will be at once called to order if attempting to do so.

Conversation. During the Session of the House, members should converse in whispers only, and refrain from indulging in any action calculated to interrupt a member in possession of the floor. When the conversation is so loud as to make it at all difficult to follow the debate, the Speaker exerts his authority to restore silence by calling "Order."

"Hear, hear." The words "Hear, hear," are often used to denote approval, but may be sometimes employed to ironically express dissent, and, if exclaimed with a loud voice, be made markedly offensive to the member who is speaking. Whenever these or similar observations are evidently intended to interfere with the proper course of debate, the Speaker will call to order, and, if the interruption is persisted in, name the offending member.

Introduction of a member. A member elected after the opening of a Parliament takes the oaths and signs the roll, as do all members, and is introduced to the Speaker, before taking his seat in the Chamber. If a member takes his seat upon a successful Petition, after a general election, introduction is unnecessary. The ceremony of introduction is brief. The new member enters the Chamber at the Bar between two other members, and the three approach the table, making a bow to the Speaker. One of them says : " Mr. Speaker, I have the honour to present to you Mr. ...., member elect for the electoral district of ...., who has taken the oaths and signed the roll, and now claims the right to take his seat." The Speaker then replies : "Let the honourable member take his seat." The new member advances to the Chair, and after shaking hands with the Speaker, takes his seat.

Admittance to the Chamber. Ex-Members of the Legislative Assembly, Senators, Members of the House of Commons, Judges, and other distinguished visitors are admitted to the floor of the House by tickets obtained from the Speaker. It is a simple act of courtesy to the Speaker, as it is of respect to the House, to inform him of the application of any person desiring such seat in the Chamber. Admission to the Speaker's Gallery is by tickets issued from the office of the Speaker, bearing his signature and the date of issue, for which day only are they accepted ; and of ladies and their escorts to the Ladies' Gallery, by cards procured from the Sergeant-at-Arms. The doors of the Visitors' Gallery are open to the public generally.

<small>When Mr. Speaker rises.</small> Whenever Mr. Speaker rises during a debate, any member then speaking or offering to speak, is to sit down, and the House is to be silent so that Mr. Speaker may be heard without interruption.

<small>Member called to order.</small> A member called to order shall sit down, and the point of order shall be stated, when he may explain.

ORDER OF PROCEDURE.

<small>Daily Routine.</small> Rule 19 provides for the ordinary Daily Routine of Business, which follows the reading of Prayers.

Presenting Petitions.

Reading and Receiving Petitions.

Presenting Reports of Standing and Select Committees.

<small>First Readings.</small> Under the head "Motions," Bills are introduced and receive their First Reading.

<small>Orders of the Day.</small> The Orders of the Day follow Routine. When Bills have advanced through the necessary stages, Third Read-
<small>Third Readings.</small> ings precede all other Orders. Bills reported from Com-
<small>Amendments to Bills.</small> mittees of the Whole, with Amendments, are considered next after Third Readings. Bills reported, after Second Reading, from a Standing or Select Committee, are on the Orders of the day following reception of the Report, for reference to Committee of the Whole, next after Bills reported from that Committee.

Monday, Wednesday and Friday are devoted primarily to the business of members not of the Government, although
<small>Private Members' Days.</small> Government Notices of Motion and Government Orders appear, after other business, on the Order Paper for Wednesday and Friday.

Government Business has precedence of all other matters on
<small>Government Days.</small> Tuesday and Thursday, which are known as Government Days. Government Orders are taken up in such rotation as the leader of the Administration may determine on the days on which Government matters have precedence.

Orders of the Day are taken up according to the precedence assigned to each, but, if not taken up when called, are dropped for that day, although set down in the Orders, after the other Orders, for the next Sitting Day.

Dropped Orders.

The Order of Business, after Daily Routine, is as follows:

Orders of Business after Routine.

Monday.

Third Readings.
Private Bills.
Questions put by Members.
Notices of Motions.
Public Bills and Orders.

Tuesday.

Third Readings.
Government Notices of Motions.
Government Orders.
Public Bills and Orders.
Questions put by Members.
Other Notices of Motions.
Private Bills.

Wednesday.

(Until the hour of six o'clock p.m.)

Third Readings.
Questions put by Members.
Notices of Motions.
Public Bills and Orders.

(From half-past seven o'clock p.m.)
Private Bills (for the first hour).
Public Bills and Orders.

Wednesday—Con.

Private Bills.
Government Notices of Motions.
Government Orders.

Thursday.

Third Readings.
Government Notices of Motions.
Government Orders.
Public Bills and Orders.
Questions put by Members.
Other Notices of Motions.
Private Bills.

Friday.

(Until the hour of six o'clock p.m.)
Third Readings.
Questions put by Members.
Notices of Motions.
Public Bills and Orders.

(From half-past seven o'clock p.m.)
Private Bills (for the first hour).
Public Bills and Orders.
Private Bills.
Government Notices of Motions.
Government Orders.

PETITIONS.

Petitions to the House may be either written or printed, although in the British House of Commons a printed or lithographed petition is not received; and the signatures of at least three Petitioners must be subscribed on the sheet containing

Signature to Petition.

the prayer of the Petition, except in the case of a single Petitioner or a Corporation. A Petition from a Corporation must have affixed thereto or impressed thereon the seal of such corporate body.

<small>Presentation.</small> A Petition is presented by a member in his place, who is answerable that it does not contain impertinent or improper matter.

<small>Endorsement.</small> A Member presenting a Petition will endorse his name thereon, and confine himself to a brief statement of its prayer, and the names of the parties from whom it comes.

<small>Must not ask money aid.</small> No petition can be received which prays for any expenditure, money grant, or charge on the Public Revenue.

<small>A prayer necessary.</small> A Petition must close with a prayer setting forth the object of the Petitioners, and a mere remonstrance cannot be received.

<small>Signatures original.</small> Signatures and even marks attached to a Petition must be written or made by the Petitioner.

<small>Chairman of public meeting an individual.</small> If a chairman of a public meeting signs a Petition in its behalf, the Petition is received as that of an individual only, and so entered on the Journals of the House.

<small>Interlineations inadmissable.</small> A Petition must be free from interlineations and erasures.

A Petition is not read when presented, unless with unanimous consent, but is "read and received" two days after presentation.

<small>Reading Petition.</small> The Speaker decided, 1st April, 1891, that "the practice of the House is that every Petition presented to it shall be at once deposited with the Clerk for examination by him, and if found to be such as, according to the rules and practice of the House, can be received, it shall be brought to the Table, by direction of the Speaker, two days after the presentation, to be read and received. It may then be read at length by the Clerk at the Table, if required, or, it may, with common consent, be read by the Clerk at the time of its presentation, but this cannot be done if any member objects. When a Petition complains of some present personal grievance, requiring an immediate remedy, it may, with common consent, be read."

The following Form of Petition may be used for a Private Bill or other purpose, the address being changed where it is for presentation to His Honor the Lieutenant-Governor in Council :

Form of petition.

Form of Petition.

TO THE HONOURABLE THE LEGISLATIVE ASSEMBLY OF THE PROVINCE OF ONTARIO, IN PARLIAMENT ASSEMBLED :

The Petition of the undersigned,   of the

HUMBLY SHEWETH : That (*here state the object of the Petitioners in soliciting the act, briefly setting forth the reasons therefor*) :

Wherefore your Petitioners humbly pray that your Honourable House may be pleased to pass an Act (*for the purposes above mentioned, or to take such other action as may be desired*), and, as in duty bound, your Petitioners will ever pray.

(*Signatures.*)

Seal in the case of existing petitioning corporation.

(*Date.*)

NOTICE OF MOTION.

Two days' notice of an intended Motion, Resolution, Address, or Amendment to a Private Bill, should be given in writing, to the Clerk, in the precise words to be proposed, not later than 5 p.m of any day when the House is in session, so that it may appear in the printed Votes and Proceedings of that date. Thus, a notice given on Monday permits the matter to be proceeded with on Wednesday, if it is then reached in the Orders of the Day. If given on Friday, it may be taken up when reached on the following Tuesday.

Two days' notice.

Notice of leave to bring in a Public Bill must precede, by two days, the introduction of the measure. Notice of a Question must be given two days before it is asked.

Bill and Question.

By Rule 32 it is provided that a Motion may be made, by unanimous consent of the House, without previous notice.

Unanimous consent.

Modification permissible. A modification of a Notice of Motion is sometimes permitted, if the Notice as amended does not exceed the scope of the original Motion, and a Motion can be amended at the direction of the mover.

May be withheld. A Notice of Motion or Question containing unbecoming expressions, or which is otherwise irregular, may, under the Speaker's authority, be corrected by the Clerk at the table, and a Notice wholly out of order may be withheld from publication.

Resuming discussion after 6 p.m. Motions on the Notice Paper under discussion at 6 p.m. on Wednesday and Friday, will be the first on the paper after 7.30 p.m., when the hour assigned to Private Bills has elapsed.

Resuming discussion after adjournment. If any Motion on the Notice Paper is under discussion when the House adjourns, it stands first on the Orders of the following day, next after any other Orders which may, by the Rules and Orders of the House, have special precedence.

No notice required for certain motions. Motions to adjourn the House or Debate, and Questions of Privilege, require no Previous Notice.

MOTIONS.

Motions must be written and seconded. A motion must be in writing or printed, and seconded, before it can be proposed from the Chair and debated, but motions to adjourn the House or a Debate are not necessarily written; and an Order of the Day may be moved without a seconder. In Committee of the Whole House, a seconder to a motion is unnecessary.

Exceptions

Motion must conform to notice. A motion, of which it was necessary to give notice, must be in the precise language in which such notice was given, any amendments thereto being made by the House after it has been moved.

Speaker will check motions contrary to rule. If a motion offered is, in the opinion of the Speaker, contrary to the Rules or Privileges of Parliament, it is his duty to apprise the House of the fact, and to quote the Rule or authority violated or relating thereto, and such motion shall not be proceeded with, unless, by an appeal to the House, the decision of the Speaker is set aside.

A member, although he has given notice, may desire not to proceed with a motion when it is called in regular order, and it is customary in such case to request that the motion may "stand," which request is usually granted.

Motions may "stand."

After a motion has been read by the Speaker or Chairman of Committee, it can be debated, amended, adopted, superseded or rejected, but can be withdrawn only on leave of the House, granted without a negative voice.

Motions withdrawn.

Sometimes the House may not be prepared to rescind a resolution, but may be willing to modify its judgment. Technically, the rescinding of a vote is the matter of a new question.

Judgment modified.

MAY says that although no question or bill can be offered which is substantially the same as one on which judgment has already been expressed during a current Session, a resolution may be rescinded, and an Order of the House discharged.

A motion upon which the judgment of the House has been expressed cannot be renewed during the current session, but a resolution may be rescinded during the Session in which it has been passed. A motion, however, which has not been seconded, or which, by leave of the House, has been withdrawn, may be revived. A motion which has been negatived cannot be afterwards moved, during the same Session, as an amendment.

Motions renewable.

No motion can be made for any appropriation of any part of the Public Revenue, creating a tax or impost, that has not been first recommended by Message of the Lieutenant-Governor.

A motion for appropriation of Public Revenue.

A question may be evaded or superseded by moving the adjournment of the House; by motion "that the Orders of the day be now read;" by moving the Previous Question; or by Amendment.

How a question may be evaded.

The question that "this House do now adjourn" may be moved by any member who obtains the floor, at any period when the House is in session, and who has not spoken during a debate then proceeding, but he cannot speak to such motion for more than ten minutes. Such adjournment of the House, during the consideration of any motion, supersedes that

Motions of adjournment.

Words taken down pleasure of the House, order them to be taken down by the Clerk, but every such objection must be taken at the time when such words are used, and not after any other member has spoken and the debate has been continued.

Objectionable words Any member having used objectionable words, and not explaining or retracting them, or offering any apologies for their use, to the satisfaction of the House, will be censured or otherwise dealt with as the House may think fit.

Naming a member When a member interrupts the proceedings of the House, and refuses to come to order, he may be called by "name" by Mr. Speaker, and directed to withdraw. The House will listen to a reasonable apology from him, or may direct the Speaker to reprimand him, the substance of which reprimand will be duly entered upon the Journal.

The member withdraws Any member against whom a charge has been made, having been heard in his place, shall withdraw while any such charge is under debate.

A motion to adjourn equivalent to speaking A member who has moved or seconded a motion to adjourn a debate is held to have spoken on the main question, and cannot again speak thereto, nor is he entitled to move an amendment. A member moving the adjournment of a debate, which motion is carried, is permitted to continue his speech when the debate is resumed, but he must have confined himself to that formal motion for adjournment while making it.

Moving adjournment of debate A member who has not spoken during a debate may move or second the adjournment of the debate, but having thus already spoken cannot afterwards move or second the adjournment of the House during the same debate.

May speak to point of order or privilege A member who has already spoken may rise and speak again upon a point of order or privilege, but may not rise to move an amendment of the adjournment of the debate or of the House, or any similar question, while the main question is still before the House, but may speak to these new questions when proposed by other members.

It is permissible, without moving any amendment, to call the attention of the House to particular subjects, on the question of

Relevancy of Debate Committee of Supply. the Speaker leaving the Chair for the purpose of going into Supply, or Committee of Ways and Means, the rules of relevancy in debate, as well as in amendments, being wholly ignored on these occasions, with the following exceptions: **Exceptions.** that (1) a member may not discuss any previous or intended votes of the Committee of Supply, or items in the Estimates; (2) nor any resolution to be proposed in the Committee of Ways and Means; (3) nor any other Order of the Day; (4) nor any motion of which notice has been given.

It has been held that, in moving a second reading of a Bill, to go through it clause by clause is to anticipate the work of the Committee to which it will be referred, and that the debate shall be confined to a discussion of the principle of the Bill. For general convenience, a departure from this course is sometimes permitted by the Speaker. **In debate on second reading discussion of clauses inadmissible.**

Rule 14 provides that any member may require the question under discussion to be read at any time of the debate, but not so as to interrupt a member while speaking. **The question to be read if necessary.**

British Parliamentary authorities set forth that a debate upon any question may be interrupted: (1) by a matter of privilege suddenly rising; (2) by words of heat between members; (3) by a motion for reading an Act of Parliament, an entry in the Journal, or other public documents relative to the question. **Interruption of debate.**

No member may speak to any question after the same has been "put" by the Speaker, and the "voices" have been given thereon in the affirmative and negative, but may be heard after the voices have been pronounced in the affirmative only. Rule 87 provides that when members have been "called in," preparatory to a division, no further debate is to be permitted. **No debate after members called in**

When two or more members rise to speak, the Speaker calls on the member who "first caught his eye." If the House dissents from his selection, a motion may be made that one of the members "be now heard." Such a course is, however, undesirable. A new member, who has not previously spoken, is generally given the preference by the Speaker and House. **Who shall speak**

AMENDMENTS.

By Rule 134 of the British House of Commons, it is declared that a question having been proposed may be amended (1) by leaving out certain words only ; (2) by leaving out certain words in order to insert or add other words ; or (3) by inserting or adding words. As it has been well put by an American writer, there are three ways of amending : by addition, elimination and substitution. By addition, when something is inserted ; by elimination, when something is stricken out ; and by substitution, when something is stricken out and other matter inserted.

What is an Amendment.

Sir R. J. D. Palgrave, Clerk of the House of Commons, England, in his "Chairman's Handbook," describes amendments to a motion as "proposals to alter an expression therein, or to add, or to omit certain words, and may be designed not to contradict, but to modify the terms or objects of the Motion." "This is effected," he adds, "by proposing a sentence defining the scope and intention of that contradiction, in lieu of those passages in the Motion which it is essential to remove ; and the usual form adopted for this mode of opposition is an Amendment, framed so as to make a coherent sentence, in combination with the first word of the Motion ; as it is obviously irregular to propose the entire omission of a sentence, which it is intended to dispose of by an alteration."

Sir R. Palgrave's definition.

The time for moving an Amendment is after a question has been proposed by the Speaker, and before it has been put.

Time of moving.

An Amendment proposed in the House, but not seconded, will not be entertained nor entered on the Journal. A seconder is not necessary when an Amendment is moved in Committee of the Whole.

Must be seconded excepting in Committee of Whole.

An Amendment to add words to the main Question having been affirmed, those words cannot be struck out by any subsequent Amendment.

Words added cannot be struck out.

No Amendment may be proposed to any part of a Question after a later part has been amended, or has been proposed to be amended, unless a proposed Amendment has been, by leave of the House, withdrawn, but words may be added to an amended Motion or Amendment. A motion to strike out

Words may be added after Amendment.

the first part of an Amendment when the amendment has been amended in the later portion, is out of order.

Repetition of Question inadmissible. No Question or Amendment may be proposed which is the same in substance as any question which, during the current Session, has been resolved in the affirmative or negative.

Substitute for Motion cannot be moved until Amendment is withdrawn. When a Member has proposed a resolution to which an Amendment is moved, he cannot substitute another Motion until the proposed Amendment has been withdrawn. A Motion and an Amendment being before the House, the Motion cannot be withdrawn until the Amendment is rejected or abandoned. A proposed Amendment may, by leave of the House, be withdrawn.

Amendment omitting matter of recital. An Amendment is not out of order because it is substantially the same as the original Motion, if it proposes to omit considerable matter of recital contained in the original Motion.

No priority because of Notice. Notice of intention to move does not give priority in moving amendments.

Further Amendment permitted. When an Amendment is carried, the question is put on the amended Motion, which is then open to the proposal of further amendments, but such proposed amendments must be to the part of the original motion subsequent to that already amended.

Must be relevant to Motion. When there is a total absence of congruity between a proposed Amendment and the main Motion, so that the Amendment is a new proposition upon a different subject, it should be ruled out of order for irrelevancy. Except on Motions for going into Committee of Supply, or of Ways and Means, an Amendment ought to be essentially analogous to the main question, and be so framed that, if agreed to, the question or Amendment as amended, would be intelligible and consistent with itself.

Cannot leave out all the words of an Amendment. An Amendment to a proposed Amendment cannot be moved if it seeks to leave out all the words of such first proposed Amendment; but in such case the first Amendment must be negatived before the second can be offered. The difficulty is avoided by moving an amendment to the Amendment which leaves out all the words of the Amendment after the first word "That."

When amendment to Amendment is not in order. An Amendment to a proposed Amendment to a Motion for the House to go into Committee of Supply is not in order.

Supply. An Amendment to a Motion for going into Committee of Supply does not require notice, and a discussion upon it is permitted to take wide latitude. In the British House of Commons, however, as in that of the Dominion, notice of intended amendments is generally given, as an act of courtesy to both sides of the House.

Amendment to Public Bill. An amendment to a Public Bill or question may be moved without previous notice, but two days' notice must be given of a proposed Amendment to a Private Bill.

Resolutions may be amended. Every resolution reported from a Committee of the Whole House may be amended, disagreed to, postponed or recommitted to the Committee. A relevant Amendment may be moved on the Second Reading.

Cannot increase proposed burthen. If it is proposed to amend a resolution from Committee of Supply, the Amendment can only effect a diminution of the proposed burthen, and not an increase.

Different appropriation of funds out of order. An Amendment (not being for an Address) proposing a different appropriation of funds to that recommended by the Lieutenant-Governor is out of order.

Amendment may leave out all but the first word "That." Amendments may be moved to the question "That Mr. Speaker do now leave the Chair," by leaving out all the words after the word "That," and substituting other words; and other Amendments often properly assume that form.

Member may speak to Amendment. Although a Member who has spoken to the main Motion cannot, at an after period, move an Amendment thereto, he may speak on an Amendment proposed by another.

Order of Amendments. In case there are several Amendments to be proposed, each should be put in the order in which, if agreed to, they would stand in the question as amended.

Withdrawn amendments. An Amendment may, with the consent of the House, be withdrawn, and proposed at some future period. But an Amendment cannot be withdrawn in the absence of the Member moving it.

Cannot speak on Motion and afterwards move an Amendment.
A Member who has already spoken, being desirous of proposing an Amendment, must place that Amendment in the hands of some other Member.

As a Member who moves an Amendment cannot speak again, so a Member who speaks in seconding an Amendment is equally debarred from speaking again upon the original question,

Cannot speak to Motion after proposing an Amendment.
after the Amendment has been withdrawn or otherwise disposed of. In both cases, the Members have already spoken while the question was before the House, and before the Amendment had been proposed from the Chair, but if another Amendment is moved by some other Member, they can speak to it.

Mover of Amendment has no right to reply.
A Member who has moved an Amendment does not, as in the case of a substantive Motion, thereby secure a right to reply.

Three months hoist.
An amendment to the proposed second or third reading of a Bill, to the effect that it shall be read at some future date, say three or six months, is always in order.

American practice.
A leading United States authority, *Jefferson's Manual*, although it may not be quotable as an authority for procedure in a Canadian Legislature, says that when a question contains several points, a division of such may be called for, as in British practice : but a question to strike out or insert shall not be divided. Rejection of a Motion to strike out and insert shall not prevent a Motion simply to strike out. Nor shall the rejection of a Motion to strike out prevent a motion to strike out and insert. In a Motion to strike out and insert, the part to be stricken out and the part to be inserted may each be regarded as a question.

FORM OF MOTION WITH AMENDMENTS.

On motion of Mr. *Clancy*, seconded by Mr. *Moore* (*Hastings*),

Motion and Amendment.
That there be laid before this House a Return, shewing with respect to the sales of timber berths in the years 1887, etc.

Mr. *Fraser* moved in amendment, seconded by Mr. *Hardy*,

That all the words of the Motion after the first word "That" be omitted and that there be inserted instead thereof the words following:—"The Government having declared that it would not be in the public interest, etc."

Mr. *Meredith* moved in Amendment to the Amendment, seconded by Mr. *Marter*,

That all the words of the Amendment after the first word "That" be struck out, and the following substituted: "There be added to the main Motion the words 'the same being information which the people's representatives should be placed in possession of.'"

And the Amendment to the Amendment, having been put, was lost on the following division: etc.

The Amendment, having been put, was carried on the following division: etc.

The main Motion, as amended, having been then put, was carried on the following division: etc.

And it was

Resolved, That the Government, having declared that it would not be in the public interest that this House should order a Return, shewing with respect to the sales of timber berths in the years 1887, 1890 and 1892, the upset or reserve price placed on each berth, and the estimates of the Crown Lands Department of the quanity and quality of the timber thereon, such Return to extend only to the berths which were and on which the purchase money has been paid; this House declines to order such a Return to be made.

DIVISIONS.

When a debate upon any Question is supposed to be closed, the Speaker asks: "Shall the Question be now put?" If no member Putting the desires to address the House, and there is no request that Question. the members shall be called in, the Speaker proceeds to put the Question by rising and reading the motion and any proposed amendments thereto in his hands, and states that "the question will be upon the amendment to the amendment," if such there be. If the amendment to the amendment prevails, he puts the amendment as amended, and this being carried, he submits the original motion as amended. He says: "The question will be upon the motion: (or amendment, as the case may be). So many as are in favor of the motion (or amendment, as the case may be) will say, "Aye.'" The "Ayes" announce themselves by responding "Aye." He will then say: "So many as are of a contrary opinion will say, 'No.'" The "Noes" having declared themselves, he will express his belief that "the 'Ayes' (or 'Noes') have it." If his opinion is not challenged, he will declare the motion carried or lost. But any five members may demand the "Yeas" and "Nays," when, if the members have not already been called in, the division bells are rung, and, after a necessary interval, the Sergeant-at-Arms enters at the Bar, makes a bow to the Speaker, and so informs him that the members are "in." The Speaker, having called order, again rises and reads the motion and proposed amendment, if the members had not been called in when the motion was first put, and says: "The 'Yeas' will be pleased to rise,"—every question being first put in the affirmative. The Clerk Assistant at the table calls the names of the "Yeas" in succession, and the Clerk marks on the Division List the name of each member voting, such list having upon it, in alphabetical order, the name of every member, under the title "Yeas," and a similar arrangement of names under the title "Nays." The members resume their seats as their names are called. The "Nays" are recorded in similar manner, and the Clerk, after counting the names on both sides of the list, announces the result of the division. If any errors have been committed in the record of the vote they are now corrected. A member is excused from voting if "paired" with an absent member, or for a reason which meets with the approval of the House, but must vote "Yea" or "Nay" if the House insists.

Aye and Noes.

Yeas and Nays.

Excused if "paired."

The Speaker announces that the motion has been lost or carried as the result of the division indicates. The names of members who have paired are then announced by the "Whips" and entered upon the Votes and Proceedings.

Result.

When a member has a direct pecuniary interest in the matter before the House, his vote is disallowed, provided that such interest is of private and not public character.

Pecuniary interest.

If a member enters the Chamber after the question is put, or is not within the Chamber at the time it is put, and which question

Must be in House when the question put. he cannot, therefore, have heard, his vote, if recorded, is struck off after the list of Yeas and Nays has been read by the Clerk. But a member not present in the Chamber during a vote upon an amendment, and entering before the main motion is put, can vote on such motion.

No record of divisions on adjournment. In divisions on the question of the adjournment of the House, or of the Debate, the numbers only, and not the names of members voting, shall be entered upon the Journal.

Members seated until result of Division is announced. After a division is taken, members must remain seated until the result thereof is determined.

COMMITTEES.

A Committee, with the exception of a Committee of the Whole House, consists of a portion of the Members, selected by the House, **Definition of a Committee.** for the purpose of considering more fully than the larger body is able to do, any matter referred to it; and, generally, is empowered, by the order of the Legislative Assembly, to call for persons and papers, and to take evidence upon oath or otherwise, as may be directed.

Chap. 12, Sec. 46, R. S. O. 1897, provides that the Legislative Assembly may at all times command and compel the attendance **Power to compel attendance of witnesses** before the Assembly, or before any Committee thereof, of such persons, and the production of such papers and things as the Assembly or Committee may deem necessary for any of its proceedings or deliberations. And Sec. 47 sets forth that the Speaker may issue his warrant or subpœna, directed to the persons named in the Order of the Legislative Assembly, requiring their attendance before the Legislative Assembly or a Committee thereof, and the production of such papers and things as may be ordered.

Oaths of witnesses. Sec. 69 provides that any Standing or Select Committee may examine witnesses upon oath administered by the Chairman or any member of the Committee, such Oath being as follows:

Form of oath. "The evidence you shall give to this Committee touching the subject of the present inquiry shall be the truth, the whole truth, and nothing but the truth: So help you God."

Powers of Assembly to punish. The Assembly has power, by sec. 57, to inquire into and punish, as breaches of privilege or as contempt of Court, any person guilty of;

Tampering with witnesses. Tampering with any witness in regard to evidence to be given by him before said Assembly or any Committee thereof;

False evidence. Giving false evidence or prevaricating or otherwise misbehaving in giving or refusing to give evidence, or to produce papers, before the said Assembly or any Committee thereof;

Disobedience to subpœna. Disobedience to subpœnas or warrants, issued under the authority of this Act, to compel the attendance of witnesses before the said Assembly or any of its Committees;

Presenting false documents. Presenting to said Assembly or to any Committee thereof, a forged or false document with intent to deceive the said Assembly or Committee; and

Falsifying records, etc. Forging, falsifying or unlawfully altering any of the records of the said Assembly, or of any Committee thereof, or any document or petition presented or filed or intended to be presented or filed before said Assembly or Committee; or the setting or subscribing by any person, of the name of another person to any such document or petition with intent to deceive.

Select Committees. Special or Select Committees are appointed by the House, and to them is directly submitted the consideration of some distinct question. By Rule 83, no Select Committee may, without leave of the House, consist of more than fifteen Members, and the House may select the names to form the Committee, unless objected to by five Members, when each Member of the House names one, and those who have most voices, with the mover, shall form the Committee.

Reference to proceedings. References in the House to the proceedings of a Committee before it has reported, are out of order.

Standing Sessional Committees. Standing Sessional Committees are appointed, on the recommendation of a Select Committee, in the early part of each Session of the Legislature, and to them are referred matters coming specially within their purview.

The Sessional Committees of the Ontario Legislative Assembly are known as the Committee on Railways, Committee on Private

Titles of Sessional Committees. Bills, Committee on Standing Orders, Committee on Privileges and Elections, Municipal Committee, Committee on Printing, and Committee on Public Accounts. A Special Standing Committee is appointed each Session for the purpose of assisting Mr. Speaker in the management of the Library, and another for the consideration of Bills appertaining to Legal Matters.

Standing Committees. In the session of a Standing Committee the proceedings are conducted, as nearly as possible, upon the same lines as those followed in a Committee of the Whole. Every member present must vote, and if he has not heard the question, the chairman will read or state it to him. The members stand when addressing the chair, and amendments are proposed as under the Rules of the House respecting the guidance of Committees of the Whole.

When Committee of Whole is necessary. The House resolves itself into Committee of the Whole, upon motion to that effect, for the purpose of considering the items of Supply, laid before the House in the form of Estimates, and accompanied by a Message from His Honour the Lieutenant Governor. The House resolves itself into a Committee of the Whole for the consideration of Ways and Means. All resolutions authorizing the expenditure of public revenues or moneys, or the imposition, reduction or abolition of a tax must originate and be discussed in Committee of the Whole. The various clauses of all Bills, Public or Private, after the second reading, and even after having been referred to a Special Committee, are subjected to the criticism of the Committee of the Whole. And any question, if referred thereto by the House, may be debated in such Committee.

Rules of Debate in Committee. The rules of debate, as to a right of reply by a member after having already addressed the House, are suspended in any Committee, and a member is at liberty to speak without restriction if he observes the usual courtesies of discussion, and makes his remarks relevant to the matter under consideration.

Question of Order in Committee. If a question of order arises in Committee of the Whole, it may be decided by the Chairman, or, on motion, referred to Mr. Speaker; and, for this purpose, the Chairman is instructed to report progress and ask leave to sit again upon that or some other day.

Seconder unnecessary. It is an established rule that a motion in Committee need not be seconded.

Previous question inadmissible. A motion for "the previous question" is not admitted in Committee of the Whole.

A Committee of the Whole has no power either to adjourn its own sittings, or to adjourn a debate to a future sitting, but it may **Cannot adjourn.** rise, report progress, and ask leave to sit again; but if a motion is carried "That the chairman do now leave the chair," or "That the Committee do now rise," without reporting, the question before the Committee is superseded.

A motion, "That the Chairman do now leave the Chair," when carried, supersedes the business of the Committee, as the adjournment of the House, during the consideration of any **A Motion by Chairman to leave Chair supersedes business of Committee.** matter, supersedes the question; and when the Speaker resumes the chair no report is made from the Committee, but no such motion can be interposed while any member is speaking.

Votes taken in Committee are by "count," the "Ayes" and **Votes in Committee** "Noes" standing up for the purpose, but no record of the names of those voting is made, unless the "Yeas" and "Nays" are called for.

Each Special or Standing Committee presents its report through its Chairman, who moves its reception and the concurrence of the **Reception of Report.** House therein, if such report makes any recommendations. If the reception of a Report is opposed, it must stand over two days before it again comes up for consideration. A report may be sent back to its Committee for reconsideration, in whole or in part.

Rule 84 provides that of the number of Members appointed **Quorum.** to compose a Committee, a majority of the same shall be a quorum, unless the House has otherwise ordered.

By long established usage in the British House of Commons, it **Disposition of existing charge.** has been determined that, where no new burden is imposed, the disposition of an existing charge is not required to originate in Committee.

On the 23rd February, 1872, Hon. T. B. Pardee was excused **Members excused from attendance.** from attending a Select Committee in consequence of illness, and another member was added to the Committee.

Although, by the Rules of the House, no Committee is permitted to sit while the House is in session, on 4th December, 1874, a Select Committee, to which had been referred certain charges against one member by another, was, by order of the House, permitted, with the unanimous consent of the Committee, to sit and continue its sittings during the sitting of the House; and on 17th December, 1874, the House ordered that any Committee of this House may, for the rest of this Session, sit during the sittings of the House.

<small>Exceptional permission to sit during sitting of the House.</small>

On 8th December, 1869, the House ordered the Standing Committee on Railways to report evidence taken before it, which had moved the Committee to report the Preamble of the Bill not proven. On 9th December, the Committee reported that it could not transmit the evidence, inasmuch as the promoters and opponents of the Bill, together with the witnesses for each, respectively, had been heard *viva voce*, and no record of their statements had been kept by the Committee.

<small>Committee ordered to report evidence.</small>

On 21st March, 1884, it was *Resolved*, That it be a Sessional Order this House that there be added to the Standing Committees of the House a Committee to be known as a Municipal Committee.

<small>Sessional Order Municipal Committee.</small>

By Rule 67 all questions before the Committee on Private Bills are decided by a majority of the voices, including the voice of the Chairman; and whenever the voices are equal, the Chairman has a second or casting vote. In Select Committees of B. H. of C. every question is determined as in the House, the Chairman voting only when there is an equality of votes.

<small>Chairman has casting vote.</small>

PUBLIC BILLS.

An Act of Parliament is the outcome of a Bill, written or printed, introduced by the courtesy and consent of the House, and carried through its various stages in compliance with its rules and orders. It is subject to change at every step of its progress after its introduction, and seldom reaches its final passage without more or less modification of its details, but no alteration can be made in it without the authority of a Committee or of the House.

<small>What is a Bill?</small>

Bills may be divided into two classes: Public and Private. Those which have a wide and general operation and concern the whole community, or a large portion of it, such as Municipal Law, Drainage Law, School Law, etc., are known as Public Bills. Those seeking an enactment calculated to advance the interest of a particular person or association of persons, or for a distinctly local purpose, or having a special private object to serve, are designated Private Bills.

Bills: Public and Private.

Perhaps there is nothing more difficult to the unprofessional mind than the drafting of a Bill, although there may be nothing more apparently easy than the conception of its main provisions and objects, and of a sharp and well-defined comprehension of the general tendency of its details. To clearly express, in legal or even ordinary phraseology, the intention of the lawmaker, is no easy task, and he who attempts it, without previous training in the technicalities of the law, runs the risk of failure in the effort to reach the end he has before him. And yet there are few men who enter the doors of our legislative halls, as representatives of the people, who do not possess practical views of immense value, and whose suggestions as to reform of existing laws and criticism of proposed changes are based upon an experience deserving high esteem. Some ideas of the difficulties of legislation may be gathered from the words of Maxwell, (whose admirable work on "The Interpretation of the Statutes" is a standard authority,) when he says: "Language is rarely so free from ambiguity as to be incapable of being used in more than one sense. * * * When the language is not only plain, but admits of but one meaning, the task of interpretation can hardly be said to arise. * * * Such language best declares, without more, the intention of the lawgiver, and is decisive of it." And again it is well to be reminded, as to the interpretation of a statute, "that the first and elementary rule of construction is that the words and phrases are used in their technical meaning, if they have acquired one, and in their popular meaning if they have not." Hence the importance of so drafting a bill that it may unmistakably express the intention of the lawmaker, and hence, too, the almost absolute necessity of a legal training on the part of those directly responsible for the legislation of our Parliaments

Drafting a Bill.

First Reading. So that publicity may be given to intended legislation, a member desiring to bring in a Public Bill will hand to the Clerk of the House, before 5 p.m. upon any day of the Session, a written notice of his intention to ask leave for its introduction, which notice will appear in the Votes and Proceedings of that day. After two days' notice, and when Mr. Speaker calls for "Motions," the member will, by written motion, ask that such leave be given, and that the Bill be now read a First time. No Bill, it must be observed, can be introduced in blank.

Unusual to oppose First Reading. The *First Reading* of a Bill is usually acceded to as a matter of courtesy without debate, although it is within the powers of the House to refuse leave. It is not unusual for the mover, upon the first reading of a Bill of more than ordinary public importance, to explain its principal provisions, but this course is confined almost altogether to Government measures. If the First Reading is in pursuance of an order of the House, it is made without amendment or debate.

First Reading refused "now." When the motion for the first reading of a Bill is negatived, the House has determined that the Bill shall not *now* be read; it is therefore permissible to renew the motion at some future date, although such an attempt would generally be futile.

Cannot revive a rejected Bill. If a Bill has been *rejected* by the House, another of the same substance cannot be brought in during the same Session.

Name of mover and date indorsed. The member introducing a Bill indorses it with his name, and when read the Clerk certifies upon it the date of its first reading, and sends it to the Law Clerk for revision before it is forwarded to the Printer.

Reading Title. In reading a Bill, the Clerk simply pronounces the title and declares it to be the First, Second or Third Reading, as the case may be.

Second Reading. The *Second Reading*, which practically determines whether the House approves of the principle of the Bill, is not made until the measure has been printed and distributed and marked *Printed* on the Orders of the Day.

A Public Bill introduced by a private member, one not of the Cabinet is generally referred, after its second reading, to a Specia

<small>Reference to Committee.</small> or Standing Committee, while Government measures are nearly always placed upon the Orders to be discussed in a Committee of the Whole House.

A Bill, after it has been reported by the Special or Standing Committee to which it has been referred, is again placed <small>After Report.</small> on the Orders for reference to a *Committee of the Whole*, where it is considered clause by clause, the Preamble being last taken up. It is then reported to the House, and, if with amendments, *Reprinted* before it is further proceeded with, this being the course pursued with respect to every Bill in which important amendments are made at any stage.

According to British practice a Bill may be re-committed, without limitation, with respect to particular clauses or amendments only ; <small>Re-committal.</small> or, on clauses or schedules offered or intended to be proposed ; or, on an instruction given to the committee that they have power to make some particular provision.

The consideration of the Preamble of a Bill is a matter of much importance, inasmuch as its words tend to make clear the prime <small>Importance of Preamble.</small> object of the measure of which it becomes, as it were, the Index. Maxwell, already quoted as an admitted authority, says that "the preamble of a statute has been said to be a good means to find out its meaning, and is, as it were, a key to the understanding of it ; and as it usually states and professes to state the general object and intention of the Legislature in passing the enactment, it may legitimately be consulted for the purposes of solving any ambiguity or in fixing the meaning of words which may have more than one, or of keeping the effect of the Act within its real scope whenever the enacting part is in any of these respects open to doubt. * * * The function of a preamble is to explain what is ambiguous in the enactment, and it may either restrain as well as extend it as best suits its intention."

A Bill reported by Committee of the Whole is forwarded to the Law Clerk, who carefully examines it, and initials it as proof that <small>Third Reading.</small> it has been amended as directed. It is in order, by direction of the House, for a *Third Reading*, and marked *Reprinted* when returned from the Printer. At this stage, the Order for the Third Reading, when called, may be discharged, and the Bill referred back to a Committee of the Whole for further amendment; but if any changes of a merely clerical character are required at the Third Reading, they are usually made at the Clerk's table while Mr. Speaker is in the chair.

The Bill having been read a third time, it is moved "That the Bill do now pass and be intituled as in the motion." An opportun-

Passing and Title. ity for amendment of the title is thus given, and often availed of, but no further amendments are generally attempted at this final stage.

The Clerk endorses upon the Bill the fact and time of its Third Reading, and forwards the document to the Law Clerk,

Bill forwarded to Law Clerk. who is responsible for the correctness of Bills if they are amended.

After a Bill has been passed, it is carefully reprinted, and a copy thereof is sent to His Honour the Lieutenant-Governor, who signs

Royal assent. it upon its face and forwards it to the Clerk of the Crown in Chancery, to be held by him until the Royal Assent is reached. At the Prorogation, or more early date if it is deemed necessary, His Honour proceeds to the House and the Royal Assent is given.

In considering a Bill in Committee of the Whole, the Chairman

Procedure in Committee. reads the number of each clause in succession, together with the short marginal notes which explain its object.

If no amendment is offered to any part of a clause, the Chairman

If no amendment. at once puts the question, "That this clause stand part of the Bill." If there is no opposition, he declares the clause carried, places his initials on its margin, and proceeds to the next.

If an amendment is offered, he states the line in which it is pro-

If amendment offered. posed that the alteration shall be made, and puts the question in the ordinary form.

MAY says that members who are desirous of offering amendments in Committee should watch carefully the progress of the Bill, and

When amendments should be offered propose them at the proper time; for if the Committee has passed on to another clause, or even amended a later line or words in the same clause, amendments cannot, without general consent, be then made in an earlier part of the Bill.

When a clause has been amended, the question put from the Chair is, "That this clause, as amended, stand part of the Bill;" and no other amendment can be proposed to a clause after this question has been put from the Chair, and declared carried.

Putting an amended clause.

A Bill reported from a Select Committee is recommitted to a Committee of the Whole House.

In the British House of Commons, verbal amendments only can be made on the Third Reading of a Bill; but by the practice of the Legislative Assembly of Ontario, a Bill can be recommitted at this stage, and material amendments made.

Amendments on Third Readings.

MAY says that "in passing Bills, a greater freedom is admitted than in proposing questions, as the object of different stages is to afford the opportunity of reconsideration, and an entire Bill may be regarded as one question which is not decided until it has passed." * * * "The same clauses or amendments may be decided in one manner by the committee, and in a second by the House on the report, and yet the inconsistency of the several decisions will not be manifest when the Bill has passed." But when Bills have been rejected, they cannot be re-introduced in the same session. And it has been held, and established by the practice of the Ontario Assembly, that the House, having resolved that a certain course shall not be taken during the then current session, a bill afterwards introduced, and seeking to effect that object, is out of order.

Open to amendments at different stages.

It is permissible to postpone the consideration of clauses, but the debate upon the proposition is limited to the simple question of such postponement. They are considered after the clauses have been disposed of, and then new clauses may be brought up, as new clauses are moved immediately after the original clauses of a Bill are disposed of.

Clauses postponed.

New clauses.

Schedules of a Bill are considered after all clauses are agreed to.

Schedules.

A Committee has power to negative or amend every clause of a Bill, and substitute new clauses for the rejected ones, if relevant to the Bill as read a second time, and in order.

New clauses

Amendments to any part of a Bill admissable.
In Committee, amendments may be made in every part of a Bill, whether in the preamble, or the clauses of the schedules; clauses may be omitted and new clauses and schedules added.

Amendment already rejected.
An amendment or new clause cannot be brought up in Committee, if substantially the same as one already negatived by the Committee.

Must be consistent.
An amendment must be consistent and coherent with the context of a Bill.

Amendments revelant.
Amendments must be relevant to the subject matter of a Bill; but the House may so instruct a Committee as to authorize the introduction of amendments to a Bill which extend its provision to objects not originally contained therein, if they are still relevant to the subject matter of such Bill.

Notice unnecessary.
No previous notice need be given of a proposed amendment of a Public Bill.

Bill may be recommitted.
A Bill may be recommitted as often as the House thinks fit without limitation, with respect to particular clauses, or for the insertion of some particular or additional provisions.

Signature of Chairman.
When a Bill has been passed through Committee, and is ready for report, the Chairman attaches thereto his signature in full.

No addition to motion for second reading.
MAY declares that no amendment can be moved on the second reading of a Bill by way of addition to the question.

Clauses initiated in Committee of Whole.
The clauses of a Public Bill, involving a charge upon the people, must be initiated in a Committee of the Whole, by the adoption of resolutions, previously recommended by Message, in the Session in which such Bill is proposed.

Amendments at Third Reading.
GREY, one of the recognized Parliamentary authorities in England, in speaking of proposed amendments at the third reading of a Bill, says: "It is with great and almost invincible reluctance that amendments are admitted at this reading, which occasion erasures or interlineations." The Canadian and British practice admit such amendments, and a decision of Mr. Speaker, 15th December, 1877, says in effect that an amendment which declares some principle adverse to the measure, or is

otherwise opposed to its progress, may be moved to the Third Reading of a Bill ; while another decision declares that no amendment to the motion for a second or third reading can be moved " by way of mere addition to the question."

Bill reinstated on Orders of Day. On 10th February, 1871, it was ordered that Bill (No. 51) to amend the Assessment Act, which had been discharged from the Orders of the Day on Monday last, be reinstated upon the Orders of the Day of Friday next, and do stand thereon for a second reading.

Passing with unusual speed. By unanimous consent, Bills have been occasionally passed with unusual speed, and instances of this, in addition to the annual Supply Bill, may be found at following dates : No. 111, 22nd March 1884 ; No. 138, 24th March, 1884 ; No. 29, 24th March, 1884 ; No. 176, 27th March, 1885 ; No. 170, 21st April, 1887 ; 21st March, 1889 ; 3rd April, 1890 ; No. 178, 9th April, 1892 ; No. 170, 11th April, 1892 ; No. 179, 11th April, 1892, No. 180, 12th April, 1892 ; No. 191, 195, 25th May, 190, 26th May, 1893, and frequently at more recent dates.

Royal Assent Refused. On 30th March, 1885, His Honour the Lieutenant-Governor, being present to give Royal Assent to various Bills, the Title to a Bill entitled " An Act to correct certain clerical errors in the Consolidated Jurors' Act of 1883," was read, and the Clerk said : " His Honour the Lieutenant-Governor doth withhold Her Majesty's assent to this Bill, the purpose thereof having been provided for by the Act for further improving the administration of the law, which Act His Honour has assented to in Her Majesty's name.

On 23rd March, 1888, the title of " An Act to incorporate the Port Arthur Water, Light and Power Company " was read, when the Clerk announced that the Lieutenant-Governor, by advice of His Executive Council, withholds the Royal Assent, on the grounds that " through inadvertence the Bill gives to the Company thereby proposed to be incorporated, important powers not mentioned in the public notices of the intention to apply for the Act, which powers may seriously affect, and it is asserted do seriously affect the rights of persons who, before the passing of the Bill, had no notice that such powers were to be applied for, and it is contrary to the intention of the Legislative Assembly in passing the Bill that the same should give such powers without the persons interested in opposing the same having an opportunity of doing so agreeably to the practice of the Legislative Assembly in that behalf."

On 29th March, 1873, the titles of two Bills intituled "An Act to Incorporate the Loyal Orange Association of Western Ontario and Eastern Ontario" were read, when the Clerk of the House, by command of the Lieutenant-Governor, said : "His Honour the Lieutenant-Governor doth reserve these Bills for the signification of the pleasure of His Excellency the Governor-General."

Bills reserved.

PRIVATE BILLS.

MAY says that "every Bill for the particular interest of any person or persons is treated in Parliament as a Private Bill, whether it be for the interest of an individual, or public company, or corporation, or parish, or city, or county, or other locality." He adds that a Private Act is an exception from the general law ; and powers are sought by its promoters which cannot be otherwise exercised, and which no other authority is able to confer. CLIFFORD in his "History of Private Bill Legislation," says that "by 'Private Bills' are commonly understood all Bills affecting the interests of individuals or particular localities, and which are not of a general public character."

What is a Private Bill.

"The British North America Act, 1867," declares by Section 92, that in each Province of the Confederation, the Legislature may exclusively make laws in relation, amongst others, to the following matters :

Powers of a Provincial Legislature as to Private Bills.

Sub-sec. 11. The Incorporation of Companies with Provincial objects.

Sub-sec. 16. Generally all matters of a merely local or private nature in the Province ;

And Local Works and undertakings other than such as seek to connect the Province with others of the Provinces, or extending beyond the limits of the Province, and such works as are declared by the Parliament of Canada to be for the general advantage of Canada, or for advantage of two or more of the Provinces.

The Legislature of Ontario divides the Private Bills submitted to it into two classes, ordinary Private Bills and Railway Bills, referring each class to its own Standing Committee.

Private and Railway Bills.

Every Private Bill is based on a petition, which should state, in general terms, the objects or privileges sought to be obtained by the parties soliciting the Bill, and be signed by them, and not by the Solicitor acting in their behalf. At least three signatures should be on the same sheet on which the petition is written or printed, except in the case of a single Petitioner, or a Corporation. If the petition is from a corporation, the seal of such body should be attached to it, and the signature of the President or Secretary, or head and Clerk of a Council.

Petitions for Private Bills.

Every petition for a Private Bill must be in duplicate, one copy to be presented to the House by the Member in charge of the Bill, and the other to be addressed to His Honor the Lieutenant-Governor, and forwarded to him through the Provincial-Secretary.

Petitions in duplicate.

Rule 56 (b) provides that, in addition to the duplicate copies required, a copy of the Petition intended to be presented to the House shall be lodged, on or before the first day of each Session, with the Clerk of the House, who shall file it in his office.

Copy of petition to Clerk.

Petitions against a Private Bill, as well as those in its favor, stand referred without motion to the Committee thereon.

Petitions against Bill.

No petition for a Private Bill is received by the House after the first ten days of each Session, unless the time for the reception of such petition has been extended, on the recommendation of two Standing Committees.

Within first ten days of Session.

No Private Bill is presented to the House after the first seventeen days of each Session, nor is the Report of a Standing or Select Committee upon a Private Bill received after the first thirty days of each Session, unless the time for such presentation and Report has been extended.

Presented within seventeen days. Reported within thirty.

After a petition for a Private Bill has been received and read, such Petition is, without further action of the House, sent to the

Sent to Committee on Standing Orders. Committee on Standing Orders, to report whether the Rules with regard to Notice have been observed, and, if not, to recommend to the House the course to be taken in consequence of such insufficiency of Notice, and omission to deposit Plans, Books of Reference, etc.

Six weeks' notice. All applicants for Private Bills shall insert a Notice, for six weeks before the consideration of the petition, in the *Ontario Gazette*, and for the same period in at least one newspaper published in the locality to be affected, and if no newspaper is therein published, then in that published nearest thereto, and send copies of such notice to the Clerk of the House, to be filed in the Room of the Standing Orders Committee.

Railway Bills. Private Bills referring to Railways running wholly within the Province of Ontario, and not forming part of a road over which the Dominion Parliament exercises control, are referred for consideration to the Railway Committee.

Notice respecting Railway Bill. In case of a Railway Bill, affecting several municipalities, the Notices of intention to apply must be published in one newspaper in each municipality, if there is such a newspaper, and, if not, in the nearest municipality thereto.

Copy of Bill and $100 to be sent to Clerk. Within two weeks of the first appearance of such notice in the *Ontario Gazette*, a copy of the proposed Bill, and the sum of one hundred dollars, for the purpose of defraying the cost of printing and the expenses attendant upon the consideration of the Bill, shall be forwarded to the Clerk of the House, and it will be the duty of that officer to get the Bill printed forthwith after the receipt of said sum.

Certain information as to tolls. Any person or persons asking for power to erect a Toll Bridge shall, upon giving the Notice, under Rule 53, also give Notice of the rates of tolls which they intend to ask, and supply certain other information required under Rule 54.

Maps and Plans, etc., to be deposited with Clerk. Before a Petition for a Bill giving powers to construct a Railway, Tramway or Canal, is received by the House, the applicants shall deposit with the Clerk a Map or Plan, of not less than half an inch to a mile, of the proposed work, and show the lines of existing or authorized works in the same locality ; a Book of Reference giving the names of municipalities in which the works are to be constructed ; the population and the ratable value of property therein : a general description of the nature and probable cost of the work ; an exhibit of capital proposed to be raised ; and an estimate of the probable revenues and annual cost of the undertaking.

When the Standing Orders Committee reports favorably upon a Petition, leave for the introduction and First Reading of the Bill prayed for may be moved, and it then stands referred to the proper Standing Committee, unless it is an Estate Bill.

<small>First Reading</small>

Sec. 68, Chap. 12, R. S. O. 1897, provides that the Lieutenant-Governor in Council may issue commissions to the Judges of the Supreme Court empowering them, or any two of them, to report to the Legislative Assembly in respect to Estate Bills or Petitions for Estate Bills which may be submitted to the Assembly.

<small>Estate Bills</small>

An Estate Bill is a Private Bill and is said to be one that affects some private fund or estate, vesting it or otherwise authorizing its disposition in a particular manner. For example : If a Bill is intended to modify a trust, or to declare the meaning of ambiguous expressions in a grant or conveyance, or to render effective provisions or conditions contained therein which, otherwise, could not be carried out by the ordinary legal tribunals, or without unreasonable expense, such a Bill would be considered an Estate Bill. The preamble of an Estate Bill must fully recite the facts upon which legislation is prayed, and the provisions of the Bill must in general be assented to by all parties concerned, and protect the just rights of all parties affected thereby.

<small>What is an Estate Bill?</small>

Every Estate Bill, when read a first time, is referred to the Commissioners of Estate Bills for their report, and any two of them may give their written opinion whether, presuming the allegations of the preamble to be proved to the satisfaction of the House, it is reasonable that the Bill do pass into law. Their report is read by the Clerk at the table, and, if it is favorable, the Bill goes at once to the Committee on Private Bills for further consideration. If the report of the Estate Commissioners is adverse. such Bill is not further considered.

<small>Report of Commissioners of Estate Bills</small>

No Private Bill is considered by a Committee thereon until after it has been printed and distributed and five days' clear notice of the sitting of such Committee has been exposed in the lobby.

Five days' notice

As a Committee on a Private Bill acts in a judicial as well as legislative capacity, full opportunity is given for promoters and opponents of the proposed measure to be heard, before a decision is reached, and counsel may appear, with the consent of the Committee, for the purpose of supporting or opposing it.

Promoters and opponents heard

By Rule 67, in case of an equal vote in Committee, the Chairman has a second or casting vote.

Chairman has casting vote

Private Bills, reported to the House by the Standing Committee to which they were referred, are placed upon the Orders of the Day following the report, for a Second Reading in the proper order, but all Private Bills reported with amendments are Re-printed before they are further proceeded with, and amendments of important character, at any stage, necessitate a Re-print.

Second Reading after report by Committee

Re-printed when amended

If further amendments are proposed to be made when the Bill is in Committee of the Whole, or at its Third Reading, two days' notice of them must have been given before they can be considered, as it is desirable, to avoid precipitate and unfair legislation, and that no new provisions may be inserted, affecting the interests of parties not represented before the Committee, that due notification should be given to all concerned, by publication in the "Votes and Proceedings."

Two days' notice of amendment.

When a Bill is abandoned by its promoters, or the Preamble be not proven, or the order for its second or third reading be discharged, the fees upon it, less the cost of printing, may be refunded, if the Committee so recommends with reasons satisfactory to the House. It is customary to remit fees, less the cost of printing, upon Bills relating to educational or ecclesiastical matters.

Fees in some cases, remitted.

Private Bills referring to railways running wholly within the Province of Ontario, and not forming part of a road over which the Dominion Parliament exercises control, are referred for consideration to the Railway Committee.

Railway Bills.

Private Bills on Orders of the Day. Private Bills are the first Order of the Day on Monday, and the last on Tuesday and Thursday. On Wednesday and Friday they are considered for an hour, from half-past seven o'clock p.m., and after "Public Bills and Orders" on the same day.

Preamble first considered. When a Private Bill is before its Standing Committee, the Preamble is first considered. and if it is rejected, the Bill is not proceeded with.

Royal Assent. A Private Bill receives the Royal Assent in the same form as a Public Bill.

In House procedure as with a Public Bill. In its passage through the House, a Private Bill is subject to the same forms of procedure as a Public Bill, with the exception already noted as to reference and amendment.

ILLEGAL PROMOTION OF BILLS.

No member shall receive remuneration for promoting a Bill. By Sec. 52, 53, Chap. 12, R.S.O. 1897, it is enacted that no member of the Legislature shall receive remuneration in any shape or manner for drafting, advising upon, revising, promoting or opposing any Bill brought before the House, or a Committee; and no barrister or solicitor, who, in the practice of his profession, is the partner of a member of the Legislative Assembly, shall accept or receive, either directly or indirectly, any fee, compensation or reward as aforesaid. Any person violating these provisions shall be subject to a penalty of $500, in addition to the amount or value of the fee or compensation and costs of action, one-half of the whole amount being payable to the person suing therefor, and the other half for the public use of the Province. Any violation of Sec. 55 shall be deemed a corrupt practice, and an election petition may be filed against the offender within six months after the offence.

The offer of money to a member for his influence a high crime. The offer of any money or other advantage to any Member of the House for the promoting of any matter whatsoever depending or to be transacted in Parliament, is declared, by Rule 116, to be a high crime and misdemeanor and tending to the subversion of the Constitution.

Offer of a bribe punishable as a breach of privilege. Chap. 12, R. S. O. 1897. enacts that the offer to, or the acceptance of a bribe by any member of the Assembly to influence him in his proceedings as such, or the offering to or acceptance of any fee, compensation or reward by any member, for or in respect of the drafting, advising upon, revising, promoting or opposing any bill, resolution, matter or thing submitted, or intended to be submitted to the Assembly, or any Committee thereof, may be punished as a breach of privilege.

BILLS DISALLOWED.

The following Acts of the Legislature of Ontario have been disallowed by the Government of the Dominion of Canada since 1st July, 1867 :

An Act to define the Privileges, Immunities and Powers of the Legislative Assembly, and to give summary protection to persons employed in the publication of Sessional Papers. Passed 19th December, 1868. Disallowed 29th November, 1869.

An Act for granting to Her Majesty certain sums of money required for defraying the expenses of civil government for the year 1869, for making good certain sums expended for the Public Service in 1868, and for other purposes. Passed 23rd January, 1869. Disallowed 20th January, 1870.

An Act to amend the law respecting escheats and forfeitures. Passed 24th March, 1874. Disallowed 1st April, 1875.

An Act respecting the administration of justice in the northerly and westerly parts of Ontario. Passed 11th March, 1879. Disallowed 12th February, 1880.

An Act for protecting the public interest in rivers, streams and creeks. Passed 4th March, 1881. Disallowed 19th March, 1881.

An Act for protecting the public interest in rivers, streams and creeks. Passed 10th March, 1882. Disallowed 20th September, 1882.

An Act for protecting the public interest in rivers, streams and creeks. Passed 1st February, 1883. Disallowed 16th March, 1883.

An Act respecting License Duties. Passed 26th March, 1884. Disallowed 30th April, 1884.

ADJOURNMENTS.

Rule respecting adjournment. Rule 30 provides that a motion to adjourn the House, or the Debate, shall always be in order; but no member shall speak to such motion for more than ten minutes; and no second motion to the same effect shall be made until after some intermediate proceeding shall have been had.

A member cannot move adjournment of Debate and House. Amendment to adjourn. A member who has moved the adjournment of the Debate cannot, before that question is decided, move the adjournment of the House; nor can he then move the adjournment of the House if motion for adjournment of Debate is negatived. The only amendment to motion that the House do adjourn to some specific hour or day is, that the House do adjourn to some other hour or day.

Cannot discuss an Order of the Day. On the motion that the House, at its rising, do adjourn until some specific day, it is irregular to discuss anything which is the subject of one of the Orders of the Day.

Reference to former debate. On the motion that the House do now adjourn, no reference can be made to a former debate of the same Session.

When irregular to move adjournment. On a motion of adjournment it is not unusual for a member to address the House on some other subject; but it is regarded as irregular for a member to move the adjournment of the House merely for the purpose of enabling another member to address the House a second time.

Amendment relating to some other matter. On the question of adjournment of the House, a member cannot make a motion on another subject by way of amendment to the question before the House.

Having spoken cannot move adjournment. A member who has once spoken in a Debate cannot move the adjournment of the House for the purpose of speaking again during the same debate. But if the motion for the adjournment be proposed by some other member, he may speak again.

Right of reply. If the motion for adjournment is made while another motion is before the House, and during the progress of the Debate, there is no right of reply on the part of its mover. But if the motion for adjournment is a substantive motion, the right of reply exists.

Adjournment may supersede a stage of a Bill. If the second reading or other stage of a Bill be superseded by adjournment, the Bill disappears from the Orders until the House appoints another day for proceeding with it.

Adjournment out of order. The adjournment cannot be moved while a member is speaking.

No record of names on motion to adjourn. No names are recorded on the Journals on a motion to adjourn the House if a vote is taken.

No Quorum. When the attention of the Speaker is called to the fact that twenty members, including himself, are not present, he may adjourn, as that number is necessary to form a quorum for the transaction of business. If at any time the House is so adjourned, the names of the members present are to be inserted in the Journal. If the House is in Committee of the Whole, **"Counting Out."** and twenty members are not present, the Chairman may count, and leave the chair, when the Speaker resumes his chair, and counts the House, adjourning if twenty members are not within the bar.

Adjournments on death of Members. The House has been adjourned at various dates as a mark of respect to the memory of a member who had died during the then current Session. On 6th January, 1869, it adjourned on the death of W. M. Shaw, Esq., South Lanark ; 12th January, 1877, on death of Peter Graham, Esq., Frontenac ; 22nd January, 1877, on death of John Fleming, Esq., South Waterloo ; in 1885, on death of W. Harkin, Esq., who died in the House ; on 20th February, 1881, on death of Abram W. Lauder, Esq., East Grey ; on 2nd March, 1885, on death of Daniel McCraney, Esq., East Kent ; and on 28th of March, 1892, on death of Henry Edward Clarke, Esq., Toronto, who died in the Chamber. The House adjourned 9th November, 1869, to attend the funeral of the Chancellor of Ontario, Hon. P. M. Vankoughnet, and in 1882 it attended the funeral of Rev. Dr. Ryerson, for many years Superintendent of Education of the Province,

ACCOUNTS AND PAPERS.

Returns of Papers relating to a public matter, over which the House or Crown has jurisdiction, may be moved for by any member, either by Order or Address. Ordinary Accounts and Papers required by members are brought down upon an Order of the House, after the adoption of a motion therefor, of which two days' notice has been given. Of this character are returns relating to public departments, or bodies incorporated by the Province of Ontario, and of all municipal, educational, and other institutions existing through and regulated by Ontario Statutes. They may be obtained from all public officers, but the information sought shall be of a public and official, and not private or confidential description. An Address to the Crown is necessary to procure Returns relating to matters connected with the exercise of the Royal Prerogative, Orders in Council, Correspondence between the Dominion and Provincial Governments, affairs of any other Province, subjects over which the Dominion or Imperial authorities have control, and other things not within the immediate jurisdiction of the Legislature of Ontario.

<small>Accounts or Papers.</small>
<small>Order of the House.</small>
<small>Address to the Crown.</small>

The following is an illustration of the use of an Address:

Resolved, That an humble address be presented to His Honour the Lieutenant-Governor praying that he will cause to be laid before this House a Return of a Copy of the Judgment of the Judicial Committee of the Privy Council in the Fisheries' Bill, and of copies of all correspondence with the Dominion Government, or any member thereof, on the question of the jurisdiction of the Dominion and Provincial Governments with respect to the Fisheries of the Province.

<small>Form of Address.</small>

The following is the Form of Notice of Motion of an Order of the House:

Mr. Beatty (Leeds).—On WEDNESDAY next.—Order of the House for a Return shewing the number of saw logs cut during the winter of 1897-1898, on the limits of the Georgian Bay and on Lakes Huron and Superior.

<small>Order of the House.</small>

MR. SPEAKER.

Sec. 38 to sec. 45, inclusive, chap. 12, R.S.O. 1897, relate to the election and duty of Speaker.

Election.
Sec. 38 provides that on its first meeting after a general election, the Legislative Assembly shall proceed with all practicable speed to elect one of its members as Speaker, while 39 declares that in case of a vacancy happening in the office from any cause, another member shall be selected for the position.

Salary.
The salary of the Speaker is such as may be voted by the Legislature.

Temporary absence.
Whenever from any cause, the Speaker finds its necessary to leave the chair during any part of the sittings of the Assembly, he may call upon any member to take the chair, and act as Speaker during the remainder of the day, or such period as he may be temporarily absent. If, upon any day, the Speaker cannot attend the Session, the Assembly may nominate a member to take the chair and preside as Speaker for that day.

Absence of forty-eight hours.
In case of the absence for any reason of the Speaker from the chair of the Legislative Assembly, for a period of forty-eight consecutive hours, the House may elect another of its members to act as Speaker, and the member so elected shall, during the continuance of the absence of the Speaker, have and execute all the powers, privileges and duties of Speaker.

Acts valid.
Every Act passed, and every Order made and thing done by the Assembly, while any member is acting or presiding as Speaker, is declared to be as valid and effectual as if done while the Speaker himself was presiding in the chair.

POWERS AND PRIVILEGES OF THE LEGISLATIVE ASSEMBLY.

Chap. 12 R. S. O. 1897, clearly defines the powers of the Legislative Assembly of Ontario:

Power to call for witnesses and papers.
The Assembly may at all times compel the attendance before it or any of its committees of such persons, and the production of such papers as may be deemed necessary for any of its proceedings.

Speaker's warrant. Whenever such attendance is required, the Speaker issues his warrant or subpoena directed to the person named in the Order of the Legislative Assembly requiring the attendance of such persons, and the production of such papers and things as may be necessary.

Warrants may command aid. No person is liable, in damages or otherwise, for any act done under the authority of the Legislative Assembly, and within its legal power, by virtue of any warrant issued under such authority; and all such warrants may command the aid and assistance of all sheriffs, bailiffs, constables and others.

Privilege of Speech. No member of the Assembly shall be liable to any civil action or prosecution, arrest, imprisonment or damages, by reason of any matter or thing done or said by him before the Assembly.

Freedom from arrest. Except for a breach of the Act, no member shall be liable to arrest, detention or molestation for any debt or cause whatever of a civil nature within the legislative authority of the Province, during a Session of the Legislature, or during the twenty days preceding or the twenty days following any Session.

Exempt from service as jurors. During the periods mentioned in the preceding paragraph, all members, officers and employees of the Assembly, and all witnesses summoned to attend before the same, or a committee, shall be exempt from serving or attending as jurors.

Members not to receive fees for drafting bills. No member of the Legislative Assembly shall accept a fee for drafting, advising upon, revising, promoting or opposing any bill, resolution, matter or thing submitted or intended to be submitted to the consideration of the Assembly or a Committee.

Barristers, partners of members, not to receive fees. No barrister or solicitor, a partner of a member of the Legislature, shall accept, directly or indirectly, a fee for promoting any bill, etc.

Penalty. A penalty of $500 or over is incurred for violation of the provisions of sections 52, 53, embodied in the preceding paragraphs.

A corrupt practice. A violation of section 52 shall be deemed a corrupt practice, and an election petition setting up the same may be filed within six months after the offence.

The election of any member violating section 52 shall become void and he is made incapable of being elected to or sitting during the then existing Legislative Assembly.

Seat voided.

By section 57, the Assembly is given the rights and privileges of a Court of Record for the purpose of punishing breaches of privilege or as contempt of Court, the acts, matters and things following :

Assembly a Court of Record for punishment of following offences.

(1). Assaults, insults or libels upon members during the Session, and twenty days before and after the same.

(2). Obstructing, threatening or attempting to force or intimidate members.

(3). Offering a bribe to a member.

(4). Assaults upon or interference with officers of the Assembly, while in the execution of duty.

(5). Tampering with any witness.

(6). Giving false evidence, or prevaricating, or otherwise misbehaving in giving or refusing evidence, or declining to produce papers before the Assembly or its Committee.

(7). Disobedience to subpœnas or warrants issued under authority of the Act.

(8). Presenting to the Assembly or to any Committee a forged or false document.

(9). Forging or falsifying any of the records of the Assembly.

(10). Bringing civil action or prosecution against any member for or by reason of any matter brought by him, by petition or otherwise, before the Assembly.

(11). The arrest, detention or molestation of a member for debt or civil cause during the session, and twenty days preceding or following it.

The Assembly is declared to possess all powers and jurisdiction necessary for enquiring into such offences and carrying into execution the punishment provided, being imprisonment for such time, during the Session then being held, as may be determined by the Assembly.

Term of imprisonment.

Sec. 67 of Chap. 12, R. S. O. 1897, declares that the Legislative Assembly shall not originate or pass any vote, resolution, address

Appropriation of revenue. or bill for the appropriation of any part of the consolidated revenue fund, or of any other tax or imposts, to any purpose which has not been first recommended by a message of the Lieutenant-Governor to the Legislative Assembly during the Session in which the vote, resolution, address or bill is proposed.

The following is the form of Warrant to be issued by the Speaker as set forth in preceding paragraphs :

Speaker's Warrant

FOR ARREST OF PARTY GUILTY OF A CONTEMPT OR BREACH OF PRIVILEGE.

Province of Ontario, ⎫ To
Dominion of Canada, ⎬
To Wit : ⎭   Sergeant-at-Arms.

Whereas, the Legislative Assembly of the Province of Ontario have this day resolved that   , having been guilty of a contempt and breach of the privileges of this House, be committed to the custody of the Sergeant-at-Arms attending this House. These are therefore to require you to take into your custody the body of the said   and him safely to keep during the pleasure of the House, for which this shall be your sufficient warrant.

Witness my hand and seal, at the City of Toronto, this   day of   , in the year of our Lord, one thousand eight hundred and ninety   .

                                         [L.S.]

                                        Speaker.

PAYMENT OF MEMBERS.

In every Session of the Legislative Assembly there shall be allowed to each Member the sum of $6 for each day's attendance, Sessional indemnity. unless the Session extends beyond thirty days, when a sessional allowance of such sum as may be appropriated for the purpose, from time to time, shall be paid. The average length of a Session is about two months, and the indemnity for many years has been fixed at $600. In addition to his indemnity, each Member receives stationery supplies to the value of $15 each Session.

A deduction, at the rate of $4 per day, shall be made from the sessional allowance of a Member for every day upon which he does not attend a sitting of the House, unless, if residing at the time within ten miles of the place where the Session is held, he is prevented by sickness from attending the sitting.

Deductions for non-attendance.

Sec. 74, Chap. 12, R. S. O. 1897, enacts that the compensation may be paid from time to time as the Member becomes entitled to it, to the extent of $4 for each day's attendance, but the remainder shall be retained by the Clerk of the House until the close of the Session, when the final payments shall be made.

Partial payment during Session.

There shall also be allowed to every Member the sum of ten cents for every mile of the distance between the place of his residence and the City of Toronto, reckoning the distance going and coming according to the nearest mail route, which distance shall be determined and certified by the Speaker.

Mileage.

Each Member, before receiving the balance of indemnity due to him at the close of each Session, must make the following declaration before the Clerk of the House, or the Accountant, or a Justice of the Peace:

Declaration as to attendance.

Declaration to obtain Sessional Allowance.

(*Rev. Stat. Ont., Chap. 12, Sec. 77, Schedule C.*)

I,   , one of the Members of the Legislative Assembly of Ontario, solemnly declare:

That I reside at   , which is distant by nearest mail route   miles, as determined by the Speaker of the Legislative Assembly, from the City of Toronto, where the Session of the Legislative Assembly of Ontario, which began on the   day of   , one thousand eight hundred and ninety-   , was held.

That the first day during the said Session on which I was present at Toronto, where the said Session was held, was the   day of   , one thousand eight hundred and ninety-   .

That on the said day, and on each day of the said Session, after the said day, on which there was a sitting of the said Legislative Assembly, I attended such sitting, or a sitting of some Committee thereof, except only on   days, on   of which I was prevented by sickness from attending as aforesaid, though I was then present at the said City of Toronto.

Declared before me at   , the
   day of   , one thousand eight hundred and
ninety-
               Clerk (or Accountant) of the Legislative
               Assembly, or Justice, of the Peace for
                    the   of   (or as the case
                    may be).

Mileage at 10 cents per mile........... $
Sessional Allowance 600 00
                                       $
Less   days absent at $4 per diem..
                                       $

Toronto,   day of   189

$
   Received from the Accountant of the Legislative Assembly, the above mentioned sum of   .

(Signature)

M.P.P.

"WHIPS."

Each party, at the commencement of a Parliament, selects one or more gentlemen to act as "Whips" and Assistant Whips. Their duties are onerous and exacting, and require those who faithfully discharge them to not only foresee but be present at all Divisions, to know the whereabouts of every member, and to take good care that the supporters of their leaders are within the sound of the Division bells when they announce that a vote is about to be taken. They are necessarily the custodians of party secrets, and become the means of communication, at times, between leaders and followers. They make "pairs" with the Whips of the opposite side, and often ascertain the names of members anxious to take part in a debate, and arrange, to some extent, the length of a protracted discussion which has gone beyond ordinary limits. They summon members to a "caucus," and attend to the many other things which must come within the scope of thorough organization. In short, what a good Adjutant is to a Regiment, a faithful Whip is to his Party.

Duties of the "Whips."

PAIRS.

A member compelled to absent himself from a division, either through sickness or other cause, ought to make an arrangement, through "the Whip" of his party, to secure him "a pair" with some member on the opposite side who may desire to be absent, or willing to good naturedly serve a fellow member. In this case, the member agreeing to pair will not vote, even if in the House, until the return of the absent member, and the relative strength of the respective parties in the House will not be affected. An official record is now kept of pairs, and, after a Division, the Whips call attention to their existence by asking that the Division List be read, and stating that several gentlemen have not voted because they had "paired" with others. This temporary suspension of the right to vote is an act of courtesy willingly extended by members to each other, but is seldom resorted to unless under pressing circumstances. The absence of the name of a member from the Division List when he is "paired" is generally reported by the press.

Pairs in case of compulsory absence.

A Select Committee was appointed in the session of 1897 to revise the Rules, Orders and Regulations of the House, and reported in favor of the addition of the following to the Rules:

88*a*. When the Yeas and Nays are taken, the Clerk shall enter upon the Votes and Proceedings, the Pairs, as may be declared (if any), and they shall also be entered in the Journals. And Pairs may be declared immediately after a vote, without re-calling the Yeas and Nays.

New Rule.

THE PREVIOUS QUESTION.

The 35th Rule of the House defines the Previous Question as precluding all amendments of the Main Question, and to be put in the words, "That this Question be now put." If this motion prevail, the original question is put forthwith without amendment or debate, and although the question of adjournment may be proposed and voted upon after a motion for the Previous Question has been placed in the hands of the Speaker, it cannot be moved when the Previous Question has carried, before the Main Question has been disposed of. The House, in adopting it, had resolved that the Original Question

The Previous Question precludes further amendments

should be *now* put, and that must be done. But the Previous Question cannot be put if an amendment is before the House. When that amendment is disposed of, the way for the Previous Question is clear. Nor can an amendment be moved to the Previous Question, although the debate upon the adoption of the Previous Question may be adjourned.

<small>No amendment moved to Previous Question</small>

No amendment should be submitted which is in the nature of a Previous Question, MAY says, nor can an amendment to an Amendment be admitted, if of this character. (See Decision of the Speaker in Ontario Legislative Assembly, 14th February, 1877.) But the more recent Practice of the Legislative Assembly, and the Speaker's rulings with reference to the same matter, have been contrary to this Decision.

<small>No amendment to be in the nature of the Previous Question</small>

THE ONTARIO CABINET.

The system of Responsible Government as prevailing in the Dominion exists in Ontario. Each member of the Executive necessarily holds a seat in the Legislature, and the Cabinet relies for its existence upon the confidence reposed in it by the representatives of the people. Its policy must be such as shall secure the approval of a majority of the Legislative Assembly, and a vote markedly adverse to it is regarded as a withdrawal of the support essential to the official existence of the then advisers of the Lieutenant-Governor. The cabinet cannot retain power in opposition to a declared want of confidence expressed by a vote of the House, although, under certain circumstances, it may advise and be granted an appeal to the electorate. Its retention of position, in such case, will depend upon the sustaining vote of a majority of the newly-elected body.

<small>Responsible Government in Ontario</small>

<small>An appeal to Electors</small>

A member of the Legislature may be called upon to enter the Cabinet, in either the Dominion or the Province, without portfolio or salary, but such an appointment is not often made, and is a departure from the general rule which apportions to each of the Executive the control of a Department.

<small>Without Portfolio</small>

In Ontario, a Minister of the Crown has frequently been compelled to undertake the management of what are practically two or three Departments, although nominally at the head of one.

A Minister has acted as Commissioner of Agriculture and of Public Works, and afterwards as Commissioner of Agriculture and Provincial Secretary. The Commissioner of Crown Lands has control of Mines and Mining, and the Provincial Secretary, in addition to his other duties, has charge of the Public Institutions of the Province. The Treasurer, while managing the Finances of the Province, superintends the License Branch, and the Minister of Agriculture discharges the duties of Registrar-General, and presides over the Bureau of Industries.

<small>Ministers combining Departments</small>

Since Confederation, the affairs of the Province of Ontario have been administered by four Cabinets, of which Hon. J. S. McDonald, Hon. E. Blake, Hon. Sir O. Mowat and Hon. A. S. Hardy have been Premiers. That of which Hon. J. S. McDonald was leader, was formed in July, 1867, and its first members were sworn in on the 16th of that month. This Government, coalition in character, remained in office until 19th December, 1871, when it resigned after adverse votes in a newly-elected Legislative Assembly. Hon. E. Blake was sworn in as Premier and President of Council, on 20th December, 1871, and held office until 25th October, 1872. In the Session of the Ontario Assembly in 1872, an Act was passed, and received the Royal Assent on 2nd March, which provided that if any person, being a member of the Legislative Assembly, should, after the dissolution of the then House of Commons of Canada, sit or vote as a member of that body, his seat in the Assembly would thereby become void ; and the House of Commons, at its Session closing 14th June, 1872, enacted that no person shall be eligible to a seat in the Commons if at the time a member of either the Legislative Assembly, or Council of a Province declaring a member of the House of Commons incapable of being appointed a member of its Legislature. In view of this legislation, Mr. Blake, a member of both the House of Commons and the Legislative Assembly, was compelled to chose one or the other as the scene of his parliamentary labors, and preferring the larger field resigned the Premiership of his native Province and his seat in its Legislative Assembly. He was succeeded by Hon. O. Mowat, who formed a Government, and took office therein as Attorney-General on 31st October, 1872.

<small>Four Cabinets since Confederation</small>

<small>Ineligibility of Members of House of Commons.</small>

First Cabinet. The First Cabinet of Ontario comprised Hons. J. S. Macdonald, Premier, S. Richards, M. C. Cameron, E. B. Wood and J. Carling.

Second Cabinet. The Second Cabinet consisted of Hons. E. Blake, Premier, A. Mackenzie, A. Crooks, A. McKellar and P. Gow.

Third Cabinet. The Third Cabinet, formed 31st October, 1872, has had amongst its members at various times, Hons. Sir O. Mowat, Premier, T. B Pardee, C. F. Fraser, A. S. Hardy, G. W. Ross, J. M. Gibson, R. Harcourt, J. Dryden, A. McKellar, S. C. Wood, A. Crooks, J. Young, A. M. Ross, C. Drury, E. H. Bronson and W. Harty.

Fourth Cabinet. The Fourth formed 14th January, 1897, has had the following members: Hon. A. S. Hardy, Premier, and Hons. G. W. Ross, J. M. Gibson, W. Harty, R. Harcourt, J. Dryden, W. D. Balfour, E. J. Davis and E. H. Bronson (without portfolio).

RESIGNATION OF A MEMBER.

May resign. A Member of the Legislative Assembly may voluntarily resign and vacate his seat, before the meeting of the House, by addressing a declaration of his intention to any two members elect, in writing, under his hand and seal, before two witnesses; and the two members so notified shall address their warrant, under **Double Election.** their hands and seals, to the Clerk of the Crown in Chancery, for the issue of a new writ. If a member has been elected for two constituencies, he can make his choice of one constituency, and resign the other.

After Election of Speaker. After the appointment of a Speaker, a member may resign by making a declaration in writing, before two witnesses, which may be delivered to the Speaker during a session, or in the interval between two sessions; or, he may resign by giving notice of his intention from his place in the House, which notice shall be duly entered on the journals, and the Speaker shall issue his warrant to the Clerk of the Crown in Chancery for the issue of a new writ.

Cannot resign. No member can tender his resignation while his election is lawfully contested, or during the time in which it may by law be contested.

If a vacancy occur by the death of a member, or by his accepting any office, commission or employment, or by becoming a party to a contract with the Government, the Speaker, on being informed of the fact by any member in his place, or under the hands and seals of two members, shall forthwith address his warrant to the Clerk of the Crown in Chancery for the issue of a writ.

<small>Acceptance of office.</small>

If at any time there is no Speaker when a vacancy is created, the Clerk of the Crown in Chancery acts upon the warrant of two members, who officially inform him of the fact.

The following is the Form of the Notice served upon the Speaker by two members of the Legislative Assembly, in case of a vacancy occasioned by the death, resignation, or acceptance of office by any member:

Notice to the Speaker of a Seat Rendered Vacant by the Death, Resignation, or Acceptance of Office by a Member.

To the Honourable Speaker of the Legislative Assembly of Ontario:

We, the undersigned, being two members of the Legislative Assembly of Ontario, do hereby give notice to you that a vacancy has happened in the Legislative Assembly of Ontario in the representation of the Electoral District of   (by the death of) (by the resignation of) (by the acceptance of an office of emolument under the Crown, that is to say, the office of   , Member of the said Electoral District of

Witness our hands and seals at   this   day of   , 189

Signed and sealed in
the presence of   A. B.   (L.S.)
  E. F.   C. D.   (L.S.)
     of

A resignation of a Member may be worded as follows:

189

To the Honourable Speaker of the Legislative Assembly of Ontario:

SIR,—I hereby declare my intention of resigning my seat in the Legislative Assembly of Ontario for the Electoral District of   and I do hereby resign the same.

And I make this declaration and resignation, under my hand and seal, and in the presence of the undersigned witnesses.

Signed and sealed in our presence
  at
  the day and year above written.   A. B.,   (L.S.)
     C. D., of
     E. F., of

OFFICERS AND SERVANTS OF THE LEGISLATIVE ASSEMBLY.

The Clerk of the House is appointed by commission from the Lieutenant-Governor, and is responsible for the safe keeping of all the Papers and Records of the House ; he has direction and control over the Officers and Clerks employed in the Legislative Chamber, subject to such orders as he may from time to time receive from the Speaker ; and by the Rules is expected to endorse, with his recommendation and approval, any new appointment of Clerk or Messenger, and send it to the Speaker for action thereon. He furnishes the Speaker every morning with the Order of the Proceedings of the Day, and forwards to the Lieutenant-Governor a copy of the Votes and Proceedings of the preceding day ; and delivers to each Member, at the beginning of each Session, a printed list of the Reports which it is the duty of any Officer or Department of the Government, or any Corporate Body to make to the House. He certifies upon all Bills the date of the readings and passing thereof, and keeps a record of their various stages ; makes all Notices as to Private Bills ; transmits Estate Bills to the Commissioners ; and posts, in some conspicuous part of the House, a list of the several Standing and Select Committees. He pays out of the Contingent Fund the fees to which witnesses before Special Committees are entitled ; records Divisions ; reads Petitions and other Documents ; admits persons to the Library ; receives Fees on Private Bills ; and discharges numerous other duties not specified in the Rules of the House.

<small>The Clerk of the House. Rule 100.
Rule 98.
Rule 101. Rule 39.
Rule 102.
Rule 46.
Rules 52, 64, 75.
Rule 62.
Rule 78.
Rule 86.
Rule 92.
Rule 110.</small>

The Clerk Assistant acts as Clerk of Votes and Proceedings ; indexes the Journals and Sessional Papers ; prepares the Orders of the Day and Notices of Motions ; indorses, enters and indexes Petitions ; calls Divisions ; keeps a record of the progress of Bills ; reads the titles of Bills for Royal Assent ; and aids generally in Sessional work, and in proof reading, indexing and other clerical labors during the recess.

<small>The Clerk Assistant.</small>

The Sergeant-at-Arms is responsible for the safe-keeping of the Mace, Furniture and Fittings of the House during the Session, and

Sergeant at-Arms. Rule 103.
Rule 6.
Rule 7.

for the conduct of the Messengers and Pages; he takes into custody any stranger admitted to the House who shall misconduct himself and not withdraw when directed; shall clear the House of strangers when directed by the Speaker; precedes the Speaker when entering and leaving the House, and issues tickets for admission to the Galleries, and invitations to the opening and closing of the Legislature.

The Law Clerk. Rule 50.

It is the duty of the Law Clerk of the House to revise all Bills after their First Reading, and to certify that they are correct: and in every subsequent stage of them he is responsible for their correctness, if amended.

Postmaster.

The Clerk in charge of the Post Office discharges all the duties of a Postmaster, and, with his assistant, receives, sorts and delivers the mail; has charge of Private Bills, Reports and other Sessional Papers for distribution; and assists in the arrangement and preservation of the Records.

Accountant of the House.

The Queen's Printer acts as Accountant to the House, and, with the Clerk, pays the Sessional Indemnity to Members; and issues stationery required for the use of the Legislature.

The Librarian.

The Library of the Legislative Assembly is in charge of a Librarian and two Assistants, one of whom at least is present from 9 a.m. to 9 p.m. daily during the Session, and later if the House continues to sit; and from 10 a.m. to 4 p.m. on every day during the recess, excepting holidays and Sundays. The Reading Room is under the control of the Librarian, and is open at the same hours. The Rules for the management of the Library are given under a separate heading.

The Housekeeper and Chief Messenger.

The Chief Messenger of the House acts as Housekeeper and has residence in the west wing of the Public Buildings. He has special charge of the cleanliness, heating and lighting of the Chamber, Committee Rooms, Speaker's Apartments, offices, corridors and entrances connected with the Legislative portion of the Building, and has control of the Messengers and other employees during the whole year, subject to the instructions of the Speaker while the Legislature is in Session. He prepares the pay-sheet for Messengers, Pages, etc., which is certified by the Clerk before it is sent to the Treasurer, and makes, under direction of the Public Works Department, purchases of necessaries.

SUSPENSION OF RULES.

Regarding extension of time. Rule 51 declares that no motion for Suspension of Rule for the extension of the time for the reception of Petitions for Private Bills, the presentation of a Private Bill, or the Report of a Standing or Select Committee thereon, shall be entertained unless after reference thereof to the several Standing Committees charged with the consideration of Private Bills, or upon report submitted by two of such Committees; but by Rule 57, it is provided that no Motion for the suspension of the Rules upon a Petition for a Private Bill is in order, unless said suspension has been reported by the Committee on Standing Orders.

Five days' notice for Private Bills. Rule 64 directs that no Private Bill is to be considered in the Committee thereon until it has been printed, distributed to Members, and five days' clear notice of the sitting of the Committee has been posted. This Rule cannot be suspended until the proper Standing Committee has reported in favor of such suspension.

In case of urgent necessity. Rule 73 says that, except in case of urgent and pressing necessity, no Motion can be made to dispense with any Standing Order relative to Private Bills, without due notice thereof.

PRAYERS.

Prayer at opening of daily Session. The proceedings in the Legislative Assembly are preceded each day by the reading, by the Speaker, of the following Prayers, adopted by the House on the report of a Special Committee, in the Session of 1878:

O Lord our Heavenly Father, High and Mighty, King of Kings, Lord of Lords, the only Ruler of Princes, who dost from Thy throne behold all the dwellers upon earth; Most heartily we beseech Thee with Thy favor to behold our Most gracious Sovereign Lady Queen Victoria, and so replenish her with the grace of Thy Holy Spirit that she may always incline to Thy will and walk in Thy way: Endue her plenteously with Heavenly gifts; grant her in health and wealth long to live; strengthen her that she may vanquish and overcome all her enemies; and finally, after this life, may attain everlasting joy and felicity, through Jesus Christ Our Lord.—Amen.

Almighty God, the Fountain of all Goodness, we humbly beseech Thee to bless Albert Edward, Prince of Wales, the Princess of Wales, and all the Royal Family: Endue them with Thy Holy Spirit; enrich them with Thy Heavenly Grace; prosper them with all Happiness; and bring them to Thine everlasting Kingdom, through Jesus Christ Our Lord.—Amen.

Most Gracious God, we humbly beseech Thee, as for the United Kingdom of Great Britain and Ireland, and Her Majesty's Dominions in general, so especially for this Province, and herein more particularly for the Lieutenant-Governor and the House of Assembly, in their Legislative capacity at this time Assembled; that Thou wouldst be pleased to direct and prosper all their consultations, to the advancement of Thy glory, the safety, honor, and welfare of our Sovereign and Her Province of Ontario, that all things may be so ordered and settled by their endeavors, upon the best and surest foundations, that peace and happiness, truth and justice, religion and piety, may be established among us for all generations. These, and all other necessaries for them, and for us, we humbly beg in the Name, and through the mediation of Jesus Christ, our Most Blessed Lord and Saviour.—Amen.

Our Father which Art in Heaven, Hallowed be Thy Name. Thy Kingdom come. Thy will be done on earth, as it is in Heaven. Give us this day our daily bread. And forgive us our trespasses, as we forgive them that trespass against us. And lead us not into temptation; but deliver us from evil.—Amen.

EXPENDITURE DURING ELECTION.

Payments other than through an agent. Chapter 12, R. S. O. 1897, declares that before a Member-elect of the Legislative Assembly is permitted to take the Oath as a Member, he shall file with the Clerk of the House the following affidavit, to be sworn before the Clerk:

Affidavit. I,   , of the   , in the County of   , elected to represent the Electoral District of   (*as the case may be*), in the Legislative Assembly of the Province of Ontario, make oath and say:

That, except in respect of my personal expenses, I have not made, before, during or since the Election, any payment, advance, loan, or deposit for the purpose of the Election last held for the said Electoral District, otherwise than through *A. B.* and *C. D.*, my agents, duly appointed under *The Ontario Election Act;* and that I will not hereafter make any payment, loan or deposit in respect of the said Election, except through an agent or agents appointed under the said Act. I further say that I have not been guilty of any corrupt practices in respect of the said Election.

Sworn before me this
day of   189   .

Clerk of the Legislative Assembly of the Province of Ontario.

OATH OF ALLEGIANCE.

Oath of Allegiance. Section 128 of *The British North America Act, 1867,* directs that every Member of a Legislative Assembly of any Province, shall, before taking his seat therein, take and subscribe before the Lieutenant Governor of the Province, or some person authorized by him, the Oath of Allegiance contained in the fifth schedule to the Act, and which reads as follows :

I, *A. B.*, do swear that I will be faithful and bear true allegiance to Her Majesty, Queen Victoria.

(NOTE.—*The name of the King or Queen of the United Kingdom of Great Britain and Ireland for the time being is to be substituted, from time to time, with proper terms of reference thereto.*)

INDEMNITY TO MEMBERS.

Sessional indemnity.
In every Session of the Legislative Assembly there is allowed to each Member the sum of $6 for each day's attendance, unless the Session extends beyond thirty days, when a sessional allowance of such sum as may be appropriated for the purpose, from time to time is paid. The average length of a Session is about two months, and the indemnity for many years has been fixed at $600. In addition to his indemnity, each Member receives stationery supplies to the value of $15 each Session.

Deduction for non-attendance.
A deduction, at the rate of $4 per day, is made from the sessional allowance of a Member for every day upon which he does not attend a sitting of the House, unless, if residing at the time within ten miles of the place where the Session is held, he is prevented by sickness from attending the sitting.

Partial payment.
Chap. 12, R. S. O. 1897, enacts that the compensation may be paid from time to time as the member becomes entitled to it to the extent of $4 for each day's attendance, but the remainder shall be retained by the Clerk of the House until the close of the Session, when the final payment is made.

Mileage.
There is allowed to every member the sum of ten cents for every mile of the distance between the place of his residence and the City of Toronto, reckoning the distance going and coming according to the nearest mail route, which distance is determined and certified by the Speaker.

Declaration as to attendance.
Each member, before receiving the balance of indemnity due to him at the close of each Session must make the following declaration before the Clerk of the House, or the Accountant, or a Justice of the Peace :

DECLARATION TO OBTAIN SESSIONAL ALLOWANCE.

(*Rev. Stat. Ont., Chap. II., sec. 68, Schedule C.*)

I,   , one of the members of the Legislative Assembly of Ontario, solemnly declare :

That I reside at   , which is distant by nearest mail route   miles, as determined by the Speaker of the Legislative Assembly, from the City of Toronto, where the Session of the Legislative Assembly of Ontario, which began on the   day of   , one thousand eight hundred and ninety-   was held.

That the first day during the said Session on which I was present at Toronto, where the said Session was held, was the   day of   , one thousand eight hundred and ninety-

That on the said day, and on each day of the said Session, after the said day, on which there was a sitting of the said Legislative Assembly, I attended such sitting, or a sitting of some Committee thereof, except only on   days, on   , of which I was prevented by sickness from attending as aforesaid, though I was then present at the said City of Toronto.

Declared before me at   , the   day of   , one thousand eight hundred and ninety-

Clerk (or Accountant) of the Legislative Assembly or Justice of the Peace for the   of   (or as the case may be).

Mileage at 10 cents per mile .... $
Sessional allowance 600 00
                                                  $
Less   days absent, at $4 per diem
                                                  $

Toronto,   day of   189

$

Received from the Accountant of the Legislative Assembly, the above mentioned sum of

(Signature)

M.P.P.

ANNUAL SESSION.

Time between Sessions.

By Sec. 4, Chap. 11, R. S. O. 1887, it is provided that there shall be a Session of the Legislature, once at least, in every year, so that twelve months shall not intervene between the last sitting of the Legislature in one Session, and the first sitting in the next.

Sec. 86 of the British North America Act, 1867, declares that there shall be a session of the Legislature of Ontario, once at least in every year.

B.N.A., 1867.

DURATION OF A LEGISLATURE.

Chap. 11 of R. S. O. enacts that every Legislative Assembly shall continue for four years from the fifty-fifth day after the date of the writs of the election, and no longer (subject to being sooner dissolved by the Lieutenant-Governor).

Four years.

The power to prorogue or dissolve the Assembly is not affected by demise of the Sovereign, nor shall the Assembly determine and be dissolved because of such demise.

On demise of the Crown.

PAYMENT OF WRITERS, MESSENGERS AND PAGES.

The amount of compensation to Sessional Writers, Messengers and Pages, is fixed by Mr. Speaker, and is generally as follows:

Sessional Writers .. $2 00 per diem
Messengers .... 1 50 "
Pages . ... $0 75 per diem.

DISTRIBUTION OF PUBLIC DOCUMENTS.

Each member of the Legislative Assembly is entitled to receive copies of Public Documents, as they are printed from time to time, in following numbers:

Votes and Proceedings, daily... 2
Orders of the Day, daily 1
Public Bills 5
Private Bills.......... 2
Sessional Papers........... 5
Departmental Reports 5

Public Bills, third reading 5
Private Bills   "   ...... †
Bound Journals of the House.... 2
  "   Sessional Papers. 1
Statutes ... .

NUMBER OF REPORTS, Etc.

The number of Reports, Votes, Orders of the Day, Bills, Sessional Papers and Journals, to be printed for the Legislative Assembly for the Province of Ontario, as per Report of Committee on Printing passed 24th March, 1885, is as follows:

---

†20 copies to the member introducing it.

	No. of copies.
1. Agriculture and Arts (including 420 for bound Sessional vols.)	2,500
2. Fruit Growers' Association (including 420 for bound Sessional vols.)	2,500
3. Agricultural College (including 420 for bound Sessional vols.)	2,500
4. Estimates (including 420 for bound Sessional vols.)	2,500
5. Public Accounts (including 420 for bound Sessional vols.)	2,500
6. Education (including 420 for bound Sessional vols.)	2,500
7. Departmental Reports (including 420 for bound vols.)	1,920
8. Votes	1,150
9. Orders of the Day	250
10. Public Bills, first reading	1,150
11. Public Bills, reprinted	250
12. Public Bills, third reading	600
13. Private Bills, first reading	600
14. Private Bills, reprinted	250
15. Private Bills, third reading	100
16. Sessional Papers (600 for immediate distribution and 420 for bound vols.)	1,020
17. Journals, bound vols	600

The number of all Departmental Reports to be 1,920, including 420 for bound volumes, excepting those numbered from 1 to 6, inclusive, which are to be 2,500.

Orders for any of the above publications required for any of the Departments must be signed by one of the members of the Executive or head of such department.

RECAPITULATION OF DISTRIBUTION.

I. — Votes.

Distribution as per list	900
Remainder	100
Total printed	*1,500

II. Orders for the Day.

Distribution as per list	230
Remainder	20
Total printed	*300

III. — Public Bills, First Reading.

Distribution as per list	1,170
Remainder	80
Total printed	*1,500

IV. — Public Bills, Reprinted.

Distribution as per list	230
Remainder	20
Total printed	250

V. — Private Bills, First Reading.

Distribution as per list	500
Remainder	100
Total printed	600

VI. — Private Bills, Reprinted.

Distribution as per list	230
Remainder	20
Total printed	250

VII.—Departmental Reports.

Distribution as per list	1,400
Remainder	100
Total printed	1,500

VIII.—Third Readings of Public Bills.

Distribution as per list	500
Remainder	100
Total printed	600

IX.—Third Readings of Private Bills.

Distribution as per list	80
Remainder	20
Total printed	100

X.—Sessional Returns.

Distribution as per list	500
Remainder	100
Total printed	600

XI.—Bound Volumes—Journals.

Distribution as per list	380
Remainder	40
Total printed	*600

XII.—Bound Volumes—Sessional Papers.

Distribution as per list	380
Remainder	40
Total printed	420

*Numbers subsequently increased by Order of Committee on Printing.

By order of

COMMITTEE ON PRINTING.

THE MACE.

In England—and a similar practice prevails in such of her dependencies as use the mace,— when a new house has been elected, and proceeds on its first meeting, to the selection of a Speaker, the mace is placed under the table of the House until a choice has been made ; when the newly-elected Speaker takes the chair it is placed upon and across the table, where it always remains while he occupies his seat. Until the Speaker-elect has been presented to the Sovereign or his representative for acceptance, he leaves the House, at adjournment, without the mace before him. The House frequently suspends its sittings, but without adjournment, and the mace remains upon the table, and, on the Speaker returning, business is gone on with as if no interruption had occurred. When the Speaker leaves the chair, upon the House going into Committee of the Whole, the mace is removed from the table and placed under it, being returned to its old position upon his resumption of the chair. When the Speaker enters or leaves the House at its adjournment, the mace is borne before him, remains with him until the next sitting, and accompanies him upon all State occasions, "in which he shall always appear in his gown." May tells us, that "in earlier times it was not the custom to prepare a formal warrant for executing the orders of the House of Commons, but the sergeant arrested persons with the mace, without any written authority, and at the present day he takes strangers into custody who intrude themselves into the House, or otherwise misconduct themselves, in virtue of the general orders of the House and without any specific instruction," and the Speaker, accompanied by the mace, has similar powers. We learn, from May again, that "when a witness is in the custody of the sergeant-at-arms, or is brought from a prison in custody, it is the usual, but not the constant, practice for the sergeant to stand with the mace at the bar. When the mace is on the sergeant's shoulder, the Speaker has the sole management ; and no member may speak or even suggest questions to the Chair." To obviate this difficulty, it is now customary to place the mace upon the table when a witness is at the bar, so that any member may propose a question to him through the Speaker. Hatsell says, "that from the earliest account of Peers being admitted into the House of Commons, the mode of receiving them seems to have been very much the same as it is at present ; that is, that they were attended from the door by the sergeant and the mace, making three obeisances to the House ; that they had a chair set for them within the bar, on the left hand as they enter, in which they sat down covered ; and if they had anything to deliver to the House, they stood up and spoke uncovered, the sergeant standing by them all the time with the mace ; and that they withdraw making the same obeisance to the House, and the sergeant with the mace accompanying them to the door." No member is at any time allowed to pass between the Chair and the Table, or between the Chair and the mace when it is taken off the table by the sergeant. It is employed, too, to enforce attendance of Committee men, sitting on special or other committees, at times when the Speaker finds it impossible to otherwise make a House at the hour for the commencement of the day's session. The appearance of the sergeant with the mace dissolves any committee then sitting, and to avoid this catastrophe, it is usual to send a messenger in advance to announce his advent, and so give the committee time to adjourn.

Of the early history of the mace used in Upper Canada, we have undoubted proof, in the present existence of that first so employed. It is in appearance as primitive as was the Parliament which assembled at the call of Governor Simcoe, at Niagara, on the 17th September, 1792. That was the day of extreme economy and simplicity, and the wooden mace, painted red and gilt, was in keeping with that small assemblage of sturdy backwoodsmen clad in homespun grey, less in number than the smallest County Council of 1898, who met to enact laws providing for the few wants of a young people. It is probable that it graced the legislative hall at Niagara, although there is no positive evidence to that effect. It was certainly used after the removal of the Upper Canada Parliament to York, for, on the 27th April, 1813, when the United States forces attacked the seat of government and captured it, they destroyed the public buildings of the embryo City of Toronto, burnt the Parliament House and carried off sundry trophies of their victory. . Amongst these was the mace used in the Assembly. Commodore Chauncey, the commander of the successful expedition, forwarded it with other spoils of war to the Secretary of the United States Navy, and it is still to be seen, with a British Standard, captured at the same time, in the United States Naval Academy, Annapolis, Maryland, in an excellent state of preservation. It may be added, that an oil painting representing this mace is to be found in the Members' Reception Room.

In the Province of Ontario, a new mace was procured by the Government of the Hon. J. Sandfield Macdonald, for the opening of the first Parliament after Confederation. It is much more modest in its appearance and value than that of the Dominion, is made of copper and is highly gilded. It was manufactured by Charles C. Zollicoffer, of Ottawa, at an expense of $200, and bears some resemblance to the much more costly one belonging to the Dominion Parliament

SALUTES TO LIEUTENANT-GOVERNORS.

When acting on behalf of the Queen. Earl Kimberley, Secretary of State for the Colonies, in reply to a question put to him, as to the ceremony to be observed at the opening and closing of Provincial Legislatures, said in a despatch to Earl of Dufferin, Governor-General of Canada, 7th November, 1872: "With reference to the question asked by Sir Hastings Doyle, and submitted by Lord Lisgar for my decision, namely, ' whether the Lieutenant-Governors are supposed to be acting on behalf of the Queen,' I have to observe that, while from the nature of their appointment, they represent, on ordinary occasions, the Dominion Government, there are, nevertheless, occasions (such as the opening or closing of a Session of the Provincial Legislatures, the celebration of Her Majesty's birthday, the holding of a levee, etc.), on which they should be deemed to be acting on behalf of Her Majesty, and the first part of the National Anthem should be played in their presence. In connection with this subject, I request you to intimate to your Ministers that it would be desirable to alter paragraph 12 of the Militia Regulations of 1870, so as to permit of the playing of the first six bars of the National Anthem in lieu of a slow march, as now prescribed by the Regulations."

By despatch, dated Downing street, 19th Oct., 1868, it was declared that Lieutenant-Governors are not entitled to salutes from Her Majesty's ships and fortifications within their respective Provinces.

Governor-General entitled to general salute.
By the Regulations and Orders for the Militia of Canada, 1887, it is provided, paragraph 470, that whenever called out for duty as a Guard of Honour, etc., the militia are to receive His Excellency the Governor-General with a "general salute," standards and colours flying, officers saluting and bands playing 'first part' of the National Anthem (six bars).

Lieutenant-Governors at opening and closing of Legislature.
By paragraph 471, it is declared that Guards of Honour, who will pay similar compliments, will be furnished to the Lieutenant-Governors of Provinces on the opening and prorogation of the Provincial Legislatures, and the applications for such Guards of Honour must be made to the D.A.G. of the District, who will order them under this authority. Such guards are, if practicable, to be furnished, and salutes fired, by any permanent force of militia stationed at the place, or by the active militia in their absence.

Lieutenant-Governors entitled to a salute of 15 guns.
Paragraph 476, sets forth that at the opening and prorogation of the Dominion Parliament, the Governor-General is entitled to a salute of 19 guns, and the Lieutenant Governors of Provinces, on the opening and closing of their Provincial Legislatures, to a salute of 15 guns.

The *Canada Official Gazette* of 3rd November, 1894, contained the following general order:

G. O., 84.

(1) An escort of cavalry will be furnished to the Lieutenant-Governor of a Province as provided in the Militia Act, sec. 79, paragraph 4a, only on the occasion of the Opening or Closing of the Legislature of the Province.

(2) The escort on such occasions will not exceed the following strength, viz.:

    1 Lieutenant.
    1 Sergeant.
    12 Rank and file.

(3) On receipt of an official notification from the Secretary of the Lieutenant-Governor, the D. A. G. commanding Military District will detail an escort of the authorized strength from the Permanent Force, or, if a unit of that force is not available, from the Active Militia, without reference to Head Quarters.

POSTAGE.

All letters subject to postage. Letters mailed by Members of the Legislative Assembly during a Session of the Legislature, and all letters from any of the Departments are subject to the usual postage rates, the postage thereon being paid by the Province.

Name of sender on envelopes. Members must initial or place their names upon the envelopes of such letters as they may send during the Session, so that the Postmaster may be satisfied of the genuine character of correspondence passing through the House Post Office. Letters not so distinguished are sent to the Dead Letter Office.

Bills not to be sealed. Members are requested not to close or seal envelopes in which Bills, etc., may be placed, as they will then be subject to letter rates. But Bills may be sent in an open envelope as free matter. Properly printed envelopes may be procured on application to the Queen's Printer.

Printed matter. All Papers printed by order of the Legislative Assembly may be sent, free of Canada postage, either singly or in packages, so put up that their contents may be known. Members sending them will mark them with their names.

Petitions, Addresses, etc. Petitions and Addresses to the Provincial Legislature of any of the Provinces of the Dominion, or to any branch thereof, and also Votes and Proceedings, and other papers printed by order of any such Legislature, or any branch thereof, may pass free of Canada postage, under such regulations as the Postmaster-General may prescribe. This does not include the Statutes of the respective Provinces, nor is the privilege conceded to Members of the Provincial Legislature, as it is to Members of the House of Commons and of the Senate, of carrying, free of postage, books to and from their respective Parliamentary Libraries.

Open on Sundays. During the Session, the post office will be open on Sundays, from 10 a.m. to 12 m.; and from 3 to 4 p.m.

Departmental Reports. Departmental Reports are allowed to pass free through Canadian territory and to the United States, where, under the existing convention between Canada and the United States, they are delivered without charge.

Closing the mails. When, during the Session, the House adjourns at or before six p.m., the Post Office closes at 9 p.m. When there is an evening Session, the mails are made up until 10.00 p.m.

STATIONERY.

On the 16th January, 1871, the House *Resolved :* That in future a Sessional allowance of Stationery of the value of ten dollars, and no more, shall be delivered to each member at the opening of the Session, and that each member may select his own stationery.

This amount has been found to be insufficient, and the allowance of stationery now represents a value of fifteen dollars.

THE CLOTURE OR CLOSURE.

The Closure. By Standing Order of the Imperial House of Commons, adopted 27th November, 1882, it was declared :

" That when it shall appear to Mr. Speaker, or to the Chairman of the Ways and Means in a Committee of the Whole House, during any debate, that the subject has been adequately discussed, and that it is the evident sense of the House, or of the Committee, that the question be now put, he may so inform the House, or the Committee ; and if motion be made, ' That the question be now put.' Mr. Speaker, or the Chairman, shall forthwith put such question ; and if the same be decided in the affirmative, the question under discussion shall be put forthwith : Provided that the question, ' That the question be now put,' shall not be decided in the affirmative, if a division be taken, unless it shall appear to have been supported by more than two hundred members, or unless it shall appear to have been opposed by less than forty members and supported by more than one hundred members."

On the 18th March, 1887, the Imperial House of Commons adopted the following Standing Order, containing further provisions for the purpose of preventing obstruction to the business of that body :

That after a Question has been proposed, a Member rising in his place may claim to put " That the Question be now put," and unless it shall appear to the Chair that such motion is an abuse of the Rules of the House, or an infringement of the rights of the minority, the Question, " That the Question be now put," shall be put forthwith, and decided without amendment or debate.

When the Motion " That the Question be now put " has been carried, and the Question consequent thereon has been decided, any further motion may be made (the assent of the Chair as aforesaid not having been withheld) which may be requisite to bring to a decision any question already proposed from the Chair; and also if a clause be then under consideration, a motion may be made (the assent of the Chair as aforesaid not having been withheld), that the Question "That certain words of the clause defined in the Motion stand part of the clause," or that the clause stand part of, or be added to the Bill, be now put, such motions shall be put forthwith, and decided without amendment or debate.

Provided always, That Questions for the Closure of Debate shall not be decided in the affirmative, if a Division be taken, unless it shall appear by the numbers declared from the Chair, that such motion was supported by more than two hundred members, or was opposed by less than forty members and supported by more than one hundred members.

Provided always, That this Rule shall be put in force only when the Speaker or the Chairman of Ways and Means is in the Chair.

TITLE OF "HONOURABLE."

By a despatch to His Excellency the Governor-General, dated Downing Street, 24th July, 1868, the following regulations for use of the title "Honourable," were laid down for observance:

"In consequence of the Confederation of the British Provinces, some revision of the former usages there about titles has been necessary, and I have the honour to inform you that Her Majesty has been pleased to approve of the adoption of the following regulations:

Governor-General.   1st. The Governor-General of Canada is to be styled "His Excellency."

Lieutenant-Governors.   2nd. The Lieutenant Governors of the Provinces to be styled "His Honour."

Privy Councillors.   3rd. The Privy Councillors of Canada to be styled "Honourable," and for life.

Senators.   4th. Senators of Canada to be styled "Honourable," but only during office, and the title not to be continued afterwards.

Executive Councillors.   5th. Executive Councillors of the Provinces to be styled "Honourable," but only while in office, and the title not to be continued afterwards.

6th. Legislative Councillors in the Provinces not in future to have that title, but gentlemen who were Legislative Councillors at the time of the Union to retain the title "Honourable" for life.

<small>Legislative Councillors.</small>

7th. The President of the Legislative Council in the Provinces to be styled "Honourable" during office.

<small>President of Legislative Councils.</small>

8th. The Speakers of the Houses of Assembly in the Provinces to be styled "Honourable" during office.

<small>Speakers of the Houses of Assembly.</small>

LIBRARY.

The following Rules, for the management of the Library of the Legislative Assembly, were adopted 1st May, 1891, and supersede all former Rules :

Rules of the Library.

<small>Catalogue.</small> 1. A proper catalogue of the books belonging to the Library shall be kept by the Librarian, or person in whom the custody and responsibility thereof shall be vested, and who shall be required to report to the House, through the Speaker at the opening of each Session, the actual state of the Library.

<small>Persons admitted.</small> 2. No person shall be entitled to resort to the Library during a Session of the Legislature, except the Lieutenant-Governor, the Members of the Executive Council and the Legislative Assembly, and the officers of the House, and such other persons as may receive a written order of admission from the Speaker of the House. Members may personally introduce strangers to the Library during the day-time, but not after the hour of six o'clock p.m.

<small>Strangers.</small>

<small>Books.</small> 3. During the Session of the Legislature no books belonging to the Library shall be taken out of the building, except by the authority of the Speaker, or upon receipt given by a member of the House.

<small>Open in Session.</small> 4. During the Session the Library shall be opened daily from 9 o'clock a.m. until 9 o'clock p.m., and should the House remain in session after such hour, the Library shall remain open until the House adjourns.

<small>Open in Recess.</small> 5. During the Recess of the Legislature, the Library shall be open every day in each week, Sundays and Holidays excepted, from the hour of ten in the morning until four in

the afternoon, and access to the Library shall be permitted to persons introduced by a member of the Legislature or admitted at the discretion of the Clerk or Librarian, subject to such regulations as may be deemed necessary for the security and preservation of the collection.

Borrowing Books.
6. During the Recess of the Legislature no member of the House shall be at liberty to borrow or have in his possession at any one time, more than three works of the Library, or retain the same for a longer period than one month. No books of reference or books of special cost or value may be removed from the seat of Government under any circumstances.

Report.
7. At the first meeting of the Library Committee in each Session of the Legislature, the Librarian shall report a list of books absent at the commencement of the Session, specifying the names of any persons who have retained the same in contravention of any of the foregoing Rules.

Books in Recess.
8. During the Recess such books may be taken out of the Library by the Lieutenant-Governor, Members of the Executive, the Speaker and Deputy Heads of Departments as may be required by them; and one volume at a time may be taken out by members of the Civil Service and by such other persons as may be named to the Librarian by a member of the Library Committee or Executive Council, and a receipt shall be given to the Librarian by each person taking out a book.

Books of Reference.
9. The following shall be deemed Books of Reference: — All books in the Law Department, Dictionaries, Encyclopedias, Manuals, Directories, Archives, Newspapers, Maps, Engravings, Pamphlet Volumes, Unbound Magazines, and books which are valuable on account of their cost, rarity or antiquity.

Applications of Works.
10. Any person wishing to obtain any book for perusal and reference in the Library must first make his selection from the catalogue and then apply for it at the desk of the Librarian. The books thus received must not be taken from the Library, but be returned to the Librarian's desk, otherwise the person shall remain responsible for the books.

Manuscripts.
11. The Librarian shall exercise a proper discrimination as to the delivery of such books as he may judge liable to be injured. Manuscripts, rare and valuable books and plates are excluded from this rule; they will be shown only on special appli-

cation to the Librarian and under such regulations as the circumstances of each case may in his judgment require.

Shelves. 12. No person, except the Librarian or his assistants, shall be permitted to take from any case or shelf or replace therein or thereon, any book, map, or other publication.

Registration. 13. No book shall be taken from the Library until its title and the name of the person taking it have been registered by the Librarian, and a receipt must be given by the person taking the book. No public officer or other person privileged to draw books, shall extend the privilege to others, or take books from the Library for the purpose of loaning them to others.

Damages. 14. Any person taking any book, map or other publication from the Library, shall be liable for all damages done thereto, while in his or her possession, which damage shall be assessed by the Librarian, and paid to him by the person taking such book, map or other publication. The leaves of books must not be turned down and no marks with ink or pencil on the margin or elsewhere will be permitted under the penalty aforesaid.

Books examined. 15. The Librarian or his assistant shall carefully examine each book returned, and if found to have sustained any injury or to have been rendered of less value by being soiled or written in, he shall require the person to whom the same was delivered, to pay the amount of damage or injury done, or otherwise to procure a new copy of equal value, and in the latter case such person shall be entitled to the damaged copy on depositing a new one.

One Book Two Weeks. 16. No person who may be privileged by card from the Speaker of the House to borrow books from the Library, shall be allowed to have in his possession more than one book at any time, or to retain the same longer than two weeks, and all such persons shall return the books so taken when required by the Librarian.

Returned before Opening. 17. All books on loan during the recess of the Legislature excepting such as may be required by the Lieutenant-Governor, Members of the Executive and the Legislative Assembly, the Speaker and the Deputy Heads of Departments, shall be returned at least ten days before the opening of the House. Should the order not be complied with, the person so offending shall forfeit all privileges to the Library.

Borrowers liable. 18. If on notice to any person that the time for which any book has been drawn from the Library by such person has expired, or if any person shall have in his or her possession any book or other article belonging to the Library, and neglect to return such book or other article to the Library for more than three days after such notice, such person shall be liable to pay for such book or books a sum equal to the value of such book or books or other article, which value shall be estimated at the cost of replacing the same.

Sundays. 19. On Sundays during the Session, the Library shall be opened to members only.

No Smoking. 20. Smoking or spitting on the floor or carpet shall not be permitted in any of the Library apartments.

Books desired. 21. A blank book shall be kept on a table or stand accessible to readers, in which may be entered the titles of any books which it may be deemed advisable to procure for the use of the Library.

TABLE OF PRECEDENCE IN CANADA.

The following official table of precedence, for use in Canada, was transmitted by the Queen's Command to the Governor-General of Canada, July 23rd, 1868, and published in the Dominion *Official Gazette:*

1. The Governor-General or officer administering the Government.

2. The senior official in command of the troops, if of the rank of General, and the officer in command of Her Majesty's naval forces on the station, if of the rank of Admiral, their own relative rank being determined by the Queen's Regulations on that subject.

3, 4, 5, 6. The Lieutenant-Governors of the several Provinces of Ontario, of Quebec, of Nova Scotia, and of New Brunswick (and in their appropriate order, the Lieutenant-Governors of Provinces afterwards added to the Dominion).

7. Archbishops and Bishops, according to seniority (of consecration).

8. Members of Cabinet, according to seniority.

9. The Speaker of the Senate.

9a. The Chief Justice of the Supreme Court.

10. The Chief Judges of the Courts of Law and Equity, according to seniority.

11. Members of the Privy Council not of the Cabinet.

12. General Officers of Her Majesty's Army serving in the Dominion, and Officers of the rank of Admiral in the Royal Navy, serving on the British North American Station, and being in the chief command ; the relative rank of such Officers to be determined by the Queen's Regulations.

13. The senior officer in command of the troops, if of the rank of Colonel or Lieutenant-Colonel, and the officer in command of Her Majesty's Naval Forces on the Station, if of equivalent rank ; their own relative rank being determined by the Queen's Regulations.

14. Members of the Senate.

15. Speaker of the House of Commons.

15a. Puisne Judges of the Supreme Court.

16. Puisne Judges of the Courts of Law and Equity, according to seniority.

17. Members of the House of Commons.

18. Members of the Executive Council (Provincial), within their Province.

19. Speaker of the Legislative Council, within his Province.

20. Members of the Legislative Council, within their Province.

21. Speaker of the Legislative Assembly, within his Province.

22. Members of the Legislative Assembly, within their Province.

Her Majesty approved of the adoption of revised regulations in respect to the style and title to be used by the following persons :

Revised regulations as to title

The Governor-General of Canada to be styled " His Excellency."

The Lieutenant-Governor of the Province, to be styled " His Honour."

The Privy Councillors of Canada to be styled " Honourable," and for life.

Senators of Canada, Executive Councillors of the Provinces, the Presidents of the Legislative Councils, and the Speakers of the Houses of Assembly in the Provinces to be severally styled " Honourable," but only during office, and the title not to be continued afterwards.

Gentlemen who were Legislative Councillors at the time of the union are permitted to retain their title of " Honourable " for life, but Legislative Councillors in the Province are not in future to have that title.

Retain title.

Decisions of the Speaker.

DECISIONS OF SPEAKER OF LEGISLATIVE ASSEMBLY OF ONTARIO.

Upon the correct interpretation of the Rules of Order by which the Legislative Assembly is governed, and the prompt and clear exposition of the numerous precedents which form the larger part of parliamentary law, depends the successful accomplishment of the work submitted to it. There are unforseen combinations of circumstances cropping up in nearly every Session, which are seldom amenable to mere rule, and can find solution only in the Practice of the legislative bodies of Canada or Great Britain. Rule 113 of the Assembly of Ontario, and a Rule of the Old Canadian Parliament, which says that: "in all unprovided cases, the rules, usages and forms of the United Kingdom of Great Britain and Ireland, as in force at the time, shall be followed," evidently indicate a recognition of difficulties which cannot be provided for in advance, and must be solved by the larger and wider experience of an older country. But it is advisable that, in so far as possible, the proceedings in any legislative body shall be governed by its own Practices and Precedents. In Ontario these are embodied, to a considerable extent, in the Decisions of the Speakers, who, since Confederation, have occupied the chair of the Legislative Assembly. Easy reference to them, when points of order suddenly arise during debate, will add eminently to their value, and it has been deemed advisable, for that purpose, to collect them from the Journals over which they are scattered, and publish them in collected and readily accessible form. In the following pages, close adherence to the language of the Journals has been maintained where thought necessary for a clearer elucidation of the Decision, and in nearly every instance a full history of each case may be found.

HON. J. STEVENSON. John Stevenson, Esq., Lennox, was the first Speaker elected in the Legislative Assembly, and was called to the Chair 27th December, 1867.

On 10th February, 1868 (page 52 of Journals), he gave his first decision.

Change of names in Preamble of Private Bill. A Private Bill was introduced for the incorporation of the Erie and Niagara Railway Company, which was duly reported by the Committees on Standing Orders and Railways, and amended in the Railway Committee, in the Preamble, by a change of names of Promoters. Exception was taken to these amendments as in excess of the prayer of the Petition on which it was based. The Speaker decided : That as it was manifest that the object of the Petitioners was to obtain authority to build a railway, the change of some of the names in the Preamble did not, in his opinion, require that the Bill should be referred back to the Committee on Standing Orders.

<small>When Amendment cannot be entertained.</small> On 25th November, 1868 (page 39), the second Reading of Bill (No. 24), To alter the Law of Dower, etc., was considered in Committee of the Whole, and reported with amendments. On motion for reception of Report, Mr. Blake moved, "That the Report be not now received, but that it be referred back to Committee of the Whole, with instructions to amend the Bill by expunging so much thereof as destroys the right of Dower in cases in which Dower is by law recoverable." This was put and lost, when Mr. Blake moved that the Report be referred back with instruction to amend the Bill by providing "That so much thereof as destroys the right of Dower, in cases in which Dower is now recoverable, shall not affect existing rights." Objection was taken by Attorney-General Macdonald that the amendment was identical in purpose with the previous amendment already declared lost, and could not therefore be properly received. Mr. Speaker decided : The latter amendment, although differing in construction, is identical in matter with the former, and cannot, therefore, I think, be received.

<small>An Amendment to a substantive Motion.</small> On December 2nd, 1868 (page 40), it was moved : "That in the opinion of this House, it is necessary and expedient, in the interests of Collegiate Education, that some comprehensive scheme be devised and adopted for giving effect to the objects, and for extending the operation of the Act, 16 Vict, cap. 89, in the establishment of a Provincial University, and the affiliation of Colleges to be supported in connection therewith." In amendment it was moved : "That all the words after 'That' in the original resolution be struck out and the following be inserted in lieu thereof : 'While the House recognizes the importance of educational interests it is still of opinion (as expressed by the Act of last Session) that no college or educational institution under the control of any religious denomination shall receive aid

from the public treasury.'" Objection was taken that the amendment contained matter irrelevant to the original motion, and could not therefore be properly received. The Speaker decided as follows: The amendment is, I think, in order, and ought to be received.

When Amendment on Third Reading out of order. On December 3rd, 1868 (page 45), it was moved that the Report of the Whole on Bill (No. 51), be adopted. It was moved, in amendment: That the Report be not now received, but that it be referred back to a Committee of the Whole for the purpose of expunging from the tenth and twenty-second sections of the Act so much as provides for the re-uniting of the City of Toronto and the County of York for judicial purposes. This was lost on a division. On December 8th (page 52), on the motion that Bill (No. 51) be read a third time, it was moved in amendment that it be referred back to Committee with instructions to amend " by expunging so much of section ten and twenty-two as provides for the re-union of the City of Toronto with the County of York for judicial purposes." The Attorney-General objected that the amendment was identical in purpose with that upon which the House had already expressed an opinion, and which could not, therefore, be properly received, and Mr. Speaker decided that : The amendment is not in order and cannot be received.

First section of a Bill must be first considered. On 9th December, 1868 (page 59), the House went into Committee on Bill (No. 88), To provide for the establishment and government of Central District Prisons, when Attorney-General Macdonald moved consideration of the second section of the Bill. Objection was taken by Mr. Blake to the consideration of the second section before the first section had been considered, contending that the Bill must be considered section by section as numbered. The Chairman ruled that the first section should be first considered. An appeal was made to Mr. Speaker, who decided: That the second section may be considered first. An appeal from the decision of the Speaker was made and sustained by a vote of 33 to 29. The House went again into Committee, when the Attorney-General moved the consideration of the first section, *Providing for expenditure.* and objection was then taken to its consideration as it involved the expenditure of money which had not been recommended by the Crown or considered in Committee of the

Whole prior to the introduction of the Bill. The Chairman decided that the consideration of the section was in order, as applying to charges to be hereafter provided for by vote in Committee of Supply.

When question as to the disposal of timber cannot be entertained.

On 14th December, 1868 (pages 66 and 67), Mr. McDougall moved :

1. That with a view to attract immigration into this Province it is expedient to provide that, on and after the first day of April, immediately subsequent to settlement on any lot, the regulations of the Government having been complied with, the locatee of such lot should have the right to cut and dispose of the timber on it, free from any Governmental charges.

2. That the right to cut pine or timber berths during at least ten years, should, subject to the foregoing resolution, be given to the license holders, under such charges for ground rent, duty, etc., and such other provisions as may be made by the Government of this Province.

And objection having been taken by Hon. Attorney-General Macdonald, that the motion could not be entertained without the recommendation of the Lieutenant-Governor having been previously obtained, Mr. Speaker decided : That, as timber affords revenue, no question as to the disposal of the same can be entertained without the approval of the Lieutenant-Governor having been previously obtained.

An appeal was made against the decision of Mr. Speaker, and the Speaker's decision was sustained by a vote of 40 to 28.

Free distribution of Statutes to Magistrates.

On 14th December, 1868 (page 67), it was moved that in the opinion of the House, it is expedient that the Statutes enacted by this House be furnished free of charge to all Magistrates who are duly qualified. Objection was taken by Attorney-General Macdonald that the motion, as it affected revenue, could not be entertained. The Speaker decided that the motion was out of order.

Interference with collection of revenue from Crown lands objected to.

On 17th December, 1868 (page 73), Mr. Lauder moved a lengthy resolution of which the gist was that it is not expedient to issue a general order directing payment of arrears upon Crown Lands until a re-valuation is made. The Commissioner of Crown Lands objected to the notice as affecting revenue, and the Speaker reserved his decision.

On 12th January, 1869 (page 97), during a debate on a Resolution from Committee of Supply, objection was taken by Mr. Ferguson to words spoken by Mr. Blake in debate as not having reference to the Resolution before the House, and as therefore out of order. Mr. Speaker decided : That as an arrangement had been made with the leave of the House, that Mr. Blake might, when this resolution came up, speak on the general policy of the Executive, Mr. Blake was in order.

<small>Arrangement made by House tantamount to an order.</small>

On 19th January, 1869 (page 113), a motion was made to recommit Bill (No. 90), respecting Tavern and Shop Licenses, for the purpose of inserting the following amendment : " By striking out all that denies an appeal from prosecutions and convictions under said Bill to and before the Chairman of the Quarter Sessions, as set forth in section thirty-six." Objection was taken, and Mr. Speaker decided : That the amendment is not in order as being indefinite and not conveying accurate instructions to the Committee as to the particular amendments to be made, and cannot therefore be entertained.

<small>An Amendment conveying accurate instructions to a Committee.</small>

Another amendment was proposed, reading : " By striking out all the words after ' Act ' in the fourth line to the word ' may ' in the sixth line of the thirty-sixth section," and objection was taken, when the Speaker decided : That the amendment, although similar in wording, differs in fact from the previous motion, and is in order, and may therefore be entertained.

<small>Amendment similar in wording, but differing in fact from one rejected in order.</small>

On 9th Nov., 1869 (page 14), objection was taken to the reception of a Petition from the Huron and Ontario Ship Canal Company, inasmuch as it had no definite prayer, and sought, if anything, a grant from the Crown without previous recommendation from the Lieutenant-Governor. The Speaker decided as follows : This Petition cannot be received, so long as the Rule of this House remains in force, whereby no Petition can be received praying for a grant not previously recommended by the Crown. The decision was appealed against, but sustained by a vote of 46 to 13.

<small>No Petition can be received praying for a grant not previously recommended by the Crown.</small>

On 8th Dec., 1869 (page 81), the Order of the Day for the second reading of Bill (No. 97), to amend the Ontario Medical

Amendment to the Ontario Medical Act, a Public Bill. Act having been read, objection was taken that the Bill was of the nature of a Private Bill and required Notices. The Speaker reserved his decision, but on 13th Dec. (page 88), declared the Bill to be of a public nature : whereupon the Bill was read a second time, and referred to a Select Committee.

On 16th Dec., 1869 (page 107), the Order of the Day for the Second Reading of Bill (No. 80) to make the Benchers of the Law Society elective by the Bar thereof, having been read, objection was taken to the Bill as of the nature of a Private Bill and requiring Notices. The Speaker decided : That the Bill was of a private nature and could not be otherwise entertained : whereupon the order was discharged and the Bill withdrawn.

Bill to make Benchers of Law Society elective by Bar thereof a Private Bill.

On 22nd Dec., 1869 (page 152), a motion was made to receive the Report of the Whole on a Bill to amend the Assessment Act. A division was had and objection was taken to the votes of certain honourable gentlemen on the ground that they had a direct pecuniary interest in the matter before the House, and were, therefore, not entitled to vote. The Speaker decided : That the Bill before the House was of a public nature, and not such as was contemplated by Rule 16 of the House.

Votes of certain Members on an Assessment Bill objected to.

On 22nd Dec., 1869 (page 157), objection was taken to a proposition to strike out a clause of a Private Bill, on the Third Reading, because no Notice had been given of such Amendment. Mr. Speaker decided : That so important an Amendment could not be entertained without previous notice given.

Notice of Amendment to Private Bill.

A further Amendment was proposed to omit certain words from said Bill and insert others, when Mr. Speaker decided that the Amendment was not in order for want of Notice.

On 27th January, 1871 (page 86), objection was taken to further consideration of Bill (No. 20), to regulate the Sale of Poisons, and respecting Chemists, Druggists and Apothecaries, as interfering with the Regulation of Trade and Commerce, and therefore beyond the powers of the Provincial Legislature, as prescribed by the B. N. A. Act, 1867. The Speaker decided : That the regulations for the sale of the articles named in

The regulation of the Sale of Poisons.

the Bill were not of such a nature as to exceed the powers of the Provincial Legislature.

On 8th Feb., 1871 (page 133), the House resolved itself into a Committee to consider Bill (No. 51) to amend the Assessment Act, and, after some time spent therein, the Committee rose without reporting, and the Speaker resumed the chair. On Feb. 9th (page 137), it was moved : That this House will at its next sitting to-day again resolve itself into a Committee to consider Bill (No. 51), and objection was taken by the Attorney-General, inasmuch as the Committee to whom the Bill had been referred had risen without reporting, and that it was contrary to precedent that the Bill shall again appear on the order paper. The Speaker reserved his decision. On 10th Feb. (page 138), the Speaker announced his decision as follows : The question, whether the fact of a Committee having risen without reporting forbids a motion to replace the measure on the Order Book to be entertained, does not appear to have been tested in Canada, and there is not any Rule of this House specially applicable to the case. But No. 102 of the Rules of this House provides that, in all unprovided cases, the rules, usages and forms of the House of Commons of Great Britain and Ireland shall be followed, and I find that the House of Commons does not admit that the fact of a Committee having risen without reporting is sufficient to take the Bill out of the control of the House. I therefore decide that the motion of the member for South Perth is in order, and that it is competent for this House to order that the Bill be replaced on the Order Book, in its proper place.

Motion for replacing a measure upon the Orders of Day.

It was therefore *Resolved*, that this House will, at its next sitting to-day, again resolve itself into a Committee to consider Bill (No. 51), to amend the Assessment Act of Ontario.

It may be interesting to note at this point that on 20th Feb., 1868, Bill (No. 10), was under consideration in Committee of the Whole, when the motion was made "that the Committee do now rise," which was carried on a division. No further action, with respect to the Bill, was taken.

Committee rising without Report.

On 2nd March, 1868, Bill (No. 92) was being considered in Committee of Whole, when the Committee rose without reporting, and the Bill was not further proceeded with.

On 9th Feb., 1871, the day before the Speaker gave his decision relative to Bill (No. 51), the House went into Committee on Bill (No. 124) for Preventing Corrupt Practices at Municipal Elections, and rose without report. The Bill did not go further.

On 28th March, 1873, the House was in Committee on Bill (No. 10), respecting the seizure and attachment of Equitable Interests, and failed to report. The Bill was allowed to drop.

On 4th March, 1881, the House considered Bill (No. 131), respecting Market Fees, and failed to report, and the Bill fell through.

On 31st January, 1883, the House, in Committee, considered Bill (No. 25), to amend the Synod and Rectory Sales Acts affecting the Diocese of Toronto, and rose without reporting. The Bill was not proceeded with.

On 24th March, 1884, the House resolved itself into Committee on Bill (No. 186), respecting the Study of Anatomy, but did not report. No attempt was made to revive the Bill.

HON. R. W. SCOTT. Hon. Richard William Scott, Ottawa, was elected Speaker of the Second Legislature, 7th December, 1871.

On 11th Dec., 1871 (page 18), on the motion for an Address in reply to the Speech from the Throne, Mr. Blake moved an amendment seeking to add further words to the first paragraph, and declaring it inexpedient to place so large a sum as $1,500,000 at the disposition of the Executive without a vote of this House appropriating the same to particular railway works. Mr. McCall moved that the following words be added to the proposed amendment : "That, inasmuch as one-tenth of the Constituencies of this Province remain at this time unrepresented in this House by reason of six of the members elected at the last election, having had their elections declared void, and a seventh having become vacant by reason of a double return, and an eighth by reason of the resignation of the member elect thereto, *it is inexpedient further to consider the said amendment*, until the said Constituencies are duly represented on the floor of this House." This was obviously out of order, as being defective in form and incongruous. But no exception was taken to it, on the ground of defective form, and it was voted down. The first paragraph of the address was amended by the addition of Mr. Blake's amendment, and when the paragraph was put as amended, Mr. Mackenzie

When amendment cannot be put.

moved that the following words be added thereto: "And we inform your Excellency that we have no confidence in a Ministry which is attempting to carry out, in reference to the control of the said fund of $1,500,000, an usurpation fraught with danger to public liberty and Constitutional Government." Mr. Macdonald, of Leeds (page 24), offered an amendment to this proposed Amendment, which repeated the whole of the words contained in Mr. McCall's rejected Amendment from the beginning thereof to and inclusive of the words "elected thereto," and then introduced the following new matter: "And that, inasmuch as the Government has declared that the Railway Fund is intact, and that it will not, *in consideration of the opinion expressed by this House in passing the said Amendment*, make any appropriation from the said fund without the same having been first submitted to Parliament, it is unfair to consider any motion declaring a want of confidence in your Excellency's present advisers, until the said Constituencies are duly represented in this House." No exception was taken to the words placed here in italics, although they would have been obviously incompatible with the amended paragraph, if adopted, and defective in form, but Mr. Speaker declared that the motion was in purport with one on which, during the present debate, the House had expressed its opinion, and that it would be irregular now again to submit this motion.

HON. JAMES GEORGE CURRIE.
Hon. James George Currie, Welland, was elected Speaker 21st December, 1871.

A motion must correspond with its notice.
On 25th Jan., 1872 (page 66), a motion was made for a Select Committee, and objection was taken thereto, and the Speaker decided: That the motion was not in order, inasmuch as it did not correspond with the notice of motion given by the Member who now introduced it.

Bill to unite the County of Perth for registration purposes a Private Bill.
On the 16th February, 1872 (page 159), a motion was made for leave to introduce a Bill intituled "An Act to unite the County of Perth for Registration purposes," and objection was taken to the Bill as being of the nature of a Private Bill. The Speaker decided: That the Bill was a Private Bill, and had not been properly introduced by notice or petition. An Act of a similar character, 27 Vict., chap. 35, had been introduced and passed as a Private Bill. An appeal was made against

the decision of the Speaker, but his decision was sustained by the House.

On the 24th February, 1872 (page 210), on a motion that a report of Committee on resolutions respecting remissions to settlers in certain free grant townships be now received, it was moved in amendment, "That the report be not now received, but that the resolution be referred to a Committee of the Whole, with instructions to amend the same by striking out of the first resolution the words 'save and except the townships of Alice, Gratton, Wilberforce and Minden.'" The Speaker decided : That the Amendment could not be entertained as it involved the necessity of an expenditure of public money without the approval of His Excellency the Lieutenant-Governor having been obtained.

<small>When Amendment cannot be entertained.</small>

On 28th February, 1872 (page 152), on the Order of the Day for receiving report of Committee of Whole on Bill (No. 152), To make further provision in aid of Railways, an amendment was moved to refer the Bill back for the purpose of providing that the Railway Aid and Subsidy Fund be so distributed as to do justice to the municipalities which have already voted large bonuses without knowledge that such fund was to be created. The Speaker decided that the Amendment was not in order, inasmuch as, if carried, the grant of money recommended by His Excellency the Lieutenant-Governor would be applied to purposes not contemplated by the resolution, to which the approval of His Excellency was announced.

<small>When Amendment cannot be passed.</small>

On 20th January, 1873 (page 38), leave was asked to introduce a Bill entitled "An Act to authorize a further expenditure of public money for Drainage Works." Objection was taken and the Speaker decided : That the Bill, as it necessitates an expenditure of public money, cannot be properly introduced until the approval of His Excellency the Lieutenant-Governor has been communicated to the House.

<small>Expenditure of public moneys must have approval of Lieut.-Gov.</small>

On 21st Jan. 1873 (page 41), objection was taken to the reception of a petition praying for an Act prohibiting the manufacture and sale of intoxicating liquors, which petition seeks for legislation affecting trade and commerce, a subject solely within the powers of the Legislature of the Dominion of Canada. The Speaker decided : That there is no

<small>Petition re prohibiting sale and use of intoxicating liquors.</small>

rule of the House infringed by the reception of the Petition ; the power of the Ontario Legislature to interfere in the matter is not at present in question.

On 21st Jan., 1873 (page 44), the Order for the Second Reading of Bill (No. 17), Respecting the University of Toronto was read, when objection was taken to the Second Reading as it necessitates an expenditure of public money, to which expenditure the approval of His Excellency the Lieutenant-Governor was necessary. The Speaker decided : That with reference to clause 51 no burden is thereby imposed or sought to be imposed on the consolidated revenue of the Province ; and with reference to clause 52 the amount of salary to be granted is left a blank ; therefore the Bill is in order.

Bill is in order which leaves amount of salary in blank.

On 16th March, 1873 (page 219), the Order for Second Reading of Bill (No. 174), To prohibit the sale of intoxicating liquors as a beverage in Ontario was read, and objection was taken to the Bill as interfering with trade and commerce. The Speaker decided : I find that the powers of the Legislature of Ontario were limited by the 90th section of the British America Act, and I have unwillingly come to the conclusion that the House has not the power to pass the Bill now before it.

Bill to prohibit sale of intoxicating liquors as a beverage not within powers of Legislature.

On 19th March, 1873 (page 263), the Order to go into Committee to consider Bill (No. 167) To amend the Act intituled An Act to amend the Act to incorporate the Fenelon Falls Railway Company was read, and objection was taken to the Bill as containing provisions not prayed for in the petition on which the Bill is founded. Mr. Speaker reserved his decision. On the 20th March (page 297), the Speaker gave his decision as follows : It appears that the Bill (No. 167), as reported by the Committee on Railways, contains a section, inserted by that Committee, not sought for by the Petition, or embraced in the notice of application for the Act. I am of the opinion that the proper course to pursue is to refer the Bill back to the Committee on Standing Orders to report as to the propriety of the suspension of Rule No. 57 in respect to the section or sections added to the Bill by the Committee on Railways, and for the House to proceed upon such report. On 21st March (page 297), the Standing Orders

A Bill amended in Railway Committee objected to.

Committee reported that they had, as directed by the House, examined the notices of application for the said Act, the Petition praying for amendments and the Bill founded thereon, and we find that the Bill embraces amendments of which no notice was given to the parties interested therein, prior to the introduction of the said Bill, but, after consideration, recommend that the Rules of the House, so far as they affect the said amendments, be suspended. On 22nd March (page 307) objection was taken to the report of the Committee on Standing Orders, and the Speaker decided: That the Order of the House to the Committee was, that the Bill was to be referred back to the Committee, with instructions to report to this House as to the propriety of the suspension of Rule No. 51, in respect to the sections added to the Bill by the Committee on Railways ; and the Committee, having strictly complied with the Order of the House, the Report is in order.

HON. R. M. WELLS. Rupert Mearse Wells, Esq., South Bruce, was elected Speaker 7th Jan., 1874.

On 9th Jan., 1874 (pages 10, 12), an amendment was moved to the 5th paragraph of the Address, which, while declaring the willingness of the House to consider a general incorporation Act for benevolent and other societies, expressed regret that two Bills for the incorporation of the Loyal Orange Association, passed in the previous session, had been reserved for the assent of the Governor-General. An amendment to this proposed amendment was moved which struck out all relative to the reservation of the Bill, and set forth that we beg to assure your Excellency that in advising your Excellency's predecessor to reserve certain Bills for the special incorporation of Orange Societies for the signification of the pleasure of his Excellency the Governor-General, the Executive Council of the Province was justified by Constitutional usage. This was carried by a vote of 38 to 24. When the twelfth paragraph was read (page 12) an amendment was moved expressing regret that his Excellency was advised to reserve, for the consideration of his Excellency the Governor-General, two Bills passed by this House, after full discussion and due deliberation, for the incorporation of the Loyal Orange Association, " in place of advising his Excellency to sanction the same, and leave to the Governor-General the responsibility, under the constitution, of

When amendment cannot be submitted.

disallowing such Bills." Objection was taken to the amendment, and the Speaker decided: That the amendment being substantially the same as the motion made in amendment to the fifth paragraph of the Address, and which has already been debated by and decided on by the House, is out of order and cannot be entertained.

Petition for grant from Public Treasury. On 14th Jan., 1874 (page 19), a motion that a Petition of John Harris and others praying for a grant from the Public Treasury in aid of St. Joseph's Hospital and Asylum at Guelph be now received and read, Mr. Speaker decided: That as the Petition asked for a grant of public money, without the consent from the Crown having been previously obtained and announced to this House, the Petition could not be received.

The Journals contain many instances of rejection of Petitions asking aid, but it will be unnecessary to quote them. Petitions of this character are frequently presented, but are not "read and received," so that their object is not stated in the Journals. They ought to be addressed to His Honor the Lieutenant-Governor in Council.

An Address for information beyond control of Provincial Government. On 4th February, 1874 (page 31), a motion was made for an Address to the Lieutenant-Governor, praying for a statement showing the number of officers and servants in the employment of the Government in the Departments and House, when an amendment was moved for the addition of words asking for a similar return of employees of the Governments of the Dominion and of Quebec. Objection was taken to the amendment, and Mr. Speaker decided: That he could not assume that it was not within the power of the Government to furnish the information sought for in the amendment, and that it was therefore in order.

A question passed in the negative cannot be again proposed. On 11th February, 1874 (page 47), a motion was made that the name of Mr. Merrick be added to the Standing Committee on Public Accounts. It was negatived on a division by 36 to 31. On 4th March (page 104), it was moved that the name of Hon. Mr. Fraser be placed on the Committee on Public Accounts, in the room of Hon. Attorney-General Mowat. On 5th March (page 107), it was moved in amendment that the words "and Mr. Merrick" be added after the word "Fraser." The Speaker decided: That the Amendment is out of order, as it is contrary to the usage and practice of the House that a question which had passed in the negative should again be proposed during the same Session. It was again moved in Amendment that the words " Mr. Hodgins and Mr. Meredith " be inserted in the motion after the word " Fraser." After some time, it was moved "That the question be now put."

<small>When previous question cannot be put.</small>

Mr. Speaker decided: That as the previous question cannot be put when an amendment is under consideration, the motion is out of order.

<small>The previous question.</small>

The amendment was put and lost, and it was moved " That the Question be now put." It was moved " That this House do now adjourn." The motion for adjournment was put and lost, and the motion " That the Question be now put " was carried, when the original motion was put and carried.

<small>No grant of money, for a specific purpose, can be put.</small>

On 11th March, 1874 (page 137), it was moved, " That, in the opinion of this House, it is expedient that provision be made by which municipalities entitled to payments under the Municipal Loan Fund Act of 1873 shall be permitted to extend their appropriations in accordance with the wishes of the ratepayers, as expressed through their councils, or by-laws, to be passed and approved of by them." Objection was taken that the motion was contrary to the express language of the *British North America Act* of 1867, section 54, and the Speaker reserved his decision, which he gave 23rd March (page 255). The Order of the Day having been read for resuming the debate on the proposed resolution and amendments, the Speaker said; The rule is perfectly clear that no important variation can be made in the purposes for which a grant of money, recommended by the Crown, has been made, without a fresh recommendation. By the English practice it is said to be possible to frame an abstract resolution on the subject of duties without going into Committee; but that is not regular. No attempt has been made in this resolution to frame it so as to take it out of the ordinary rule. I see no difference whatever between such an important change in the distribution of the fund as is now contemplated, and a resolution which would assume to appropriate any part of the public revenue. The one is just as objectionable in principle as the other, and the same reasoning as applicable to one as to the other throughout all the cases which I have consulted. But it is said that this resolution only proposes an abstract opinion. Sir Erskine May says that such resolutions have been allowed, but he proceeds to say that "they are objectionable, and being an evasion of a wholesome rule, are discouraged as much as possible." Mr. Todd says that "abstract resolutions in regard to particular branches of taxation have been submitted to the House by private members, but they have been uniformly resisted as being inexpedient and impolitic." These abstract resolutions are, in fact, growing more and more into disfavour in England, as tending to embarrass the executive, etc. The language of the 54th section of the British North America Act seems also to be more stringent than the rule in England. " It shall not be lawful for the House to adopt or pass any vote, resolution, address or Bill for the appropriation of any part of the public revenue, or of any tax or impost to any purpose that has not been first recommended," etc. But whatever might have been my own opinion upon this subject, I consider myself bound by a precedent which I find in the Journals of this House (1868, page 66) An abstract resolution was proposed affecting the revenue from timber. The Attorney-General, Macdonald, objected that it could not be entertained without the recommendation of His Excellency. A long discussion followed, in which the propriety of permitting abstract resolutions was fully discussed. The Speaker ruled against the resolution, and upon an appeal to the House his ruling was sustained. Believing, as I do, that there is in principle no difference between a resolution which proposes a grant of money, and one which proposes to apply a grant already made to an entirely different purpose from that recommended by the Crown, and finding an express decision not only by the Speaker but of the House itself against such motions, and finding also that abstract resolutions are so much condemned and discouraged in England, I cannot do otherwise than rule in favour of the objection.

Abstract resolutions on taxation inadvisable.

A case in point.

On 12th March, 1874 (page 154, 155), an amendment was moved to the question that " Mr. Speaker do now leave the Chair," for the purpose of going into a Committee of Supply, when an amendment to the Amendment was proposed. Objection was taken and the Speaker decided: That the rule is well settled in this country that it is not in order to

Amendment to an Amendment to go into a Committee of supply not in order.

move an amendment to an Amendment to the motion to go into Supply. Mr. Speaker Smith gave two contradictory decisions upon the question, but Mr. Speaker Wallbridge afterwards gave a more formal decision, expressly stating his opinion to be that, according to the English practice, only one amendment can be moved. But it is hardly accurate to say that only one amendment can, in England, be moved to a motion to go into Supply. It is true that, if the first amendment is lost, no further amendment can be moved; but it is also true that, if the amendment is carried, further amendments can be moved. The reason why no further amendment can be moved when the first is negatived is, that the form of putting the question, "shall the words proposed to be left out stand part of the question" entirely precludes it. If that question is carried, the House has declared that the original question shall stand unaltered, and it is therefore irregular to propose any amendment. It must also be borne in mind that under no circumstances can an amendment to an amendment be moved in England until the first amendment has been carried, and so has become a substantive motion. I recognize the importance to the minority of having some one occasion—and going into Supply being the recognized time for stating grievances, is no doubt the most convenient time—when they may be permitted to offer, for the consideration of the House, a proposition, with the assurance that it shall not be superseded by an amendment. But it must be remembered that they have no such privilege in England, for no matter what the amendment may be, the question first put to the House is "That the Speaker do now leave the Chair." It is perfectly clear, therefore, that this rule, which has been adopted in this country, is not justified by Parliamentary practice in England. But the rule has been so firmly settled, so frequently acted upon, and so well recognized by all parties, and by all Parliaments in this country, that I cannot take upon myself the responsibility of reversing it, without an express resolution of this House, and I therefore hold the proposed amendment to the Amendment to be out of order.

On 21st March, 1874 (page 240), on the Order of the Day for the consideration of the amendments made in Committee on Bill (No. 11), Respecting the Railway Fund and the Railway Subsidy Fund, having been read, Mr. Rykert took objections to the introduction of any clause in the Bill altering the amount to be paid to any railway under Railway Subsidy Act, as follows :

Where new recommendation not required.   1st. Because the Railway Subsidy Act having provided that no less than $120 or more than $240 per mile per annum shall be paid any railway company it is not competent for this House, by a subsequent Act, to insert a clause providing for the payment of any greater sum than $240 out of the said fund without a recommendation from the Crown.

2nd. That in no case can a motion or Act of Parliament interfere with the distribution of public money already voted, unless recommended by the Crown.

The Speaker decided : The rule, no doubt, is that no new duties can be imposed, nor can the public expenditure be increased, unless the same has been recommended by a message from His Excellency. In the present case there is no new duty imposed, nor is the public expenditure increased ; but it is objected that the Bill proposes a material variation in the mode of distributing the public moneys from that which has been recommended. The cases cited from Laperriere's decisions, No. 50, 54, 112 and 161, are quite decisive upon that point : but they do not decide that a recommendation is necessary for the purpose of enabling Parliament to alter the mode of distributing the fund in the manner proposed by this Bill. In the present case two funds have been appropriated in aid of railways, one payable *en bloc*, the other by way of an annual payment for twenty years. This Bill merely proposes to declare what sum per mile, by way of an annual grant for twenty years, shall be equivalent to a present grant of $2,000 per mile, etc., and gives the Governor-in-Council power to pay out of either fund at his option. There is here no variation of the fund, no change in the purpose for which it was originally intended, and I, therefore, overrule the question of order.

Motion to commit to a future expenditure out of order.   On 11th December, 1874 (page 125), the House considered the fourth resolution for Committee of Supply, respecting Hospitals and Charities, when it was moved that the following words be added thereto: This House, while concurring in the Resolution, desires to express the opinion that so long as the policy of granting Provincial aid to charitable institutions, of the character of those mentioned in the schedules to the

"Charity Aid Act of 1874" continues, justice demands that such aid should not be confined to the institutions mentioned in the said schedules, but that it should be extended to other institutions of the like character and usefulness, which have come into existence since the passing of the Act.

Objection was made to the motion as being out of order, on the ground that it contemplates a further grant of public money without the consent of the Crown ; but no exception was taken to the expressed concurrence of the House in the Resolution, on the ground that it partook of the character of the Previous Question.

The Speaker decided : That this Motion seeks to commit the House to a future expenditure of public money. There are in the Journals numerous instances of abstract resolutions of this sort, but the current of modern decision has been against them. MAY says that such resolutions have grown into disfavour, and should be discouraged. I feel bound to follow my decision of last Session upon this subject, following a decision confirmed by this House upon appeal in 1869 as to the Crown Timber dues. The effect of these decisions is practically to put an end to abstract resolutions of this character, and I therefore feel bound to rule this Motion out of order.

Notice to a Private Bill required. On 27th January, 1876 (page 184), on the Motion for Third Reading of a Private Bill, an important Amendment was moved, of which no notice had been given. Objection was taken thereto and the Speaker decided : That the Amendment was not in order, the notice required by Rule 67 not having been given.

A bill fixing the date for meeting of the Legislature, an interference with Prerogative of Crown. On 3rd February, 1876 (page 210), the Order of the Day for the Second Reading of Bill (No. 147), to fix and declare the period of the annual meeting of the Legislative Assembly of Ontario having been read, the Hon. Mr. Fraser took exception to the Bill on the ground that it was unconstitutional, and the Speaker decided : That the Bill interferred with the Prerogative of the Crown, and could not be proceeded with.

Amendment to divert Public Revenue out of order. On 7th February, 1876 (page 228), on the Order for Third Reading of Bill (No. 158), to amend the law respecting the sale of Fermented or Spirituous Liquors, it was moved that the following words be added to the Motion : That this House cannot help expressing regret that the Lieutenant-Governor has not been advised to recommend to the House that, as the issue of licenses is by the Bill restricted, and the revenue of the Municipalities thereby lessened, the whole amount payable for licenses, less the expenses incurred by the Government in respect thereof, should be paid by the Government to the Treasurers of the Municipalities for the use of such Municipalities. The Speaker decided that it was out of order.

When an amendment to an amendment out of order. On 14th February, 1877 (page 141), upon the reading of the fiftieth Resolution respecting Unforeseen and Unprovided Expenses, it was moved in amendment "that the sum be reduced to twenty thousand dollars, so that the large sum of fifty thousand dollars may not be left to be expended at the sole discretion of the Executive Government." It was moved in amendment "that all the words after the word 'That' be struck out and the following substituted therefor : 'this House is of opinion that the experience of former Governments of this Province shows that the sum now to be granted is required by the Public Service, and that the said Resolution be concurred in.'" Objection was taken to the Amendment by the Hon. Mr. Cameron as merely affirming the original Motion. The Speaker decided : Referring to a case which occurred in 1873, when, upon a Motion for the Third Reading of a Bill, an amendment to an Amendment was moved concluding with the words "and that the Bill be now read a third time," he decided that if such an Amendment were carried it would preclude all further Amendments. Such a Motion differed in no way from "the previous question," and even that Motion could not be moved upon an Amendment. Mr. Cameron's objection must therefore prevail.

Although the decision of Mr. Speaker was not objected to by the House, the Practice of the Assembly, both before and since it was given, has been in direct opposition to it. As illustrations of this see Journals for following years, and at pages specified : 1878, pages 145, 150, 151, 153, 158 ; 1879, pages 169, 184, 194, 195, 197, 198 ; 1880, pages 139, 153, 157 ; 1881, pages 155, 159 · 1883, pages 119, 133 ; 1885, pages 137, 156, 157, 158 ; 1887, page 138 ; 1886, page

154; 1893, page 184. Similar amendments have been moved, without objections, since the latter date.

On 15th February, 1877 (page 14), on the Motion for Third Reading of Bill (No. 103), to give the right of voting to Farmers' Sons in certain cases, an Amendment was proposed to strike out all the words after the word "That" and to substitute others, declaring that to confer the privilege of the franchise upon them, solely in right of their fathers' property, would be to confer special privileges upon them. The question of order was raised that no Amendment could be moved to the Third Reading of a Bill except an amendment relating to time. The House had ordered the Bill to be read the third time to-day, and no question touching the merits of the Bill could now be raised. Mr. Speaker referred to MAY, page 487, and decided: That it is competent for any member who desires to place on record any special reasons for not agreeing to the Second or Third Reading of a Bill, to move as an Amendment to the question a Resolution declaratory of some principle adverse to or differing from the principle of the Bill, or otherwise opposed to its progress. There are numerous modern instances of such amendments, therefore the Amendment is in order.

When Amendment may be moved to Third Reading.

On the 19th February, 1877 (page 149), on the Order of the Day for the House to resolve itself into a Committee on Bill (No. 53), respecting the Street Railway Company, the Hon. Mr. Fraser took objection to the Bill as containing conditions in excess of the original notices, and asked Mr. Speaker to refer the Bill back to the Committee on Standing Orders, for the purpose of reporting as to the sufficiency of the notice. The Speaker doubted whether he had power to make an arbitrary order of that sort. But, even if his power were undoubted, he would hesitate to exercise it at this late period of the Session, unless forced upon him by clear and distinct authority. He should prefer to follow the course adopted in a case which is reported in the Journals of Canada, 1868 (page 242), where, upon a similar objection being taken, it was, by direction of the Speaker, moved as an Amendment: That the Bill be referred back to the Committee on Standing Orders, with instructions to report, etc. That is also the course adopted in many other cases reported in the

Bill amended in Private Bills Committte referred to Committee on Standing Orders.

Journals. In this way the matter is fully discussed and the House has no difficulty in arriving at an intelligent decision. It is open to any Member to make a similar Motion in the present case by way of Amendment to the Motion which has been put from the Chair.

An Amendment to the effect suggested was put and lost.

When a Debate upon a Motion cannot be entered upon.

On 22nd February, 1877 (page 160), the House resolved to go into Committee to-morrow on certain proposed Resolutions relating to a Railway Subsidy Fund. The Hon. Mr. Cameron proceeding to speak to the Resolutions, an objection was taken, and the Speaker decided : That if any Motion be made in the House involving a charge upon the people, the debate shall not be presently entered upon, but shall be adjourned until a future day.

Abstract Resolutions affecting Revenue.

On 27th February, 1877 (page 174), on resumption of debate on Resolutions respecting Railway Aid, it was moved in Amendment of Motion to agree that the following be added thereto : "This House regrets that the Government has not recommended for the consideration of the people's representatives the expediency of granting further aid to the Toronto, Grey and Bruce Railway, in respect of the portion of the line between Weston and Orangeville, which portion has not heretofore received Government aid."

The Speaker said that this was an Abstract Resolution, tending to an appropriation of part of the Public Revenue. The question of the right of private members to move abstract resolutions of a certain character seems to have been decided in a case reported in this House, 1868-8, p. 67, when a Motion that it was expedient to attract immigration into this Province by granting certain privileges as to cutting and disposing of timber was ruled out of order, not only by the Speaker, but, on appeal, by the House. By a reference to the *Globe* report, it will be found that the question of Abstract Resolutions upon matters affecting the Revenue was fully discussed. See also 7 Jour. *Ont.*, 255 ; 8 *ibid*, 125 ; see also 1 *Todd*, p. 252, *May*, p. 585, 161 *Hans*, 1448 ; 205 *ibid*, 394. The form of the present Motion—expressing regret, etc.—differs from those referred to, and perhaps involves other considerations. At all events the matter was of so much importance, that, with the permission of the

House, he would postpone further consideration of it until the Third Reading of the Bill, when the same Amendment could be moved.*

<small>No Amendment to Private Bill on its Third Reading without notice.</small>
On 12th, February, 1877 (page 128), the Order of the Day for the Third Reading of Bill (No. 42), respecting the Credit Valley Railway Company having been read, it was sought to amend by adding certain words to a clause therein. Objection was taken that the proposed Amendment was irregular for want of notice. The Speaker decided : That as no notice had been given, he sustained the objection.

<small>When amendment out of order.</small>
On 6th March, 1878 (page 156), the Speaker ruled a proposed amendment out of order as identical with a question upon which the House had, during the Session, pronounced an opinion.

On 12th February, 1878 (pages 79-80), the Order of the Day for the Second Reading of Bill (No. 87), Respecting the Magistracy <small>Amendment must relate to some provision of the Bill.</small> having been read, it was moved in amendment that all the words after "That" be struck out, and the following inserted in lieu thereof : " In the opinion of this House it is inexpedient to authorize the appointment of Police Magistrates in the Counties for the purpose of enforcing any special law on the ground that the existing Magistracy is either unable or unwilling to act ; that no sufficient proof of such unwillingness or misconduct has been laid before this House ; that the proper course for the Government to pursue in such a case is to suspend or dismiss the offending Magistrate, and not to supersede the whole Bench of Magistrates in the County, by a special appointee of the Government, with instructions to fine, imprison and punish a particular class of delinquents against whom the Government of the day may entertain a special dislike or enmity."

And objection having been taken to such an amendment at this stage of the Bill, the Speaker said : "That the first part of the Amendment relating to the appointing of Police Magistrates in Counties was undoubtedly in order. Upon the second or third reading of a Bill resolutions may be moved declaratory of any principle adverse to the Bill, or opposed to its further progress ; numer-

---

*The Amendment was not moved at the Third Reading, and no decision upon the question of order was therefore given.

ous instances of such resolutions are to be found in the Journals, both in England and in this country. But it is doubtful whether the remainder of the amendment is in order, inasmuch as it does not relate to any provision of the Bill, but rather to matters which arose during the argument.

On 18th February, 1879 (pages 105, 109), Mr. Clarke (Wellington), reported from Committee of the Whole : That Mr. Bell having proposed to read a letter, or portion of a letter, upon his own responsibility as to contents, Mr. Bethune objected, for the following reason : That no member of this House has a right to read a letter unless prepared to read the whole of the document, and so place the House in possession of the whole of the said letter, including the signature; and that the Chairman having ruled against the objection, the Committee had appealed against the decision to the House.

<small>Members reading letters without signature must assume responsibility for contents.</small>

A debate arose which was adjourned until to-morrow.

On 19th February (page 109), the Order of the Day for resuming the Debate relative to the appeal to the House from the Committee of the Whole House, on the 18th, having been read, the Debate was resumed ; and, after some time, the decision of the Chairman, Mr. Clarke (Wellington), was sustained by the House. (See MAY upon similar point, p. 379, edition, 1883).

On 7th March, 1879 (page 181), a motion was made to refer back a Resolution to Committee of Supply with instructions to strike out the item of $400, being the salary of the Clerk of the Crown in Chancery, no good reason being shewn for the continuance of that officer in his present capacity, the opinion of this House being that the light duties of the office should be attached, at a reduced figure, to the office of the Clerk Assistant of the House.

<small>No interference with expenditure of public money recommended by Crown.</small>

An objection being taken to the amendment, on the ground that it interfered with an expenditure of public money recommended by the Crown, the Speaker decided that the amendment was out of order.

<small>Ibid.</small>

On the 8th March, 1879 (page 194), an amendment was moved for the purpose of recommitting a Resolution with instructions to reduce the salary of the Superintendent of Industries. The Speaker decided that the motion was not in order.

HON. CHARLES CLARKE, Charles Clarke, Esq., Centre Wellington, was elected Speaker, 7th Jan., 1880.

Advisers of Lieutenant-Governor responsible for communications on matters of Supply. On 27th February, 1880 (page 111), on a motion for Committee of Supply, it was moved in amendment that the following words be added to the main motion: "And this House, desiring to comply with the expressed wish of His Honour the Lieutenant-Governor in that behalf, directs the Committee of Supply to reduce the proposed item of $5,571 22, for the payment re visit of His Honour to the Northwest, etc., by the sum of three hundred and fifty dollars, which last mentioned sum appears to be more than sufficient to cover any of the said expenses that might be considered personal."

Mr. Morris objected to the proposed amendment as being irregular, in that it referred to an expressed wish of His Honour, the Lieutenant-Governor, made to the House in a private letter, whereas any such communication should have been made through a responsible Minister of the Crown, and recorded on the Journals of the House.

The Attorney-General, by command of the Lieutenant-Governor, informed the House that the Lieutenant-Governor desires that the Committee of Supply do reduce the proposed item of supply of $5,571.22, for the payment of the expenses of His Honour's visit to the Northwest, by the sum of three hundred and fifty dollars, which amount His Honour transmits to cover what might be considered as personal expenses.

The Speaker, having been referred to, decided: That, inasmuch as the Attorney-General had stated in his place that the responsibility of the communication from His Honour had been assumed by his advisers, the objection could not be entertained.

No Bill in order affecting Revenue unless recommended by Crown. On 15th Jan., 1883 (page 41), the Order of the Day for the Second Reading of Bill (No. 69), to establish Public Creameries, having been read, objection was taken that the Bill involved the expenditure of public money, and required the previous assent of His Honour, and the Speaker reserved his decision. On the 17th Jan. (page 58), he gave the following decision: Objection has been taken to the second reading of this Bill on the ground that it involves the expenditure of public money, and ought to have received the previous assent of His

Honour. It is the practice that all Bills directly imposing a charge upon the people do originate in a Committee of the Whole House, and that no such charge shall be proposed without the expressed sanction of the Crown, but it has been equally the practice here, and in the Imperial Parliament, to take initiatory steps towards expenditure, and not involving actual expenditure, upon the responsibility of a Minister of the Crown, without direct and specific concurrence of the Crown being expressed by message. In 1868, a Bill was introduced in this Legislature by the Hon. J. S. Macdonald, then Attorney-General, providing for the establishment of Central District Prisons, and, when in Committee, objection was taken by Mr. E. Blake to the first section, giving power to the Lieutenant-Governor to purchase and acquire lands, and erect two or more buildings to be known as Central Prisons, inasmuch as it had not been based on resolutions recommended by His Honour the Lieutenant-Governor. The objection was overruled by the Chairman, as the first section applied to charges to be thereafter provided by a Committee of Supply, and Mr. Blake did not appeal from the decision. The Bill was ultimately abandoned, but reintroduced in the same Parliament in 1870-1, without precedent resolutions, and passed without renewal of the objections originally taken. In the Imperial Parliament, on 2nd March, 1865, Mr. Cowper, a Member of the Government, moved for leave to bring in a Bill to enable the Commissioner of Her Majesty's Works and Public Buildings to acquire additional lands for improving the site of the new public offices in Downing Street, and the approaches thereto, when Mr. Lygon submitted as a point of order that this was a Bill which should be originated in Committee of the Whole House. Mr. Cowper said that the Bill was of exactly the same character as five or six Acts which were upon the Statute Books, all of which had been introduced in the same manner, and which indeed could not, by the Rules of the House, have been introduced in any other way. Mr. Speaker said that the Bill was to enable the Government to take ground for certain purposes. It did not give them the power to purchase the property; the funds for that purpose should be voted afterwards in Committee of the Whole House. There was, therefore, no question of order.

Referring to the Rules of this House, I find that Rule 93 provides that if any motion shall be made for any public aid or charge upon the people, it shall be referred to Committee of the Whole House before any vote of the House does pass thereupon, and by the 54th section of 'The British North America Act' it is provided that the House shall not pass any Bill for the appropriation of any part of the public revenue to any purpose that has not first been recommended by a message in the Session in which such Bill is proposed. The 93rd Rule, which deals with motions exclusively, I regard as inapplicable to the Bill, and the 54th section of the B. N. A. Act cannot be held as fatal to the second reading of a measure which, in its present form, makes no definite appropriation of or charges upon any part of the public revenue. But if, in the further progress of the Bill through the House, it seeks to impose a specific charge upon the people through a distinct appropriation of public moneys, such changes in it can be made only after a recommendation of the expenditure by His Honour, communicated to this House in the usual manner. I am of opinion that there is now no question of order.

On 10th January, 1883 (pages 123-124), the Order of the Day for the Third Reading of Bill (No. 77), for amending the Election Act, *Amendment similar to one already passed upon during the same Session out of order.* was read, when Mr. Meredith moved in amendment: That the said Bill be not now read a third time, but be referred back to the Committee of the Whole, with instructions to amend the same so as to confer upon the sons of mechanics and others, not now entrusted with a franchise, the same privileges as are now conferred upon farmers' sons. Objection was taken, and the Speaker decided : That the proposition contained in the amendment, being in substance, if not in precise form, the same as already passed upon by this House, during the present session, cannot now be submitted to this House, and is therefore out of order.

Objection was taken to the decision of Mr. Speaker, and the same, being submitted to a vote, he was sustained by a vote of 49 to 25.

Mr. Meredith then proposed to strike out all the works after the word " That," and insert the following in lieu thereof : " The *Motion extending Franchise out of order.* policy of the law is to exempt from taxation for municipal purposes incomes below $400 ; that large numbers of persons, particularly among the young men and of the industrial portion of the people, who are by their intelligence and otherwise justly entitled to vote at Parliamentary elections, are, by reason of the existence of the property qualification required by law, excluded from the exercise of the franchise unless as income franchise voters ; that the existing law which requires persons in receipt of incomes to waive their exemption from taxation in respect of such income to entitle them to the franchise, ignores the true principle upon which the income franchise rests, and excludes from the benefits of the franchise almost the whole of those whom it was the ostensible object of the Act creating the income franchise vote to invest with it, and is therefore unjust, and ought, so far as relates to Parliamentary elections, to be changed, and to that end, that the said Bill be not now read the third time, but be forthwith referred back to the Committee of the Whole House, with instructions to amend the same, by repealing, so far as the same relates to Parliamentary elections, the provisions of the law requiring persons otherwise qualified to vote in respect of income, to be rated for income exempt from taxation, and to pay taxes upon such income in order to entitle them to vote in respect of income.

Objection was taken to the amendment, and the Speaker decided : That inasmuch as this House has declared during the present Session* that a considerable extension of the franchise is especially a subject upon which the people ought to be consulted, and that the approaching general election will offer an opportunity for so consulting and ascertaining the wish of the people, any proposition to admit large numbers of persons to the franchise, as proposed in the amendment, cannot be now entertained, and that this proposed amendment is therefore out of order.

The Speaker's decision was appealed against, and sustained by a vote of 47 to 25.

---

* On 27th January, 1883, the House

Resolved : That the Liberal Party of this Province stands pledged to extend the franchise ; that if this House should now legislate to extend the franchise, any law passed for that purpose could not be brought into operation in time for the coming general election ; that any considerable extension of the franchise is especially a subject upon which the people ought to be consulted ; that the approaching general election will afford an opportunity of so consulting and ascertaining the wishes of the people ; but the House meanwhile does not hesitate to affirm its opinion that no such extension of the franchise will prove satisfactory which does not, with proper checks and safeguards, give the right to vote to all classes who can fairly and reasonably claim to be endowed therewith.

An amendment was then moved that "the said Bill be not now read the third time, but be forthwith referred back to the Committee of the Whole House, with instructions to amend the same by reducing the qualification of income franchise voters in cities, towns and villages to three hundred dollars, and in townships to two hundred dollars." Objection was taken, and the Speaker decided : That the amendment was out of order on the ground that the question involved had been already decided upon by the House.

<small>A question already decided cannot be again put.</small>

On 14th February, 1884 (page 66), it was moved, "That by reason of the incurable mental condition of the Honourable Adam Crooks, Member-elect for the South Riding of the County of Oxford, as stated in the Report of the Committee on Privileges and Elections, this day presented to and adopted by this House, the representation of the said Riding in this House is hereby declared to be vacant, and that a new Writ do forthwith issue for the election of a Member to fill the vacancy, and to serve in this present Parliament for the said Riding in the room and stead of the said the Honourable Adam Crooks',

<small>When no notice of motion for issue of Writ necessary.</small>

Mr. Morris raised the following point of order :—

Whether, in view of the fact that the motion for the Writ now proposed to be issued arises from an extraordinary occasion unprovided for by Statute, and in which the procedure depends upon the practice of the Parliament of Great Britain, notice is not required of the motion therefor.

The Speaker decided : That in view of the absence of Canadian precedents for the guidance of this House, and of any distinct rule bearing upon the question before it, he had carefully examined the Journals of the English House of Commons, and had found five cases of seats vacated by the incurable sickness of those representing them, and that in each case a Writ had issued upon the day on which the Committee on Privileges and Election had reported the facts to the House, and he was of the opinion, therefore, that no notice of motion was required.

Mr. Morris then raised the following further point of order :

Whether the Report of the Committee on Privileges and Elections, in the case in question, should not have been printed and placed in the hands of Members for their information before motion was made for the issue of a new Writ ?

The Speaker decided : That, as the Report in question had been adopted by the House, it was presumed to be in the hands of Members ; and that, as no notice was required for the introduction of a motion for the issue of a Writ, the motion of the Attorney-General was in order.

On 10th February, 1885 (page 35), Mr. Meredith tendered to be laid on the Table of the House, and required that the same be read,
Proposal to lay on the Table and be read, irregular. a paper purporting to be a certified copy of a decision of the Court of Appeal, in the case of an Election Petition against the return of Charles Drury, Esquire, as Member for the East Riding of the County of Simcoe, and objection being taken thereto, the Speaker decided : That the course proposed to be taken by the Honourable Member was irregular.

On 9th March, 1885 (page 97), Mr. Broder moved : That in the opinion of this House it is expedient that the Government shall
When amendment to Amendment, adding words, carried, motion to strike out first part not in order. make some suitable recognition to the Volunteers of 1837-8, residing in the Province of Ontario, for the valuable services they rendered in defence of their country at that time.

The Attorney-General moved an amendment : That all the words of the Motion after the first word "That" be omitted, and that instead thereof there be inserted the following : "This House cordially recognizes the loyalty and services of the Volunteers of 1837-1838, who responded to the call then made upon them by the lawfully constituted authorities, and recognizes also the services rendered to this Province through the efforts of the Reformers of the same period, which secured for the same people of Canada the blessing of true Constitutional Government ; but this House deems it inopportune to make any declaration that might excite hopes and expectations which this House may not be in a position to fulfil."

Mr. Ross moved that as an amendment to the Amendment there be added to it these words : " This House, however, would be remiss in a plain duty if it did not avail itself of this opportunity to place on record its high and grateful appreciation of the services of those other Volunteers who, in 1866, loyally and cheerfully rallied to defend this Province against the lawless horde of intruders who then threatened our shores with invasion.

And this amendment to the Amendment was put and carried.

Mr. Meredith then moved in amendment to the Amendment, as amended "That all the words in the amendment of the Attorney-General after the first word "That" be struck out and the following words be added to the amendment of the Minister of Education : " And this House feels that this may be done without impugning the conduct or the motives of those who, by constitutional means, contended for principles, the adoption of which they believed to be in the interest of the country."

Objection was taken to this proposed amendment, and the Speaker decided : That, inasmuch as the amendment to the Amendment confirmed the subject matter of the Amendment, and the amendment of the Member for London proposed to strike out the former portion of the Amendment, his motion was out of order. It was competent to the Member to vote against the Amendment as amended, or to propose the addition of relevant words thereto.

Mr. Meredith appealed to the House against this decision, and it was sustained by a vote of 37 to 28.

On 19th March, 1886 (page 126), the House resolved itself into a Committee of the Whole to consider Bill (No. 41), respecting the City of Toronto, a Private Bill. An important amendment was proposed in Committee, and objected to because no Notice had been given as required by Rule 72. The Chairman of the Committee, Mr. Baxter, being appealed to, decided that the proposed amendment was out of order. An appeal from his decision was taken, and the Speaker decided : That the proposed amendment, being an important and distinct amendment, of which no notice had been given, was out of order, and that he sustained the ruling of the Chairman.

Amendment to a Private Bill without Notice out of order.

HON. JACOB BAXTER. Jacob Baxter, Esq., Haldimand, appointed Speaker, 10th February, 1887.

On 8th March, 1888 (page 97), the Order of the Day for resuming the adjourned debate on the Concurrence Resolutions

When Amendment and Motion passed no further Amendment of non-concurrence can be put. respecting amendments in the British North America Act was read, and it was moved in amendment, that all the words in the Motion after the first "That" be struck out and the following substituted: "The proposed plan of dealing with the constitution of the Senate of Canada does not afford a satisfactory solution of the objections urged to that body as it now exists under the provisions of the British North America Act."

It was moved in amendment to the Amendment, that all after the first word "That" in the Amendment be omitted, and there be inserted instead thereof, the following: "there be added to the original Motion these words: 'and that an humble address be presented to His Honour the Lieutenant-Governor, requesting him to communicate to His Excellency the Governor-General, and to the Secretary of State for Canada, the concurrence of this House in the said Resolution.'"

And the amendment to the Amendment having been put was carried, and the original Motion as amended was also carried.

Mr. Meredith rose to a point of order, and inquired of Mr. Speaker whether or not the amendment to the proposed Amendment, as carried, precluded any further motion to amend the Resolution?

The Speaker decided: That as the House by the words added to the main Motion had expressed concurrence in the Resolutions, no such further amendment declaring, or by its terms involving, non-concurrence of the House in the said Resolutions could be proposed.

Similar Amendment yet going further than Motion, in order. On 20th March, 1889 (page 140), the Order of the Day for the House to resolve itself into Committee to consider certain proposed Resolutions respecting Aid to Railways was read, and it was moved that "Mr. Speaker do now leave the Chair." It was moved in amendment that all the words after the word "That" be struck out, and the following substituted: "This House regrets that in opening the question of aiding out of Provincial funds the building of railways, a more just, equitable and satisfactory scheme had not been submitted for its consideration." After several amendments to this proposition had been voted down, it was moved in amendment to the proposed Amendment : That all the words after the first word "That" be omitted, and instead thereof there be inserted these words : "All words of the original question after the word "That" be struck out, and instead thereof the following be inserted : This House, while approving of a reasonable amount of Provincial aid being given to needful and deserving colonization railways within this Province, do forthwith resolve itself into a Committee to consider Resolutions relating to Railway Aid heretofore ordered to be considered in committee of the Whole House, and that Mr. Speaker do accordingly now leave the Chair.' "

Objection was taken to the proposed amendment to the Amendment, in that it only affirmed the original Motion, and nothing more.

Mr. Speaker decided : That as the amendment was framed, it proposed to go much further than the original Motion, and was, therefore, fully in order.

HON. T. BALLANTYNE. Thomas Ballantyne, Esq., elected Speaker 11th February, 1891

1st April, 1891 (page 66), in the matter of the Petition of Archibald McKellar, of Hamilton, which Mr. Wood (Hastings) had desired read on a previous day, and to the reading of which objection had been taken as irregular,

The Speaker decided : In case of the Petition in question, an objection having been taken, and there having been no motion made for the reading of the Petition, it could not then be read. Although a member presenting a Petition is by Rule 89 answerable that it shall not contain impertinent or improper matter, the practice of the House is, that every Petition presented to it shall at once be deposited with the Clerk for examination by him, and if found to be such as, according to the Rules and Practice of the House, can be received, it shall be brought to the Table by direction of the Speaker, two days after the presentation, to be read and received. It may then be read by the Clerk at the table, if required, or it may, with common consent, be read by the Clerk at the time of its presentation, but this cannot be done if any member objects. When a Petition complains of some present personal grievance requiring an immediate remedy, it may, with common consent, be at once read.

Petition may be read by Clerk two days after presentation.

On the 2nd of April, 1891 (page 70), the Speaker, in the matter of concurrence in the Ninth Report of the Standing Committee on Standing Orders, presented to the House on Thursday last, decided as follows : A Special or Standing Committee having recommended the suspension of a Rule, for the extension of time for the reception of Petitions ; or the course to be taken in consequence of the insufficiency of notice ; or other action for some particular purpose,—it is proper that concurrence therein should be moved in the House, which can be done by common consent upon presentation of the report. If this consent is not given, the report stands for further consideration. If no special recommendation is made, the report is regarded as concurred in, unless opposition is offered to its reception. If a member objects to a report in any particular, it is in order for him to move that either the whole or part thereof be referred back to the Standing Committee for further consideration. When more than one report is made by the Committee, each single report shall be entered on the Journal under its special designation as the second, third or other report.

When motion for concurrence in Report of a Committee necessary.

On 18th March, 1892 (page 96), in the matter of a ruling of Mr. Speaker, in the Session of 1891, relative to a point of order raised on the question of the presentation and reading of a Petition, and of a case cited on Monday last bearing upon such ruling, the Speaker addressed the House as follows :

When petitions may be read on presentation.

From his place in this House, the honourable member from London, on Monday last, called my attention to the fact that, on the 23rd July last, Mr. Atkinson, member for Boston in the British House of Commons, attempted to read a Petition which he presented to that body. Although Mr. Atkinson was prevented by Mr. Speaker from proceeding beyond the presentation of the Petition, it was read by the Clerk of the House, no opposition to such reading having been made. The unanimous consent of the House in this reading did not imply the existence of the right of any member to a compliance with his demand for such reading. Like the irregular introduction of a Bill or a Motion, it was done by " common consent." In this particular, Canadian Legislatures follow the practice of Great Britain, and the ruling made by me on 1st April, last Session, is in strict accordance with the rules and action of the British House of Commons.

Bourinot says: "A member presenting a Petition has no right himself to read it at length, but he may have it done by the Clerk at the Table, with the consent of the House. Petitions may be at once read and received by common consent, chiefly in order to refer them to a Committee; if a member objects, it cannot be done."

"Previous to 1885," says Bourinot, "a very loose practice existed with respect to the reading of Petitions, when required by a member, but in that year it was decided that the consent of the House was necessary, in accordance with the English rule, which is the same literally as the Canadian Rule 86."

On the 16th of May, 1885, a discussion arose in the Dominion House of Commons on an attempt on the part of Mr. Charlton to read the allegations of a Petition. Mr. Speaker declared it irregular for an honourable member to read a Petition when he was presenting it, and added that if he wished to have it read, the Clerk would read it. He said: "I think it is the right of an honourable member to ask to have the Petition read, though, of course, if the House refuses its consent, it cannot be read."

Sir John A. Macdonald said: "If the House assents, it is read; if the House dissents, or any one member, I take it, dissents, it must be postponed."

Hon. E. Blake said: "I quite agree with the honourable gentleman that there have been cases in which Petitions have been read and received at once, but that has always been on a motion, and always with the unanimous consent of the House."

Sir Hector Langevin said: "But is it the privilege of a member to have it read without the consent of the House, for, if so, I must say that after 28 years experience in Parliament this is the first time it has been done within my experience."

Mr. Chapleau said: "This is the question. Can a Petition be read by a member presenting it, or can it be read as a matter of right, by the Clerk of the House, at the request of a member? I say, No. Not only can it not be received, but it can not be read."

Although not bearing directly upon our practice, it may be interesting to know that pursued in Congress:

Cushing says: "If the Petition is to be read in full or as a Petition, it must first be received by the House, and upon the reading being ordered, be read by the Clerk at the Table. If the House refuses to allow a Petition to be read, it is effectually rejected ; if decided in the affirmative, the Petition is read by the Clerk at the Table, and the contents of it are then fairly in possession of the House."

On 25th May, 1893, it was moved,

When concurrence not necessary. That this House do now concur in the report of the Standing Committee on Public Accounts.

And a Debate having arisen,

Exception was taken to the continuance of the Debate on the grounds of irregularity, in that the Report contained nothing that required either concurrence therein or adoption thereof, by the House, and that a motion for concurrence in, or adoption of, the Report was unnecessary and irregular.

And Mr. Speaker being appealed to, decided,

That the motion for concurrence was out of order, and that, therefore, the Debate could not continue.

When an Amendment to amendment not in order. On 25th May, 1893, the Order of the Day for the House to resolve itself into a Committee of the Whole to consider certain proposed Resolutions relating to Railway Aid, having been read,

The Attorney-General acquainted the House that His Honour the Lieutenant-Governor, having been informed of the subject matter of the proposed Resolutions, recommends them to the consideration of the House.

Mr. Hardy then moved,

That Mr. Speaker do now leave the Chair.

Mr. Meredith moved in amendment, seconded by Mr. Clancy,

That all the words in the Motion after the word "that" be struck out and the following substituted therefor :—" This House, while it approves of the grants proposed by the Resolutions in aid of railways therein mentioned, regrets that His Honour has not been advised to submit, for the approval of this House, a liberal scheme for developing the mineral and mining resources of the Province."

Mr. Fraser, moved in amendment to the Amendment, seconded by Mr. Gibson (Hamilton).

That all the words of the Amendment after the first word "that" be omitted, and instead thereof there be inserted these words, "all words of the original question after the word 'that'" be struck out, and instead thereof the following be inserted : 'This House, approving of a reasonable amount of Provincial Aid being given to needful and deserving Railways intended to develop the Colonization and Mining interest of this Province, do forthwith resolve itself into a Committee to consider the Resolutions relating to Railway Aid heretofore ordered to be considered in Committee of the Whole House, and that Mr. Speaker do accordingly now leave the Chair.'"

Mr. Meredith objected that the amendment to the Amendment was not in order because (1), On a motion to go into Committee on the Resolutions only one amendment to the Motion "That Mr. Speaker do now leave the Chair" can be moved, and (2), The amendment to the Amendment is a mere re-affirmation of the original Motion. And Mr. Speaker, being appealed to, decided that,

(1) An amendment to an Amendment, upon the motion "That Mr. Speaker do now leave the Chair" is in order, excepting when the House is going into Committee of the Whole upon Supply. (2), The proposed amendment to the Amendment is not a mere affirmation of the main motion, but a permissible expression by the House of its approval of the policy of extending reasonable aid to Colonization and Mining interests. The objections raised by the honourable member cannot, therefore, be entertained.

No addition can be made to motion for second reading of Bill. On 25th May, 1893, on the proposed Third Reading of Bill (No. 199), Respecting Aid to certain railways, it was moved,

That the following words be added to the Motion :—

"And it is, in the opinion of this House, expedient that during the recess the Government consider and be prepared to submit to the House at its next Session some measure looking to the development of the mineral resources of the Province."

And objection being taken to the proposed Motion in amendment as contravening all established rules of Parliamentary Practice in cases of motions of the third reading of a Bill.

Mr. Speaker being appealed to decided.

That the objection must prevail, as in his opinion no amendment can be moved on the second reading or other stage of a Bill by way of mere addition to the question.

On 25th May, 1893, on the motion that Bill (No. 156) to enable the electors of the Province to pronounce upon the desirability of prohibiting the importation, manufacture and sale, as a beverage, of intoxicating liquors be now read a third time, it was moved in amendment.

<small>What an Amendment should consist of.</small>

"That this House regrets that provision has not been made for the expense of taking the vote of the electors, being paid by the Province, instead of requiring that expense to be defrayed by the municipalities."

Exception was taken to the proposed amendment,

And Mr. Speaker being requested to rule, decided that an Amendment should be so framed as to leave out certain words: to leave out certain words in order to insert or add others; or to insert or add certain words. Inasmuch as the proposed amendment does not comply with any of these conditions it is out of order.

<small>HON. A. F. E. EVANTUREL.</small> Hon. A. F. E. Evanturel, Prescott, was elected Speaker of the Eighth Legislature, and of the Ninth Legislature, August 3rd, 1898.

On August 19th, 1898, Mr. Whitney raised a point of Order, and quoted Rule 16 as to the right of certain Members to vote upon the Second Reading of Bill 2, "An Act respecting the Election Laws," in consequence of the fact that they had a pecuniary interest in the subject matter of the proposed legislation, and placed upon the Table certified copies of certain Election Petitions then pending before the Courts.

<small>When pecuniary interest of members involved.</small>

Mr. Speaker ruled that no objection to a vote can be raised on the ground of pecuniary or personal interest, except upon a substantive motion to be dealt with by the distinct action of the House. Such substantive motion, he conceived, could not be entertained in this instance, after a vote had been taken, inasmuch as the Members named had no direct pecuniary interest in the proposed legislation, which was based solely upon public policy. And the Return of Members having been duly made by the Clerk of the Crown in Chancery, and they having taken the oaths and their seats, their right to vote could not be questioned on other grounds than that of pecuniary interest.

DECISION BY THE CLERK.

On 7th December, 1871, at the opening of the Second Parliament, Mr. Blake, addressing himself to the Clerk, Col. Gillmor, drew attention to the fact that certain members, declared by the Judges not to have been duly elected, had taken the oath and their seats ; and that the reports of the Judges having been sent to the Clerk, it was his duty to lay the reports before the House at the earliest practicable opportunity, the Clerk being, for the purposes of the Act, the Speaker.

<small>Documents cannot be received until election of Speaker.</small>

The Clerk, being referred to, said, That the Clerk of the Crown in Chancery had handed him a roll containing the names of the members duly returned to the present Parliament, and that the members so named having taken the oath and subscribed the roll before him, he, as Clerk of the House, could not presume to question the fact of their right to take their seats.

That he was of opinion that it was not competent for him to lay any papers on the Table, His Excellency having informed the House that he would not declare the causes of his calling the Parliament together until a Speaker had been elected, and until the orders of His Excellency have been obeyed, the House would not be properly constituted, so that it would be practicable to lay the reports on the table.

RULES, ORDERS

AND

FORMS OF PROCEDURE.

RULES, ORDERS,

AND

FORMS OF PROCEEDING

OF

LEGISLATIVE ASSEMBLY OF ONTARIO.

I.—REGULATION AND MANAGEMENT OF THE HOUSE.

1. The time for the Ordinary Meeting of the House is at Three o'clock in the afternoon of each sitting day ; and if at that hour there be not a Quorum, the Speaker may take the Chair and adjourn. When the House rises on Friday, it shall stand adjourned, unless otherwise ordered, until the following Monday.

2. If at the hour of six o'clock p.m., the Business of the Day be not concluded, the Speaker shall leave the Chair until half past seven.

3. When the House adjourns, the Members shall keep their seats until the Speaker has left the Chair.

4. The presence of at least Twenty Members of the House, including the Speaker, shall be necessary to constitute a meeting of the House for the exercise of its powers.

5. Whenever the Speaker shall adjourn the House for want of a quorum, the time of the adjournment, and the names of the Members then present, shall be inserted in the Journal.

6. Any Stranger admitted to any part of the House or Gallery, who shall misconduct himself, or shall not withdraw when Strangers are directed to withdraw, while the House or any Committee of the Whole House is sitting, shall be taken into custody by the Sergeant-at-Arms ; and no person so taken into custody is to be discharged without the special Order of the House.

7. Any Five Members may require the House to be cleared of Strangers, and the Speaker shall immediately give directions to the Sergeant-at-Arms to execute the Order without debate.

8. The Speaker shall preserve Order and Decorum, and shall decide questions of Order, subject to an appeal to the House; in explaining a point of Order or Practice, he shall state the Rule or Authority applicable to the case.

9. The Speaker shall not take part in any Debate before the House. In case of an equality of Votes, the Speaker gives a casting Voice, and any reasons stated by him are to be entered in the Journal.

II.—RULES OF DEBATE.

10. Every Member desiring to speak is to rise in his place, uncovered, and address himself to the Speaker.

11. When two or more members rise to speak, the Speaker calls upon the Member who rose first in his place; but a motion may be made that any Member who has risen "be now heard" or "do now speak."

12. A Member called to Order shall sit down, but may afterwards explain. The House, if appealed to, shall decide on the case, but without debate. If there be no appeal, the decision of the Chair shall be final.

13. No member shall speak disrespectfully of Her Majesty, nor of any of the Royal Family, nor of the Governor, or person administering the Government of Canada, nor of the Lieutenant-Governor of the Province; nor shall he use offensive words against any member of the House; nor shall he speak beside the Question in Debate. No Member may reflect upon any Vote of the House, except for the purpose of moving that such a Vote be rescinded.

14. Any Member may require the Question under discussion to be read at any time of the Debate, but not so as to interrupt a Member while speaking.

15. No member may speak twice to a Question, except in explanation of a material part of his speech in which he may have been misconceived, but then he is not to introduce new matter. A reply is allowed to a Member who has made a substantive Motion to the House, but not to any Member who has moved an Order of the Day, an Amendment, the Previous Question, or an Instruction to a Committee.

III.—CONDUCT OF MEMBERS.

16. No Member is entitled to vote upon any Question in which he has a direct pecuniary interest, and the vote of any Member so interested shall be disallowed.

17. When the Speaker is putting a Question, no Member shall walk out of or across the House, or make any noise or disturbance; and when a Member is speaking, no Member shall interrupt him except to a Question of Order, nor pass between him and the Chair; and no Member may pass between the Chair and the Table, nor between the Chair and the Mace, when the Mace has been taken off the Table by the Sergeant.

18. Every Member is bound to attend the service of the House, unless leave of absence has been given him by the House.

IV.— BUSINESS OF THE HOUSE.

Routine Business.

19. The ordinary daily Routine of business of the House shall be as follows :—

    Presenting Petitions.
    Reading and Receiving Petitions.
    Presenting Reports of Standing and Select Committees.
    Motions.

The Order of Business for the consideration of the House, day by day, after the above Daily Routine, shall be as follows :

MONDAY.

    Private Bills.
    Questions Put by Members.
    Notices of Motions.
    Public Bills and Orders.

TUESDAY.

    Government Notices of Motions.
    Government Orders.
    Public Bills and Orders.
    Questions Put by Members.
    Other Notices of Motions.
    Private Bills.

WEDNESDAY.

(Until the hour of six o'clock p.m.)

    Questions Put by Members.
    Notices of Motions.
    Public Bills and Orders.

(From half past seven o'clock p.m.)

    (For the first hour) Private Bills.
    Public Bills and Orders.
    Private Bills.
    Government Notices of Motions.
    Government Orders.

THURSDAY.

    Government Notices of Motion.
    Government Orders.
    Public Bills and Orders.
    Questions Put by Members.
    Other Notices of Motions.
    Private Bills.

FRIDAY.

(Until the hour of six o'clock p.m.)

Questions Put by Members.
Notices of Motions.
Public Bills and Orders.

(From half-past seven p.m.)

(For the first hour) Private Bills.
Public Bills and Orders.
Private Bills.
Government Notices of Motions.
Government Orders.

20. Orders for the Day for the Third Reading of Bills shall take precedence of all other Orders for the same day, except Government Orders, or Orders to which the House has given priority.

21. Bills reported from Committees of the Whole House, with amendments, shall be placed on the Orders of the Day for consideration by the House next after Third Readings.

22. Bills reported, after Second Reading, from any Standing or Select Committee, shall be placed on the Orders of the Day following the reception of the Report, for reference to a Committee of the Whole House in their proper order, next after Bills reported from Committee of the Whole House.

23. All items standing on the Orders of the Day shall be taken up according to the precedence assigned to each on the Order Book; the right being reserved to the Administration of taking up Government Orders, in such rotation as they see fit, on the days on which Government Bills have precedence.

24. Items not taken up when called shall be dropped. Dropped Orders shall be set down in the Order Book, after the Orders of the Day, for the next day on which the House shall sit.

25. All Orders undisposed of at the adjournment of the House shall be postponed until the next Sitting Day, without a motion to that effect.

26. If, at the hour of six p.m. on a Wednesday or Friday, a Motion on the Notice Paper be under consideration, that question will stand first on the Orders of that evening, after the hour assigned to Private Bills has elapsed.

27. If, at the time of the adjournment of the House, a Motion on the Notice Paper be under consideration, that question shall stand first on the Orders of the following day, next after Orders to which a special precedence has been assigned by Rule or Order of the House.

28. A Motion for Reading the Orders of the Day shall have preference of any Motion before the House.

Questions put by Members.

29. Questions may be put to Ministers of the Crown relating to Public Affairs; and to other Members relating to any Bill, Motion or other public matter connected with the business of the House, in which such Members may be concerned,—but, in putting any such question, no argument or opinion is to be offered, nor any fact stated; and, in answering any such question, a Member is not to debate the matter to which the same refers.

Motions and Questions.

30. A Motion to adjourn the House or the Debate shall always be in order; but no Member shall speak to such Motion for more than ten minutes; and no second motion to the same effect shall be made until after some intermediate proceeding shall have been had.

31. Two days' notice shall be given of a Motion for leave to present a Bill, Resolution or Address; for the appointment of any Committee; or for the putting of a Question; but this Rule shall not apply to Bills after their introduction, or to Private Bills, or to the times of the meeting, or Adjournment of the House; such Notice to be laid on the Table before five o'clock p.m., and to be printed in the Votes and Proceedings of that day.

32. A Motion may be made, by unanimous consent of the House, without previous notice.

33. All Motions shall be in writing, and seconded, before being debated, or put from the Chair. When a Motion is seconded, it shall be read by the Speaker before debate.

34. A Member who has made a Motion may withdraw the same by leave of the House; such leave being granted without any negative voice.

35. The Previous Question, until it is decided, shall preclude all amendment of the Main Question, and shall be in the following words: "That this Question be now put." If the Previous Question be resolved in the affirmative, the Original Question is to be put forthwith, without any amendment or debate.

36. A Motion to commit a Bill, or Question, until decided, shall preclude all amendment of the Main Question.

37. Whenever the Speaker is of opinion that a Motion offered to the House is contrary to the Rules and Privileges of Parliament, he shall apprise the House thereof immediately, before putting the Question thereon, and quote the Rule or Authority applicable to the case.

Privilege.

38. Whenever any matter of Privilege arises, it shall be taken into consideration immediately.

Votes and Proceedings.

39. A copy of the Votes and Proceedings of the House, certified by the Clerk, shall be delivered each day to the Lieutenant-Governor.

Proceedings on Bills.

40. Every Bill shall be introduced upon Motion for leave, specifying the Title of the Bill, or upon Motion to appoint a Committee to prepare and bring it in.

41. No Bill may be introduced either in blank or in an imperfect shape.

42. When any Bill shall be presented by a Member, in pursuance of an Order of the House, the Question, "That this Bill be *now* read a first time," shall be decided without amendment or debate.

43. No Bill shall be read the second time until it has been printed and distributed, and has been subsequently marked on the Orders of the Day—thus, PRINTED (*Signifying that it has been printed and distributed*).

44. When a Bill has been amended in Committee of the Whole House, or by any Select or Standing Committee, it shall be re-printed as amended ; the amendments to be in *Italics* ; and when the Bill has been sent to be re-printed, it shall be marked on the Orders of the Day—thus, NOT RE-PRINTED ; and shall not be further proceeded with until that mark has been removed and the word PRINTED substituted (*Signifying that the Bill has been re-printed and distributed*).

45. Every Bill shall receive three several readings, on different days, previously to being passed. On urgent or extraordinary occasions, a Bill may be read twice or thrice, or advanced two or more stages in one day.

46. When a Bill is read in the House, the Clerk shall certify upon it the Readings, and the time thereof. After it has passed, he shall certify the same, with the date at the foot of the Bill.

47. Every Public Bill shall be read twice in the House before committal or amendment.

48. In proceedings in Committee of the Whole House upon Bills, the Preamble shall be first postponed, and then every clause considered by the Committee in its proper order, the Preamble and Title to be last considered.

49. All amendments made in Committee shall be reported by the Chairman to the House which shall receive the same forthwith. After Report, the Bill shall be open to debate and amendment, before it is ordered for a Third Reading. But when a Bill is reported without amendment, it is forthwith ordered to be read a Third time, at such time as may be appointed by the House.

50. It shall be the duty of the Law Clerk of the House to revise all Bills after their First Reading, and to certify thereon that the same are correct; and in every subsequent stage of such Bills the Law Clerk shall be responsible for the correctness of Bills, should they be amended. And he shall prepare a Breviat of every Bill previous to the Second Reading thereof.

Private Bills.

51. No petition for any Private Bill is received by the House after the first ten days of each Session; nor may any Private Bill be presented to the House after the first seventeen days of each Session; nor may any report of any Standing or Select Committee upon a Private Bill be received after the first thirty days of each Session. And no Motion for the general suspension or modification of this Rule shall be entertained by the House, unless after reference made thereof, at a previous Sitting of the House, to the several Standing Committees charged with consideration of Private Bills, or upon report submitted by two or more of such Committees.

52. The Clerk of the House shall, during each recess of Parliament, publish weekly in the *Ontario Gazette* the following Rules respecting Notices of intended applications for Private Bills; and shall also, immediately after the issue of the Proclamation convening Parliament for the Despatch of Business, publish in the *Ontario Gazette*, until the opening of Parliament, the day on which the time limited for receiving petitions for Private Bills will expire, pursuant to the foregoing Rule; and the Clerk shall also announce, by Notice affixed in the Committee-rooms and Lobbies of the House, by the first day of every Session, the time limited for receiving Petitions for Private Bills and Reports thereon.

53. All applications for Private Bills properly the subject of legislation by the Legislative Assembly of Ontario within the purview of "The British North America Act, 1867," whether for the erection of a Bridge, the making of a Railroad, Turnpike Road or Telegraph Line; the construction or improvement of a Harbour, Canal, Lock, Dam or Slide, or other like work; the granting of a right of Ferry; the incorporation of any particular Trade or Calling, or of any Joint Stock Company; or otherwise for granting to any individual or individuals any exclusive or particular rights or privileges whatever, or for doing any matter or thing which in its operation would affect the rights or property of other parties, or relate to any particular class of the community; or for making any amendments of a like nature to any former Act, shall require a Notice, clearly and distinctly specifying the nature and object of the application, and, where the application refers to any proposed work, indicating generally the location of the work, and signed by or on behalf of the applicants, such Notice to be published as follows, viz:

A Notice inserted in the *Ontario Gazette*, and in one Newspaper published in the County, or Union of Counties, affected, or if there be no Newspaper published therein, then in a Newspaper in the next nearest County in which a Newspaper is published.

Such Notice shall be continued in each case for a period of at least six weeks, during the interval of time between the close of the next preceding Session, and the consideration of the Petition ; and copies of such Notice shall be sent by the parties inserting such Notice to the Clerk of the House, to be filed in the Standing Orders Committee-rooms.

And within two weeks from the first appearance of such Notice in the *Ontario Gazette*, a copy of said Bill, with the sum of one hundred dollars, shall be placed by the applicant in the hands of the Clerk of the House, whose duty it shall be to get the said Bill printed forthwith.

54. Before any Petition praying for leave to bring in a Private Bill for the erection of a Toll Bridge is received by the House, the person or persons intending to petition for such Bill shall, upon giving the Notice required by the preceding Rule, also at the same time and in the same manner, give notice of the rates which they intend to ask, the extent of the privilege, the height of the arches, the interval between the abutments or piers for the passage of rafts and vessels, and mentioning also whether they intend to erect a drawbridge or not, and the dimensions of the same.

55. Before any petition praying for leave to bring in a Bill for the construction of Railways, Tramways, or Canals, is received by the House, the person or persons petitioning for such Bill shall deposit with the Clerk the following documents :—

(1) A Map or Plan upon a scale of not less than half an inch to the mile, showing the location upon which it is intended to construct the proposed work, and showing also the lines of existing or authorized works of a similar character within, or in any way affecting the district or any part thereof which the proposed work is intended to serve. Such map or plan to be signed by the Engineer or other party making the same.

(2) A Book of Reference, in which shall be clearly set out the following information, in separate Schedules, namely :

Schedule A.—The name of each Municipality within which the proposed works, or any part thereof, are intended to be constructed ; the population of each such Municipality, as returned by the next preceding census ; the ratable value of the property within each such Municipality, as returned by the next preceding assessment rolls thereof ; and this Schedule may contain in a separate statement similar information as to the adjoining districts intended to be served by the proposed work.

Schedule B. A general description of the nature, extent and proposed character of the contemplated works, and an estimate of the probable cost thereof, distinguishing the general items of construction, and the cost thereof respectively, as well as the nature, extent and probable cost of all engines and car stock, or other outfit or equipment necessary to the use and operation of the proposed undertaking, such Schedule to be signed by the Engineer, or other person preparing the same.

Schedule C.—An exhibit showing the total amount of capital proposed to be raised for the purposes of the undertaking, and the manner in which it is proposed to raise the same, whether by ordinary shares, bonds, debentures or other securities, and the amount of each respectively.

Schedule D.—An estimate of the probable revenues of the proposed undertaking showing the sources whence the same are expected to be derived ; the annual earnings thereof respectively ; the probable annual cost of operation or working expenditure ; and the annual net revenue applicable to the payment of interest on the proposed investments. Such Schedules to be signed by the person preparing the same.

56. Petitions for Private Bills, when received by the House, are to be taken into consideration (without special reference) by the Committee on Standing Orders ; which is to report, in each case, whether the Rules with regard to Notice have been complied with ; and in every case where the notice shall prove to have been insufficient, either as regards the petition as a whole, or any matter therein which ought to have been specially referred to in the Notice, the Committee is to recommend to the House the course to be taken in consequence of such insufficiency of Notice.

56. (a) The promoter of any Private Bill shall lodge with the Clerk of the House a statement as to the compliance by them with the Standing Orders of the House, in relation to such Bill, on or before the first day of each Session.

56. (b) A copy of the Petition intended to be presented to the House, praying for the passage of any Private Bill, shall be lodged, on or before the first day of each Session, with the Clerk of the House, who shall file the same in his office, and shall prepare for the Committee on Standing Orders, at the first meeting thereof, a report, in which he shall state the result of his examination into the facts required to be proved before the Committee relating to the compliance or non-compliance with the Standing Orders of the House.

56. (c) The Committee may determine, upon the facts so reported, or certified by the Clerk, whether the Standing Orders have been complied with in respect to each Petition, and whether the Stand-

ing Orders ought or ought not to be dispensed with, and shall report the same to the House.

57. No Motion for the suspension of the Rules upon any Petition for a Private Bill is entertained, unless the same has been reported upon by the Committee on Standing Orders.

58. All Private Bills are introduced on Petition and presented to the House upon Motion for leave, and after such Petition has been favorably reported on by the Committee on Standing Orders.

59. When any Bill for confirming by Letters Patent, or Agreement, is presented to the House, the copy of such Letters Patent, or Agreement, shall be attached to it.

60. The expenses and costs attending on Private Bills giving any exclusive privilege, or for any object of profit, or private, corporate or individual advantages ; or for amending, extending or enlarging any former Acts, in such manner as to confer additional powers, ought not to fall on the public ; accordingly the parties seeking to obtain any such Bills shall be required to pay the sum of one hundred dollars, as provided by Rule 53.

61. Every Private Bill, when read a first time, shall, unless it be an Estate Bill, stand referred to the proper Standing Committee, and all Petitions before the House, for or against the Bill, are considered as referred to such Committee.

62. Every Estate Bill, when read a first time, shall, without special reference, stand referred to the Commissioners of Estate Bills for their Report ; and a copy of such Bill, and of the Petition on which the same is founded, shall be forthwith transmitted by the Clerk of the House to the said Commissioners, or one of them, in order that they, or any two of them, may, after perusing the Bill, without requiring any proof of the allegations thereof, report to the House their opinion thereon under their hands ; and whether, presuming the allegations contained in the preamble to be proved to the satisfaction of the House, it is reasonable that such Bill do pass into a law ; and whether the provisions thereof are proper for carrying its purposes into effect ; and what alterations or amendments, if any, are necessary in the same ; and in the event of their approving the said Bill, they are to sign the same ; and the said Report, with the said Bill and Petition, are to be transmitted by the said Commissioners to the Clerk ; and the report shall be read by the Clerk at the Table, and shall be entered on the Journals of the House ; and the Bill, together with the Report, shall stand referred to the Standing Committee on Private Bills, which is not to consider the said Bill, before the delivery of the said Report, Bill and Petition to the Chairman of the said Committee.

63. In the event of the Commissioners of Estate Bills reporting that, in their opinion, it is not reasonable that the Bill submitted to them shall pass into law, such Bill shall not be further considered.

64. No Committee on any Private Bill, of which notice is required to be given, is to consider the same until such Bill has been printed and distributed to Members, and five days' clear Notice of the sitting of such Committee has been affixed in the Lobby. And no Motion for any suspension or modification of this Rule shall be entertained by the House, unless after reference made thereof, at a previous Sitting of the House, to the Proper Standing Committee, or upon Report submitted by such Committee.

(2) On the day of posting of any Bill under this Rule, the Clerk of the House shall append to the printed Votes and Proceedings of the Day, a Notice of such posting; and also a Notice of Meetings of any of the Standing Committees charged with the consideration of Private Bills or Petitions therefor, that may have been appointed for the following day.

65. A copy of the Bill containing the Amendments proposed to be submitted to the Standing Committee, shall be deposited in the Private Bill Office two clear days before the meeting of the Committee thereon.

66. All persons whose interest or property may be affected by any Private Bill shall, when required so to do, appear before the Standing Committee touching their consent, or may send such consent in writing, proof of which may be demanded by such Committee. And in every case the Committee upon any Bill for incorporating a Company may require proof that the persons whose names appear in the Bill, as composing the Company, are of full age, and in a position to effect the objects contemplated, and have consented to become incorporated.

67. All questions before Committee on Private Bills are decided by a majority of voices, including the voice of the Chairman; and whenever the voices are equal the Chairman has a second or casting vote.

68. It is the duty of a Select Committee to which any Private Bill may be referred by the House, to call the attention of the House specially to any provision inserted in such Bill that does not appear to have been contemplated in the Notice for the same, as reported upon by the Committee on Standing Orders.

69. The Committee to which a Private Bill may have been referred, shall report the same to the House in every case; and when any material alteration has been made in the Preamble of the Bill, such alteration, and the reasons for the same, are to be stated in the Report.

70. When the Committee on any Private Bill report to the House that the Preamble of such Bill has not been proved to their satisfaction, they must also state the grounds upon which they have arrived at such a decision; and no Bill so reported upon shall be

placed upon the Orders of the Day, unless by special order of the House.

(2) Private Bills, otherwise reported to the House by such Committee, shall be placed upon the Orders of the Day following the reception of the Report, for a Second Reading in their proper order.

71. The Chairman of the Committee shall sign with his name, at length, a printed copy of the Bill, on which the amendments are fairly written, and shall also sign, with the initials of his name, the several Amendments made and Clauses added in Committee, which shall be filed in the Office of Routine and Records ; and another Bill, with the amendments written thereon, shall be prepared by the Clerk of the Committee, and attached to the Report.

72. No important Amendment may be proposed to any Private Bill in a Committee of the Whole House, or at any Third Reading of the Bill unless two days' notice of the same shall have been given.

73. Except in case of urgent and pressing necessity, no Motion may be made to dispense with any Standing Order relative to Private Bills, without due notice thereof.

74. A Book, to be called the Private Bill Register, shall be kept in the Private Bill Office, in which Book shall be entered, by the Clerk appointed for the business of that Office, the name, description, and place of residence of the parties applying for the Bill, or of their Agent, and all the proceedings thereon, from the Petition to the passing of the Bill ; such entry to specify briefly each proceeding in the House, or in any Committee to which the Bill or Petition may be referred, and the day on which the Committee is appointed to sit ; such Book to be open to public inspection daily, during Office hours.

75. The Clerk of the House shall prepare, daily, lists of all Private Bills and Petitions for such Bills, upon which any Committee is appointed to sit, specifying the time of meeting and the room where the Committee shall sit ; and the same shall be hung up in the Lobby.

76. Every Parliamentary Agent conducting Proceedings before the House shall be personally responsible to the House and to the Speaker for the observance of the Rules, Orders, and Practice of Parliament, and Rules prescribed by the Speaker, and also for the payment of all fees and charges ; and he shall not act as Parliamentary Agent until he shall have received the express sanction and authority of the Speaker, who may revoke the same at pleasure.

77. Any Agent who shall wilfully act in violation of the Rules and Practice of Parliament, or any Rules prescribed by the

Speaker, or who shall wilfully misconduct himself in prosecuting any proceedings before the House, shall be liable to an absolute or temporary prohibition to practice as a Parliamentary Agent at the pleasure of the Speaker.

Committees.

78. The Clerk of the House shall cause to be affixed, in some conspicuous part of the House, a list of the several Standing and Select Committees appointed during the Session.

79. There shall be appointed in each Session a Permanent Chairman of Committees of the Whole House, who, when the Speaker leaves the chair, shall, if present, preside over and maintain order in the Committee.

(2) The Rules of the House shall be observed in Committee of the Whole House so far as may be applicable, except the Rule limiting the number of times of speaking.

80. Questions of Order arising in Committee of the Whole House shall be decided by the Chairman, subject to an appeal to the House ; but disorder in a Committee can only be censured by the House on receiving a report thereof.

81. A Motion that the Chairman leave the chair shall always be in order, and shall take precedence of any other Motion.

82. Bills which may be on the Order of the Day for consideration in Committee on the same day, may be referred together to a Committee of the Whole House, which may consider all the Bills so referred to it without the Chairman leaving the Chair on each separate Bill.

83. No Select Committee may, without leave of the House, consist of more than fifteen members, and the Mover may submit the names to form the Committee, unless objected to by five members; if objected to, the House may name the Committee in the following manner :—Each member to name one, and those who have most voices, with the mover, shall form the same ; but it shall be always understood that no member who declares or decides against the Principle or substance of a Bill, Resolution or matter to be committed, can be nominated of such Committee.

84. Of the number of Members appointed to compose a Committee, a majority of the same shall be a Quorum, unless the House has otherwise ordered.

85. Reports from Standing and Select Committees may be made by Members standing in their places, and without proceeding to the Bar of the House.

85 (a) The Special Committee to prepare and report lists of Members to compose the Standing Committees of the House, and

the said several Standing Committees, may be appointed, and thereafter may proceed to organize and sit, and report at any time after an Address to His Honour the Lieutenant-Governor in reply to the Speech shall have been moved in the House, although the Debate on such Address may not have been concluded.

Witnesses.

86. The Clerk of the House is authorized to pay out of the Contingent Fund to Witnesses summoned to attend before any Select Committee of the House, except in the case of Private Bills, a reasonable sum per diem, to be determined by the Speaker, during their attendance, and a reasonable allowance for travelling expenses, upon a certificate or order of the Chairman of the Committee before which such witnesses have been summoned; but no witness shall be so paid unless a certificate shall first have been filed with the Chairman of such Committee, by some member thereof, stating that the evidence to be obtained from such witness is, in his opinion, material and important; and no such payment shall be made in any case without the authority of the Speaker, which will be signified by the endorsement of the Speaker upon the aforesaid certificate; and when any witness shall have been in attendance during three days, if his presence is still further required, recourse shall again be had to the Chairman of the Committee, and so on, every three days; and no witness residing at the Seat of Government shall be paid for his attendance.

Divisions.

87. When Members have been called in, preparatory to a Division, no further debate is to be permitted.

88. Upon a Division, the Yeas and Nays shall not be entered upon the Minutes, unless demanded by five Members; and on Questions of Adjournment of the House, or of the debate, the numbers only shall be entered.

88 (a) When the Yeas and Nays are taken, the Clerk shall enter upon the Votes and Proceedings, the Pairs, as may be declared, (if any), and they shall also be entered in the Journals. And Pairs may be declared immediately after a vote, without re-calling the Yeas and Nays.

Petitions.

89. Petitions to the House shall be presented by a Member, in his place, who shall be answerable that they do not contain impertinent or improper matter.

90. Every Member offering to present a petition to the House, shall endorse his name thereupon, and confine himself to a statement of the parties from whom it came, the number of signatures

attached to it, and the material allegations it contains. Petitions may be either written or printed; provided always that the signatures of at least three petitioners are subscribed on the sheet containing the prayer of the petition, except in the case of a single petitioner, or a corporation.

91. No Petition can be received which prays for any expenditure, grant or charge on the public revenue, whether payable out of the Consolidated Revenue Fund, or out of moneys to be provided by the House.

92. Every Petition not containing matter in breach of the Privileges of the House, and which according to the rules or practice of the House can be received, is brought to the Table by direction of the Speaker, who cannot allow any debate, or any Member to speak upon, or in relation to, such petition; but it may be read by the Clerk at the Table, if required; or if it complain of some present personal grievance, requiring an immediate remedy, the matter contained therein may be brought into immediate discussion.

Aid and Supply.

[By the 54th Section of the Imperial Act, 30 Vict. c. 3, "The British North American Act, 1867," it is provided that the House shall not adopt or pass any Vote Resolution, Address or Bill for the appropriation of any part of the Public Revenue, or of any Tax or Impost, to any purpose that has not been first recommended by a message of the Lieutenant-Governor in the Session in which such Vote, Resolution, Address or Bill is proposed.]

93. If any Motion be made in the House for any public aid or charge upon the people, the consideration and debate thereof may not be presently entered upon, but shall be adjourned till such further day as the House shall think fit to appoint; and then it shall be referred to a Committee of the Whole House, before any resolution or vote of the House do pass thereupon.

94. The Committee of Supply and of Ways and Means are appointed on motion, without previous notice, at the commencement of each Session, as soon as an address has been agreed to in answer to the Speech of the Lieutenant-Governor.

Printing.

95. On motion for Printing any Paper being offered, the same shall be first submitted to the Standing Committee on Printing, for Report, before the question is put thereon.

VI.—OFFICERS AND SERVANTS OF THE HOUSE.

96. The Hours of attendance of the respective officers of the House, and the extra clerks employed during the Session, shall be fixed from time to time by the Speaker.

97. Before filling any vacancy in the service of the House by the Speaker, inquiry shall be made touching the necessity for the continuance of such office ; and the amount of salary to be attached to the same shall be fixed by the Speaker, subject to the approval of the House.

98. No Clerk or Messenger shall be employed, nor any new appointment made, until the Clerk of the House shall have set forth the necessity for such appointment, and shall have delivered such requisition to the Speaker endorsed with his recommendation and approval.

99. It shall be the duty of all the Permanent Officers of this House to complete and finish the work remaining at the close of the Session.

100. The Clerk of the House shall be responsible for the safe keeping of all the Papers and Records of the House and shall have the direction and control over all the officers and clerks employed in the offices, subject to such orders as he may from time to time receive from the Speaker of the House.

101. The Clerk of the House shall place on the Speaker's table, every morning, previous to the meeting of the House, the Order of the Proceedings for the Day.

102. It shall be the duty of the Clerk to make and cause to be printed, and delivered to each Member at the commencement of every Session of Parliament, a List of the Reports, or other periodical Statements which it is the duty of any officer or department of the Government, or any corporate body, to make to the House, referring to the Act or Resolutions and page of the volume of Laws or Journals wherein the same may be ordered ; and placing under the name of such officer or corporation a List of the Reports or Returns required of him, or it, to be made, and the time when the Report or Periodical Statement may be expected.

103. The Sergeant-at-Arms attending the House shall be responsible for the safe keeping of the Mace, Furniture, and Fittings thereof, and for the conduct of the Messengers and inferior Servants of the House.

104. No stranger who shall have been committed by Order of the House to the custody of the Sergeant-at-Arms, shall be released from such custody until he has paid a fee of four dollars to the Sergeant-at-Arms.

105. No allowance shall be made to any person in the employ of the House, who may not reside at the Seat of Government, for travelling expenses in coming to attend his duties.

VII. LIBRARY.

106. A proper Catalogue of the Books belonging to the Library shall be kept by the Librarian, or person in whom the custody and

responsibility thereof shall be vested, and who shall be required to report to the House, through the Speaker, at the opening of each Session, the actual state of the Library.

107. No person shall be entitled to resort to the Library during a Session of Parliament, except the Lieutenant-Governor, the Members of the Executive Council and Legislative Assembly, and the officers of the House, and such other persons as may receive a written order of admission from the Speaker. Members may personally introduce strangers to the Library during the day time, but not after the hour of six o'clock p.m.

108. During a Session of Parliament, no Books belonging to the Library shall be taken out of the building, except by the authority of the Speaker, or upon receipt given by a Member of the House.

109. During the Session the Library shall be open daily, from nine o'clock a.m. until nine o'clock p.m.; and should the House remain in Session after such hour, the Library shall remain open until the House adjourns.

110. During the Recess of Parliament, the Library shall be open every day in each week, Sundays and Holidays excepted, from the hour of ten in the morning until four in the afternoon, and access to the Library shall be permitted to persons introduced by a Member of the Legislature, or admitted, at the discretion of the Clerk or Librarian, subject to such regulations as may be deemed necessary for the security and preservation of the collection.

111. During the Recess of Parliament, no Member of the House shall be at liberty to borrow, or to have in his possession at any one time, more than three works from the Library, or to retain the same for a longer period than one month. No books of reference, or books of special cost or value, may be removed from the Seat of Government under any circumstances.

112. At the first meeting of the Library Committee, in each Session of Parliament, the Librarian shall report a list of Books absent at the commencement of the Session, specifying the names of any persons who have retained the same, in contravention of any of the foregoing rules.

Unprovided Cases.

113. In all unprovided cases, the Rules, Usages and Forms of the House of Commons of the United Kingdom of Great Britain and Ireland, as in force at the time, shall be followed.

114. The Votes and Proceedings of this House shall be printed, having first been persued by the Speaker, and he shall appoint the printing thereof, and no person but such as he shall appoint shall presume to print the same.

114 (a) If anything shall come in question touching the Return or Election of any Member, he is to withdraw during the time the matter is in debate, and all Members returned upon double Returns are to withdraw until their Returns are determined.

115. If it shall appear that any person hath been elected or returned a Member of this House, or endeavored to be, by bribery, or any other corrupt practices, this House will proceed with the utmost severity against all such persons as shall have been wilfully concerned in such bribery or corrupt practices.

116. The offer of any money or other advantage to any Member of this House, for the promoting of any matter whatsoever depending or to be transacted in Parliament, is a high crime and misdemeanor, and tends to the subversion of the Constitution.

INDEX TO RULES, ORDERS AND FORMS OF PROCEEDING.

Absence of Members. Not permitted without leave, Rule 18.
Adjournment of the House. On Friday, Rule 1—For want of a quorum, 1—Without disposing of Orders, 25—Or of Motion under discussion, 25, 27—Yeas and Nays not to be entered on Questions of adjournment, 88.
Adjournment of the House, or Debate. Motions for, always in order, Rule 30. May be made without giving Notice, 31.
Agreements. Bills for confirming, Rule 59.
Aid and Supply. See *Supply.*
Amendments to Private Bills. Notice to be given of any important amendment proposed in Committees, or at Third Reading, Rules 65, 72.
Annual Reports to Legislature. List of, to be prepared by the Clerk, Rule 102.
Appointments to office. Rules relative to, 97, 98.
BILLS :
   Precedence in daily Routine, regulated, Rules 19-23 Rules as to introduction of, and proceedings upon, 40-45.
   See also *Private Bills.*
Bribery Practices. Rule 116.
Business of the House. Ordinary daily Routine, Rule 18—How disposed of, 20-28.
CANAL BILLS :
   Require Special Notice, Rule 55.
Casting Vote. To be given by the Speaker on an equal division, Rule 9—by the Chairman, in Private Bills Committees, 67.
Chairman of Committees. Permanent Chairman of Committees of the Whole House to be appointed each Session, Rule 79.
CLERK OF THE HOUSE :
   To certify readings of Bills, Rule 56 To publish Rules respecting applications for Private Bills, before every Session, 52 To set up lists of Committees appointed, 78 To pay Witnesses before Select Committees, 86—His responsibility and jurisdiction, 100 Certain duties required of him, 98, 101, 102.
Clerks and Servants. See *Officers and Servants of the House.*
Commitment, Motion of. Precludes amendment of the Main Question, Rule 36.

Committees of the Whole House. How formed and regulated, Rule 79, 82—Permanent Chairman to be appointed, 79—On Bills reported from Select Committees, 22—Proceedings in Committee on Bills, 48, 72—Proceedings on Report, 49—Several Bills may be referred to the same Committee, Rule 82.

Committees, Select. How appointed, Rule 83—Quorum, 84—Reports from, 85—Payment of Witnesses, 86—Lists of Committees to be hung up, 78.

Committees (Standing) on Private Bills and Standing Orders. Their duties, Rules 55, 56 (a), 56 (b), 56 (c), 57, 61-71, 85—Must report on every Bill referred, 69.

Committees (Standing). May be appointed after Address is proposed, 85 (a).

DEBATES :

Rules regulating, 9-15—No Member to speak twice except in certain cases, 15— To cease after Members are called in for Division, 87.

Divisions. Rules concerning, 87, 88.

Double Returns. Members returned upon Double Returns to withdraw till their Elections are determined, Rule 116.

Dropped Orders of the Day. How disposed of, Rule 24.

Elections. A Member to withdraw during the discussion of any question touching his election, Rule 114 (a).

Employés. See *Officers and Servants of the House.*

Estate Bills. Proceedings thereon before the Commissioners of Estate Bills, Rules 62, 63.

Evening Sittings of the House. Rule 2.

Extra Clerks, Employment of. Rules 96, 98.

Fee to the Sergeant : For custody of Strangers, Rule 104.

Fee on Private Bills. Payment thereof, Rules 53, 60.

First Reading of Bills. Questions for, to be decided without amendment or debate, Rule 42.

Government Orders. To have precedence on certain days, Rules, 19, 20, 23.

GOVERNOR-GENERAL :

No Member to speak disrespectfully of, Rule 13.

House of Commons of Great Britain. Rules of, to be followed, in unprovided cases, Rule 113.

Journal, Matters to be specially entered therein Names of Members present at adjournment for want of a quorum, Rule 5 Reason given by The Speaker on a Casting Vote, 9—Yeas and Nays upon a Division (not being upon a question of adjournment), when demanded by five Members, 88.

Law Clerk. His duties, Rule 50.

Letters Patent. Bills for confirming, Rule 59.

Librarian. His duties and responsibility, Rules 106-112.

Library of Parliament. Regulation of, during Session, Rules 106-112.

Lieutenant-Governor. No Member to speak disrespectfully of, Rule 13—A copy of the Journal to be sent to him daily, 39 To originate, by Message, all supply votes, page 32—To have access to the Library, Rule 107.

Meeting of the House. At three o'clock p.m. each sitting day, Rule 1—Evening Sittings, 2—Motions respecting, may be made without Notice, 32.

MEMBERS :

To remain seated (upon adjournment) until Speaker retires, Rule 3—Rules and Order in Debate, 10-15—Not to reflect on any Vote of the House, Rule 13 Not to speak twice to a Question, 15—A Reply allowed in certain cases, Rule 15—Not to vote if pecuniarily interested, 16 To preserve decorum in the House, 17—Not to be absent without leave, 18—Answerable for propriety of Petitions, 89, 90 - To endorse Petitions, and not to debate them on presentation, 90—Privileges with respect to the Library, 107-111.

To withdraw if their Elections be discussed, or if returned upon double returns, 114 (*a*)—Bribery practices to be severely punished, 113 And the offer of Money, etc., to a Member, 116.

Messengers. See *Officers and Servants of the House.*

Motions and Questions. Rules concerning, 28-37.

Notices of Motion. Undisposed of at adjournment of the House, Rule 26, 27—Mode of giving Notices, 31—Dispensed with, by unanimous consent, 32.

Notices of Private Bills. Rules relative thereto to be published, Rule 53—Forms to be observed in intended application for Private Bills, 53-55- Committee on Standing Orders to report thereon, without special reference, 56- If Bills contain provisions not contemplated in Notice, Committee thereon is to call the attention of the House thereto, 68.

Notice of Sitting of Committee on any Private Bill. To be affixed in the Lobby and appended to the Votes, Rule 64 No Motion for a general suspension of such Notice to be entertained except after Report by Committee, 64.

Offensive Words. Against the Queen, or Royal Family, or the Governor, or either House, or any Member, not permitted, Rule 13.

OFFICERS AND SERVANTS OF THE HOUSE :

Hours of attendance, Rule 96 Vacancies among, how filled, 97 — New appointments, how made, 98 To finish the work of the

Session, 99—Authority of the Clerk in respect of, 98-100—To have access to the Library, 107—Messengers, etc., under the control of the Sergeant-at-Arms, 103—Travelling expenses not to be allowed to employés, 105.

ORDER :
In Adjournments of the House, Rule 3—To be preserved by Mr. Speaker, 8—Points of Order to be decided by Mr. Speaker, with an appeal to The House, *ib*—In debate, 12—In the House, 17—In Committee of the Whole House, 79-91.

ORDERS OF THE DAY :
Precedence thereon regulated, Rules 19-28—Undisposed of at adjournment of the House, 25, 26—Questions superseded by Motion to read Orders of the Day, 28—To be placed on Speaker's Table every morning, 101.

Pairs. Rule 88a.

Parliamentary Agents. Rules respecting, 76, 77.

Pecuniary Interest. No Member having a pecuniary interest in any question may vote thereon, Rule 16.

Personal Advantage offered to Members. Rule 116.

Petitions. Presentation and Reception of, Rules 88-92—May be either written or printed, 90—If complaining of present personal grievance, may be immediately discussed, 92—Cannot be received if praying for grant of charge on Revenue, 91.

Petitions for Private Bills. Rules concerning, 51-56—To be considered by Committee on Standing Orders without special reference, 56.

Previous Question. Rule 35.

Printing. Of Bills, Rules 43, 44—Of other documents, to be sanctioned by Printing Committee, 95.

Private Bills. Rules concerning. 51-75.

Private Bill Register. Rule 74.

PRIVATE BILL :
Privilege. Questions of, having precedence, Rule 38.

QUEEN, HER MAJESTY THE
No Member to speak disrespectfully of, Rule 13.

QUESTIONS :
Members not to speak beside the Question, Rule 13—May be read when required, 14—Superseded by Motion to read the Orders of the Day, 28—Questions and Motions, Rules concerning, 30-37.

Questions put by Members. Rule as to Questions to Ministers of the Crown, and others, 29—Two days' Notice thereof required, 31.

Quorum. Twenty Members required to form a Quorum, Rule 4—Adjournment for want of, 1—If no Quorum, names of Members present to be recorded, 5—Quorum of Select Committee, 84.

Railway Bills. Require Special Notice, Rule 55.

Reports. How made, Rule 85—Reports on Private Bills, 68-71.

Royal Family. No Member to speak disrespectfully of any member thereof, Rule 13.

Saturday. House does not ordinarily sit on, Rule 1.

Select Committees. See *Committees, Select.*

SERGEANT-AT-ARMS :

To apprehend Strangers acting improperly, Rules 6—To clear The House of Strangers when required, 7—His responsibility and jurisdiction, 103—Entitled to a Fee for custody of Strangers, 104.

Servants. See *Officers and Servants.*

SPEAKER :

His duties at the Meeting and Adjournment of the House, Rules 1-5 To direct Strangers to withdraw, when required by five Members, 7.

To preserve Order, and decide questions of Order, Rule 8—Not to debate, and only to give a Casting Vote, 9—To read Motions before debate thereon, 33—To apprize the House of Unparliamentary Motions, 37—To determine allowances to Witnesses, 88—Not to allow discussion on presenting Petitions, 92—To have full control over Parliamentary Agents, 76, 77—To fix hours of attendance of Officers and Clerks, 96 To fill up vacancies in the Offices, and fix salaries of new Employés, 97, 98—His authority in respect to the Library, 106, 108—Orders printing of Votes and Proceedings, 114.

Speeches. See *Debates.*

Strangers. If guilty of misconduct, or not withdrawing when directed, to be taken into custody, Rule 6—Not to be discharged without special order, *ib*—Strangers to withdraw when required by five Members, 7—Strangers committed, not to be discharged until payment of a Fee to the Sergeant, 104.

SUPPLY :

Supply votes to be first recommended by the Governor, Page 31 Motions for Supply not to be presently entered upon ; To be first discussed in Committee of the Whole House, Rule 93 Committees of Supply, and Ways and Means appointed at the commencement of each Session, 94.

Suspension of Rules. On Petitions for Private Bills, Rules 51, 57—On Private Bills, 64, 73.

Third Readings of Bills. When to take place, Rules 20, 49.

Toll Bridge Bills. Require Special Notices, Rule 54.

Tramway Bridges Bills. Require Special Notice, Rule 55.

Travelling Expenses of Employés. Not to be allowed to them, Rule 105.

Unparliamentary Motions. Rule 37.

Unprovided Cases. Rule 113.

Votes of The House. Not to be reflected on by Members, Rule 13.

Votes and Proceedings. Certain Notices to be appended thereto, Rules 31, 64—Certified Copy to be sent daily to the Lieutenant-Governor, Rule 39—Shall be printed, 114.

Withdrawal of Motions. Is permitted with unanimous consent of the House, Rule 34.

Witnesses. Before Select Committees, how paid, Rule 86.

Yeas and Nays. Not to be recorded (upon a Division) unless demanded by five Members, nor upon questions of adjournment, Rule 88.

APPENDIX.

MEMBERS OF FIRST LEGISLATIVE ASSEMBLY OF ONTARIO.
Met 27th December, 1867.

Addington : E. J. Hooper.
Algoma : Fred. W. Cumberland.
Bothwell : Archibald McKellar.
Brant, N. : Hugh Finlayson.
Brant, S. : E. B. Wood.
Brockville : W. Fitzsimmons.
Bruce, N. : Donald Sinclair.
Bruce, S. : Edward Blake.
Cardwell : Thomas Swinarton.
Carleton : Robert Lyon.
Cornwall : Hon. J. S. Macdonald.
Dundas : Simon Cook.
Durham, E. : A. T. H. Williams.
Durham, W. : John McLeod.
Elgin, E. : Solomon Wigle.
Elgin, W. : Nicol McColl.
Essex : Daniel Luton.
Frontenac : Hon. Sir H. Smith.
Grenville, S. : James Craig.
Grey, S. : A. W. Lauder.
Grey, N. : Thomas Scott.
Haldimand : Jacob Baxter.
Halton : William Barber.
Hamilton : James M. Williams.
Hastings, W. : Ketchum Graham.
Hastings, E. : Henry Corby.
Hastings, N. : Geo. H. Boulter.
Huron, N. : W. T. Hays.
Huron, S. : Robert Gibbons.
Kent : John Smith.
Kingston : M. W. Strange.
Lambton : Timothy Blair Pardee.
Lanark, N. : Daniel Galbraith.
Lanark, S. : W. M. N. Shaw.
Leeds and Grenville : Henry D. Smith.
Leeds, S. : Benjamin Tett.
Lennox : John Stevenson.
Lincoln : John C. Rykert.
London : Hon. J. Carling.
Middlesex, N. : Jas. L Smith.
Middlesex, W. : Nathaniel Currie.
Middlesex, E. : James Evans.
Monck : George Secord.
Niagara (with township) : Donald Robertson.
Norfolk, S. : Simpson McCall.
Norfolk, N. : James Wilson.
Northumberland, E. : John Eyre.
Northumberland, W. : Alex. Fraser.
Ontario, N. : Thomas Paxton.
Ontario, S. : William McGill.
Ottawa : R. W. Scott.
Oxford, N. : George Perry.
Oxford, S. : Adam Oliver.
Peel : John Coyne.
Perth, N. : Andrew Monteith.
Perth, S. : James Trow.
Peterboro', W. : John Carnegie, Jr.
Peterboro', E. : George Read.
Prescott : James Boyd.
Prince Edward : Absolom Greeley
Renfrew, S. : J. L. McDougall.
Renfrew, N. : John Supple.
Russell : W. Craig.
Simcoe, S. : Thos. R. Ferguson.
Simcoe, N. : W. Lount.
Stormont : W. Colquhoun.
Toronto, W. : John Wallis.
Toronto, E. : Hon. M. C. Cameron.
Victoria, N. : A. P. Cockburn.
Victoria, S. : Thos. Matchett.
Waterloo, N. : Moses Springer.
Waterloo, S. : Isaac Clemens.
Welland : William Beatty.
Wellington, N. : Robt. McKim.
Wellington, C. : A. D. Ferrier.
Wellington, S. : Peter Gow.
Wentworth, N. : Robt. Christie.
Wentworth, S. : Wm. Sexton.
York, E. : H. P. Crosby.
York, W. : Thomas Graham.
York, N. : Hon. John McMurrich.

Afterwards Added.

3rd November, 1868.
Frontenac : D. D. Calvin.

14th December, 1868.
Brant, S. : Isaac Carling.

3rd November, 1869.
Lanark, S.: Abraham Code.

7th December, 1870.
Prince Edward : W. Anderson.

SECOND LEGISLATIVE ASSEMBLY.
Met 7th December, 1871.

Addington : H. M. Deroche.
Algoma : F. W. Cumberland.
Bothwell : A. McKellar.
Brant, N. : Hugh Finlayson.
Brant, S. : Hon. E. B. Wood.
Brockville : W. Fitzsimmons.
Bruce, N. : Donald Sinclair.
*Bruce, S. : Edward Blake.
Cardwell : Geo. McManus.
Carleton : W. G. Monk.
Cornwall : Hon. J. S. Macdonald.
Dundas : Simon S. Cook.
Durham, E.: A. T. H. Williams.
Durham, W. : Edward Blake.
Elgin, E. : J. H. Wilson.
Elgin, W. : Thos. Hodgins.
Essex : Albert Prince.
Frontenac : D. D. Calvin.
Glengarry : Jas. Craig.
Grenville, S.N. : Macneil Clarke.
Grey, S. : A. W. Lauder.
Grey, N. : Thos. Scott.
Haldimand : Jacob Baxter.
Halton : W. Barber.
Hamilton : J. M. Williams.
Hastings, W.: Ketcham Graham.
Hastings, E. : Henry Corby.
Hastings, N. : G. H. Boulter.
Huron, N. : Thos. Gibson.
Huron, S. : Robt. Gibbons.
Kent : James Dawson.
Kingston : William Robinson.
Lambton : T. B. Pardee.
Lanark, N. : David Galbraith.
Lanark, S. : Abraham Code.
Leeds and Grenville, N.: Henry Merrick.
Leeds, S. : H. S. Macdonald.
Lennox : J. T. Grange.
Lincoln : J. C. Rykert.
London : Hon. John Carling.
Middlesex, N. : J. S. Smith.
Middlesex, W.: Alex. McKenzie.
Middlesex, E. : Richard Tooley.
Monck : L. McCallum.
Niagara : Hon. Stephen Richards.
Norfolk, S. : S. McCall.
Norfolk, N. : John Clarke.
Northumberland, E. : W. W. Webb.
Northumberland, W. : Alex. Fraser.
Ontario, N. : Thos. Paxton.
Ontario, S. : Abram Farewell.
Ottawa : Hon. R. W. Scott.
Oxford, N. : Geo. Perry.
Oxford, S. : Adam Oliver.
Peel : John Coyne.
Perth, N. : A. Monteith.
Perth, S. : Thos. D. Guest.
Peterborough, W. : Thos. M. Fairbairn.
Peterborough, E. : Geo. Read.
Prescott : J. W. Hamilton.
Prince Edward : Gideon Striker.
Renfrew, S. : Eric Harrington.
Renfrew, N. : Thos. Deacon.
Russell : William Craig.
Simcoe, S. : Thos. R. Ferguson.
Simcoe, N. : W. D. Ardagh.

---

*Mr. Blake elected to sit for South Bruce ; Mr. McLeod elected for Durham West.

Stormont: W. Colquhoun.
Toronto, W.: Adam Crooks.
Toronto, E.: Hon. M. C. Cameron.
Victoria, N.: Duncan McCrea.
Victoria, S.: S. C. Wood.
Waterloo, N.: Moses Springer.
Waterloo, S.: I. Clemens.
Welland: Hon. J. G. Currie.
Wellington, N.: Robt. McKim.
Wellington, C.: Charles Clarke.
Wellington, S.: Peter Gow.
Wentworth, N.: Robt. Christie.
Wentworth, S.: W. Sexton.
York, E.: H. P. Crosby.
York, W.: P. Patterson.
York, N.: Alfred Boultbee.

— 82.

Afterwards Added.

18th January, 1872.
Simcoe, N.: W. D. Ardagh.
Durham, W.: John McLeod.
Northumberland, W.: Charles Gifford.

19th January, 1872.
Stormont: James Bethune.

8th January, 1873.
Prince Edward: J. T. McCuaig.
Cornwall: G. S. Snetzinger.
Bruce, S.: R. M. Wells.
Oxford, N.: O. Mowat.
Monck: H. N. Haney.
Lanark, N.: W. C. Caldwell.
London: W. R. Meredith.
Middlesex: John Watterworth.
Leeds and Grenville: C. F. Fraser.

7th January, 1874.
Peel: Kenneth Chisholm.

Grenville, S.: C. F. Fraser.
Brant, S.: Arthur S. Hardy.
Simcoe, S.: D'Arcy Boulton.
Leeds, S.: John Godkin Giles.

8th January, 1874.
Huron, S.: Arch. Bishop.

3rd February, 1874.
Oxford, S.: Adam Oliver.

5th February, 1874.
Ottawa: Dan. O'Donoghue.

24th February, 1874.
Perth, N.: T. M. Daly.

2nd February, 1874.
Wellington, N.: John McGowan.

12th November, 1874.
Peterborough, W.: W. H. Scott.

THIRD LEGISLATIVE ASSEMBLY.
Met 24th November, 1875.

Addington: H. M. Deroche.
Algoma: Simon J. Dawson.
Brant, N.: Hugh Finlayson.
Brant, S.: A. S. Hardy.
Brockville: W. H. Cole.
Bruce, N.: Donald Sinclair.
Bruce, S.: R. M. Wells.
Cardwell: John Flesher.
Carleton: G. W. Monk.
Cornwall: A. F. McIntyre.
Dufferin: John Barr.
Dundas: Andrew Broder.
Durham, E.: John Rosevear.
Durham, W.: John McLeod.
Elgin, E.: J. H. Wilson.
Elgin, W.: Malcolm G. Munro.
Essex, S.: Lewis Wigle.
Essex, W.: J. C. Patterson.
Frontenac: Peter Graham.
Glengarry: Alex. J. Grant.
Grenville, S.: C. F. Fraser.
Grey, S.: James H. Hunter.

Grey, N. : Thomas Scott.
Grey, E. : Abram W. Lauder.
Haldimand : Jacob Baxter.
Halton : W. Barber.
Hamilton : J. M. Williams.
Hastings, W. : Thomas Wills.
Hastings, E. : A. S. Appleby.
Hastings, N. : Geo. H. Boulter.
Huron, W. : A. McLagan Ross.
Huron, E. : Thomas Gibson.
Huron, S. : Archibald Bishop.
Kent, W. : Alexander Coutts.
Kent, E. : Archibald McKellar.
Kingston : William Robinson.
Lambton, W. : T. B. Pardee.
Lambton, E. : Peter Graham.
Lanark, N. : W. Mostyn.
Lanark, S. : Abraham Code.
Leeds and Grenville, N.: Henry Merrick.
Leeds, S. : Robert H. Preston.
Lennox : John Thos. Grange.
Lincoln : Sylvester Neelon.
London : W. R. Meredith.
Middlesex, N. : John McDougall.
Middlesex, W. : John Watterworth.
Middlesex, E. : Richard Tooley.
Monck : Henry R. Haney.
Muskoka and Parry Sound: John C. Miller.
Norfolk, S. : Richard Richardson.
Norfolk, N. : John Clarke.
Northumberland, E. : Jas. M. Ferris.

Northumberland, W. : W. Hargraft.
Ontario, N. : Thomas Paxton.
Ontario, S.: Nicholas W. Brown.
Ottawa : Daniel J. O'Donoghue.
Oxford, N. : O. Mowat.
Oxford, S. : Adam Oliver.
Peel : K. Chisholm.
Perth, N. : David D. Hay.
Perth, S. : Thomas Ballantyne.
Peterborough, W.: Geo. A. Cox.
Peterborough, E. : J. C. Sullivan.
Prescott : W. Harkin.
Prince Edward : Gideon Striker.
Renfrew, S. : James Bonfield.
Renfrew, N. : Thomas Deacon.
Russell : Adam Jacob Baker.
Simcoe, S. : D'Arcy Boulton.
Simcoe, E. : John Kean.
Simcoe, W. : Thomas Long.
Stormont : James Bethune.
Toronto, W. : Robert Bell.
Toronto, E. : M. C. Cameron.
Victoria, N. : John D. Smith.
Victoria, S. : S. C. Wood.
Waterloo, N. : Moses Springer.
Waterloo, S. : John Fleming.
Welland : J. G. Currie.
Wellington, N.: John McGowan.
Wellington, C. : Charles Clarke.
Wellington, S. : Peter Gow.
Wentworth, N. : Thomas Stock.
Wentworth, S. : W. Sexton.
York, E. : John Lane.
York, W. : Peter Patterson.
York, N.: Joseph H. Widdifield.

Afterwards Added.

3rd January, 1877.
Wellington, S. : James Massie.

14th January, 1877.
Frontenac : D. D. Calvin.

23rd February, 1877.
Waterloo, S. : Isaac Master.

9th January, 1879.
Simcoe, S. : Wm. J. Parkhill.
Monck : Richard Harcourt.
Essex, N. : Solomon White.
Elgin, W. : David M. Laws.
Algoma : R. A. Lyon.
Toronto, E. : Alex. Morris.

FOURTH LEGISLATIVE ASSEMBLY.

Met 7th January, 1880

Addington : H. M. Deroche.
Algoma : Robert A. Lyon.
Brant, N. : James Young.
Brant, S. : Hon. A. S. Hardy.
Brockville : Hon. C. F. Fraser.
Bruce, N. : Donald Sinclair.
Bruce, S. : R. M. Wells.
Cardwell : Charles Robinson.
Carleton : Geo. W. Monk.
Cornwall : Wm. Mack.
Dufferin : John Barr.
Dundas : Andrew Broder.
Durham, E. : John Rosevear.
Durham, W. : J. W. McLaughlin.
Elgin, E. : Thomas M. Nairn.
Elgin, W. : John Cascaden.
Essex, N. : Solomon White.
Essex, S. : Lewis Wigle.
Frontenac : D. D. Calvin.
Glengarry : Donald Macmaster.
Grenville, S. : Fred. F. French.
Grey, N. ; David Creighton.
Grey, E. : A. W. Lauder.
Grey, S. : James H. Hunter.
Haldimand : Jacob Baxter.
Halton : David Robertson.
Hamilton : John Morison Gibson.
Hastings : W. Alexander Robinson.
Hastings, E. : N. S. Appleby.
Hastings, N. : Geo. H. Boulter.
Huron, E. : Thomas Gibson.
Huron, S. : Arch. Bishop.
Huron, W. : A. M Ross.
Kent, E : Daniel McCraney.
Kent, W. : Edward Robinson.
Kingston : James Henry Metcalfe.
Lambton, E. : Peter Graham.
Lambton, W. : Hon. T. D. Pardee.
Lanark, N. : Wm. C. Caldwell.

Lanark, S. : Wm. Lees.
Leeds and Grenville : Henry Merrick.
Leeds, S. : Wm. Richardson.
Lennox : George D. Hawley.
Lincoln : Sylvester Neelon.
London : W. R. Meredith.
Middlesex, E. : Richard Tooley.
Middlesex, N : John Waters.
Middlesex, W. : John Watterworth.
Monck : Richard Harcourt.
Muskoka and Parry Sound : John C. Miller.
Norfolk, S. : Wm. Morgan.
Norfolk, N. : John B. Freeman.
Northumberland, E. : J. M. Ferris.
Northumberland, W. ; John C. Field.
Ontario, N. : Thomas Paxton.
Ontario, S. : John Dryden.
Ottawa : Patrick Baskerville.
Oxford, N. : Hon. O. Mowat.
Oxford, S. : Hon. Adam Crooks.
Peel : Kenneth Chisholm.
Perth, N. : D. D. Hay.
Perth, S. : Thomas Ballantyne.
Peterborough, E. · Thomas Blezard.
Peterborough, W. : William H. Scott.
Prescott : William Harkin.
Prince Edward : Gideon Striker.
Renfrew, S. : James Bonfield.
Renfrew, N. : Thomas Murray.
Russell : Ira Morgan.
Simcoe, E. : Herman H Cook.
Simcoe, S. : W. James Parkhill.
Simcoe, W. : Thomas Long.
Stormont : Joseph Kerr.
Toronto, E. : Hon. A. Morris.
Toronto, W. : Robert Bell.

Victoria, N.: Samuel Stanley Peck.
Victoria, S.: Hon. S. C. Wood.
Waterloo, N.: Moses Springer.
Waterloo, S.: James Livingston.
Welland : Daniel Near.
Wellington, W.: Robert McKim.
Wellington, C.: Charles Clarke.
Wellington, S.: James Laidlaw.
Wentworth, N.: Jas. McMahon.
Wentworth, S.: J. M. Carpenter.
York, E.: T. W. Badgerow.
York, W.: Peter Patterson.
York, N.: J. H. Widdifield.

Afterwards Added.

16th January, 1880.
Dufferin : Wm. Jelly.

12th January, 1882.
Durham, E.: Chas. H Brenton.
Ontario, N.: Frank Madill.
Prescott : Albert Hagar.
Waterloo, N.: Elias W. D. Snider.

19th January, 1882.
Peterborough, W.: R. Kincaid.

9th December, 1882.
Simcoe, E.: Charles Drury.
Essex, S.: W. D. Balfour.
Hastings, W.: Battis Rose.
Waterloo, S.: Isaac Master.
Renfrew, N.: W. B. McAllister.
Glengarry : James Rayside.

15th December, 1882.
Bruce, S.: H. P. O'Connor.
Muskoka and Parry Sound : I. H. Bettes.

FIFTH LEGISLATIVE ASSEMBLY.

Met 23rd January, 1884.

Addington : George Denison.
Algoma : R. A. Lyon.
Brant, N.: James Young.
Brant, S.: A. S. Hardy.
Brockville : C. F. Fraser.
Bruce, N.: John Gillies.
Bruce, S.: H. P. O'Connor.
Cardwell : W. H. Hammel.
Carleton : G. W. Monk.
Cornwall : Alex. P. Ross.
Dufferin : Robert McGhee.
Dundas : Andrew Broder.
Durham, E.: C. H. Brereton.
Durham, W.: J. W. McLaughlin.
Elgin, E.: Charles Oaks Ermatinger.
Elgin, W.: John Cascaden.
Essex, N.: Solomon White.
Essex, S.: W. D. Balfour.
Frontenac : Henry Wilmot.
Glengarry : James Rayside.
Grenville, S : Fred. J. French.
Grey, N.: David Creighton.
Grey, E.: A. W. Lauder.
Grey, S.: John Blythe.
Haldimand : Jacob Baxter.
Halton : Wm. Kerns.
Hamilton : J. M. Gibson.
Hastings, W.: Eph. Geo. Sills.

Hastings, E.: Wm. P. Hudson.
Hastings, N.: A. F. Wood.
Huron, E.: Thomas Gibson.
Huron, S.: Arch. Bishop.
Huron, W.: A. M. Ross.
Kent, E.: Daniel McCraney.
Kent. W.: James Clancey.
Kingston : James H. Metcalfe.
Lambton, W.: T. B. Pardee.
Lambton, E.: Peter Graham.
Lanark, N.: W. C. Caldwell.
Lanark, S.: William Lees.
Leeds, S.: Robert H. Preston.
Lennox : A. Hale Roe.
Lincoln : Sylvester Neelon.
London : W. R. Meredith.
Middlesex, E.: D. McKenzie.
Middlesex, N.: John Waters.
Middlesex, W.: Alex. Johnston.
Monck : Richard Harcourt.
Muskoka and Parry Sound : F. G. Fauquier.
Norfolk, S.: Wm. Morgan.
Norfolk, N.: John B. Freeman.
Northumberland, E.: J. M. Ferris.
Northumberland, W.: R. Mulholland.
Ontario, N.: Isaac J. Gould.
Ontario, S.: John Dryden.
Ottawa : P. Baskerville.
Oxford, N.: Oliver Mowat.
Oxford, S.: Adam Crooks.
Peel : Kenneth Chisholm.
Perth, N.: George Hess.
Perth S.: Thomas Ballantyne.
Peterborough, E.: Thomas Blezard.
Peterborough, W.: John Carnegie.
Prescott : Albert Hagar.
Prince Edward : James Hart.
Renfrew, S.: John F. Dowling.
Renfrew, N.: Thomas Murray.
Russell : Honore Robillard.
Simcoe, E.: Charles Drury.
Simcoe, S.: Geo. R. McKay.
Simcoe, W.: Orson J. Phelps.
Stormont : Joseph Kerr.
Toronto, E.: Alex. Morris.
Toronto, W.: H. E. Clarke.
Victoria, N.: John Fell.
Victoria, S.: D. J. McIntyre.
Waterloo, N.: E. W. B. Snider.
Waterloo, S.: Isaac Master.
Welland : James E. Morin.
Wellington, W : Robert McKim.
Wellington, C.: Chas. Clarke.
Wellington, S.: James Laidlaw.
Wentworth, S.: Nicholas Awrey.
York, E : Geo. W. Badgerow.
York, W.: John Gray.
York, N.: J. H. Widdifield.

Afterwards Added.

7th March, 1884.
Oxford, S.: George A. Cooke.

24th March, 1884.
Grey, E.: Neil McColman.

3rd February, 1885.
Muskoka and Parry Sound : J. W. Dill.
Renfrew, S.: J. F. Dowling.

28th January, 1886.
Muskoka and Parry Sound, James Conmee.

29th January, 1886.
Lennox : George D. Hawley.
Kent, E.: Robert Ferguson.

2nd February, 1886.
Algoma : Robert Adam Lyon.

SIXTH LEGISLATIVE ASSEMBLY.
Met 10th February, 1887.

Addington. John S. Miller.
Brant, N.: Wm. B. Wood.
Brant S.: A. S. Hardy.
Brockville: C. F. Fraser.
Bruce, N.: J. W. S. Biggar.
Bruce, S.: H. P. O'Connor.
Bruce, C.: W. M. Dack.
Cardwell: W. H. Hammell.
Carleton: Geo. W. Monk.
Cornwall & Stormont: William Mack.
Dufferin: F. C. Stewart.
Dundas: Theo. J. Chamberlain.
Durham, E.: Thos. D. Craig.
Durham, W.: J. W. McLaughlin.
Elgin, E.: Thos. M. Nairn.
Elgin, W.: A. B. Ingram.
Essex, N.: Gaspard Pacaud
Essex, S.: W. D. Balfour.
Frontenac: Henry Wilmot.
Glengarry: Jas. Rayside.
Grenville: F. J. French.
Grey, N.: D. Creighton.
Grey, C.: Joseph Rorke.
Grey, S.: John Blyth.
Haldimand: Jacob Baxter.
Halton: William Kerns.
Hamilton: J. M. Gibson.
Hastings, W.: G. W. Ostrom.
Hastings, E.: W. P. Hudson.
Hastings, N.: A. F. Wood.
Huron, E.: Thos Gibson.
Huron, S.: A. Hyslop.
Huron, W.: A. M. Ross.
Kent, E.: Robt. Ferguson.
Kent, W.: Jas. Clancy.
Kingston: J. H. Metcalfe.
Lambton, E.: Peter Graham.
Lambton, W.: T. B. Pardee.
Lanark, N.: Daniel Hilliard.
Lanark, S.: William Lees.
Leeds: Robert H. Preston.
Lennox: Walter W. Meacham.
Lincoln: William Garson.
London: W. R. Meredith.
Middlesex, E.: Richard Tooley.
Middlesex, N.: John Waters.
Middlesex, W.: Geo. W. Ross.
Monk: Richard Harcourt.
Muskoka: Geo. Fred. Marter.
Norfolk, S.: William Morgan.
Norfolk, N.: John B. Freeman.
Northumberland, E.: W. A. Willoughby.
Northumberland, W.: C. C. Field.
Ontario, N.: Isaac J. Gould.
Ontario, S.: John Dryden.
Ottawa: Erskine H. Bronson.
Oxford, N.: Oliver Mowat.
Oxford, S.: Angus McKay.
Parry Sound: Sam Armstrong.
Peel: Kenneth Chisholm.
Perth, N.: George Hess.
Perth, S.: Thos. Ballantyne.
Peterborough, E.: T. Blezard.
Peterborough, W.: James R. Stratton.
Prescott: Alfred Evanturel.
Prince Edward: J. A. Sprague.
Renfrew, S.: J. A. McAndrew.
Renfrew, N.: Thos. Murray.
Russell: Alex. Robillard.
Simcoe, E.: Chas. Drury.
Simcoe, W.: Thos. Wylie.
Simcoe, C.: C. J. Phelps.
Toronto: H. E. Clarke.
Toronto: E. F. Clarke.
Toronto: John Leys.
Victoria, E.: John Fell.
Victoria, W., J. S. Cruess.
Waterloo, N.: E. W. B. Snider.
Waterloo, S.: Isaac Master.
Welland: James E. Morin.
Wellington, S.: Donald Guthrie.
Wellington, E.: Chas. Clarke.
Wellington, W.: A. S. Allan.
Wentworth, N.: Jas. McMahon.
Wentworth, S.: Nicholas Awrey.
York, E.: Geo. B. Smith.
York, W.: John T. Gilmour.
York, N.: J. H. Widdifield.

Afterwards Added.

31st January, 1888.
Algoma : R. A. Lyon. James Conmee.

10th February, 1888.
Dundas : J. P. Whitney.

13th February, 1888.
Northumberland : Rich. Clarke.

24th January, 1889.
Simcoe, E. : Charles Drury.
York, N. : E. J. Davis.

Frontenac : Hugh Smith.
Elgin, E. : Jas. Chas. Dance.
Northumberland, E. : W. A. Willoughby.

30th January, 1889.
Lambton, W. : Chas. Mackenzie.

31st January, 1889.
Lanark, N. : W. C. Caldwell.

1st February, 1889.
Hamilton : J. M. Gibson.

SEVENTH LEGISLATIVE ASSEMBLY.
Met 11th February, 1891.

Addington : James Reid.
Algoma, E. : A. F. Campbell.
Algoma, W. : James Conmee.
Brant, N. : W. B. Wood.
Brant, S. : A. S. Hardy.
Brockville : C. F. Fraser.
Bruce, N. :
Bruce, S. : H. P. O'Connor.
Bruce, C. : W. M. Dack.
Cardwell : W. H. Hammell.
Carleton : Geo. W. Monk.
Dufferin : John Barr.
Dundas : J. P. Whitney.
Durham, E. : Geo. Campbell.
Durham, W. : W. T. Lockhart.
Elgin, E. : H. T. Godwin.
Elgin, W. : Dugald McColl.
Essex, N. : Solomon White.
Essex, S. : W. D. Balfour.
Frontenac : Hugh Smith.
Glengarry : James Rayside.
Grenville : Orlando Bush.
Grey, N. : James Cleland.
Grey, C. : Joseph Rorke.
Grey, S. : J. H. Hunter.
Haldimand : Jacob Baxter.
Halton : William Kerns.
Hamilton :

Hastings, W. : W. H. Biggar.
Hastings, E. : W. P. Hudson.
Hastings, N. : A. F. Wood.
Huron, S. : Arch. Bishop.
Huron, W. : Jas. T. Garrow.
Huron, E. : Thos. Gibson.
Kent, E. : Robt. Ferguson.
Kent, W. : James Clancy.
Kingston : J. H. Metcalfe.
Lambton, E. : Hugh McKenzie.
Lambton, W. : C. Mackenzie.
Lanark, N. : W. C. Caldwell.
Lanark, S. : N. McLanaghan.
Leeds : Robert H. Preston.
Lennox : W. W. Meacham.
Lincoln : James Hiscott.
London : W. R. Meredith.
Middlesex, E. : Rich. Tooley.
Middlesex, N. : John Waters.
Middlesex, W. : Geo. W. Ross.
Monck : Richard Harcourt.
Muskoka : G. F. Marter.
Nipissing : John Loughrin.
Norfolk, N. : W. A. Charlton.
Norfolk, S. : E. C. Carpenter.
Northumberland, E. : W. A. Willoughby.

Northumberland, W. : C. C. Field.
Ontario, N. : Jas. Glendinning.
Ontario, S. : John Dryden.
Ottawa : E. H. Bronson.
Oxford, N. : Oliver Mowat.
Oxford, S. : Angus McKay.
Parry Sound : James Sharpe.
Peel : Kenneth Chisholm.
Perth, N. : Thos. Magwood.
Perth, S. : Thos. Ballantyne.
Peterborough, E. : T. Blezard.
Peterborough, W. : James R. Stratton.
Prescott : Alfred Evanturel.
Prince Edward : J. A. Sprague.
Renfrew, S. : J. F. Dowling.
Renfrew, N. : Arunah Dunlop.
Russell : Alex. Robillard.
Simcoe, E. : A. Miscampbell.
Simcoe, W. : Thos. Wylie.
Simcoe, C. : Robert Paton.
Stormont : Wm. Mack.
Toronto, E. - H. E. Clarke.
Toronto, W. : E. F. Clarke.
Toronto, C. : Joseph Tait.
Victoria, E. : John Fell.
Victoria, W. : John McKay
Waterloo, N. : E. W. D. Snider.
Waterloo, S. : John D. Moore.
Welland : Wm. McCleary.
Wellington, S. : Don. Guthrie.
Wellington, E. : Chas. Clarke.
Wellington, W. : A. S. Allan.
Wentworth, N. : Jas. McMahon.
Wentworth, S. : Nicholas Awrey.
York, E. : Geo. B. Smith.
York, W. : John T. Gilmour.
York, N. : E. J. Davis.

Afterwards Added.

10th March, 1891.
Hamilton : J. M. Gibson.

13th March, 1891.
Bruce, N. : David Porter.

6th April, 1891.
Grey, S. : Gilbert McKechnie.

11th February, 1892.
Wellington, E. : Jas. Kirkwood.

1st March, 1892.
Renfrew, N. : Henry Barr.
Kingston : William Harty.

31st March, 1893.
Toronto, E. : G. S. Ryerson.

4th April, 1893.
Peel : John Smith.

14th February, 1894.
Bruce, N. : D. McNaughton.

15th February, 1894.
Lambton, E. : Peter D. McCallum.

27th February, 1894.
Lanark, S. : J. M. Clarke.

EIGHTH LEGISLATIVE ASSEMBLY.
Met 21st February, 1895.

Addington : James Reid.
Algoma, E. : C. F. Farwell.
Algoma, W. : James Connee.
Brant, N. : W. B. Wood.
Brant, S. : Hon. A. S. Hardy.
Brockville : Geo. A. Dana.
Bruce, N. : Daniel McNaughton.
Bruce, S. : Reuben E. Truax.
Bruce, C. : J. Stevenstone McDonald.

Cardwell : E. A. Little.
Carleton : Geo. N. Kidd.
Dufferin : William Dynes.
Dundas : J. P. Whitney.
Durham, E. : W. A. Fallis.
Durham, W. : W. H. Reid.
Elgin, E. : Chas A. Brower.
Elgin, W. : Donald Macnish.
Essex, N. : W. J. McKee.
Essex, S. : W. D. Balfour.
Frontenac : Joseph T. Haycock.
Glengarry : D. M. McPherson.
Grenville : Orlando Bush.
Grey, N. : James Cleland.
Grey, C. : Thos. Gamey.
Grey, S. : David McNicol.
Haldimand :
Halton : William Kerns.
Hamilton, W. : Hon. J. M. Gibson.
Hamilton, E. : J. T. Middleton.
Hastings, W. : W. H. Biggar.
Hastings, E. : Alex. McLaren.
Hastings, N. : Jas. Haggarty.
Huron, E. : Thomas Gibson.
Huron, S. : Murdo Y. McLean.
Huron, W. : Jas. T. Garrow.
Kent, E. : Robert Ferguson.
Kent, W. : Thomas L. Pardo.
Kingston :
Lambton E : P. D. McCallum.
Lambton, W. : Alfred T. Gurd.
Lanark. N. : R. F. Preston.
Lanark, S. : A. J. Matheson.
Leeds : Walter Beatty.
Lennox : W. W. Meacham.
Lincoln : James Hiscott.
London : Thos. S. Hobbs.
Middlesex, E. : William Shore.
Middlesex, N. : W. H. Taylor.
Middlesex, W. : Hon.G.W. Ross.
Monck : Hon. Richard Harcourt.
Muskoka : Geo. E. Langford.
Nipissing : John Loughrin.
Norfolk, S. : W. A. Charlton.
Norfolk, N. : Ed. C. Carpenter.

Northumberland, E. : W. A. Willoughby.
Northumberland, W. : C. C. Field.
Ontario, N. : Thos. W. Chapple.
Ontario, S. : Hon. John Dryden.
Ottawa : {Hon. E. H. Bronson. (George O'Keefe.
Oxford, N. : Hon. Sir O. Mowat.
Oxford, S. : Angus McKay.
Parry Sound : W. R. Beatty.
Peel : John Smith.
Perth, N. : Thomas Magwood.
Perth, S. : John McNeil.
Peterborough, E. : Thos. Blezard.
Peterborough, W. : James R. Stratton.
Prescott : F. E. A. Evanturel.
Prince Edward : John Caven.
Renfrew, S. : R. A. Campbell.
Renfrew, N. : Henry Barr.
Russell : Alex. Robillard.
Simcoe, E. : A. Miscampbell.
Simcoe, W. : Archibald Currie.
Simcoe, C. ; Robert Paton.
Stormont : John Bennett.
Toronto, W. : Thomas Crawford.
Toronto, E. : Geo. S. Ryerson.
Toronto, N. : Geo. F. Marter.
Toronto, S. : Oliver A. Howland.
Victoria, E. : John Carnegie.
Victoria, W. : John McKay.
Waterloo, N. : A. B. Robertson.
Waterloo, S. : John D. Moore.
Welland : W. M. German.
Wellington, S. : John Mutrie.
Wellington, E. : John Craig.
Wellington, W. :
Wentworth, N. : John Ira Flatt.
Wentworth, S. : Nicholas Awrey.
York, E. : John Richardson.
York, W. : J. W. St. John.
York, N. : E. J. Davis.

Afterwards Added.

4th February, 1896.
Wentworth, S.: John Dickenson.
Brant, N.: Daniel Burt.

11th February, 1896.
Kingston : William Harty.

10th February, 1896.
Wellington, W.: James Tucker.

9th February, 1897.
Oxford, N.: Andrew Pattullo.

21st March, 1895.
Haldimand : J. Baxter.

NINTH LEGISLATIVE ASSEMBLY.

Met 3rd August, 1898.

Addington : James Reid.
Algoma, East : Charles Franklin Farwell
Algoma, West : James Conmee.
Brant, N.R.: Daniel Burt.
Brant, S. R.: Hon. Arthur Sturgis Hardy.
Brockville : George P. Graham.
Bruce, N.R. : Charles Martin Bowman.
Bruce, S.R.: Reuben E. Truax.
Bruce, C.R.: Andrew Malcolm.
Cardwell: Edward Alfred Little.
Carleton : George Nelson Kidd.
Dufferin : John Barr.
Dundas : James Pliny Whitney.
Durham, E. R. : William A. Fallis.
Durham, W.R.: William Henry Reid.
Elgin, E. R.: Charles Andrew Brower.
Elgin, W.R.: Finlay G. McDiarmid.
Essex, N.R.: William J. McKee.
Essex, E.R.: John Allan Auld.
Frontenac : John S. Gallagher.
Glengarry : Donald Robert McDonald.
Grenville : Robert L. Joynt.
Grey, N.R. : George Milward Boyd.
Grey, C.R.: Isaac B. Lucas.
Grey, S.R.: David Jamieson.

Haldimand : Jose W. Holmes.
Halton : John Roaf Barber.
Hamilton, West : Andrew Alexander Colquhoun.
Hamilton, East : Henry Carscallen.
Hastings, W.R. : M. B. Morrison.
Hasting,, E.R.: Samuel Russell.
Hastings, N.R.: William John Allen.
Huron, E.R.: Archibald Hislop.
Huron, S.R.: Henry Eilber.
Huron, W.R.: James Thompson Garrow.
Kent, E.R.: Robert Ferguson.
Kent, W. R. : Thomas Letson Pardo.
Kingston ; Hon. Wm. Harty.
Lambton, E. R. : Henry John Pettypiece.
Lambton, W.R. : Frederick F. Pardee.
Lanark, N.R. William C. Caldwell.
Lanark, S. R. : Arthur James Matheson.
Leeds : Walter Beatty.
Lennox : Bower Ebenezer Aylsworth.
Lincoln ; Elisha Jessop.
London : Francis Baxter Leys.
Middlesex, E. R. : Thomas D. Hodgins.

Middlesex, N.R.: William Henry Taylor.
Middlesex, W.R.: Hon. George William Ross.
Monck: Hon. Richard Harcourt.
Muskoka: Samuel Bridgland.
Nipissing: John Loughrin.
Norfolk, S. R.: William A. Charlton.
Norfolk, N.R.: E.C, Carpenter.
Northumberland, E. R.: John H. Douglas.
Northumberland, W.R.; Samuel Clarke.
Ontario, N. R.: Wm. H. Hoyle.
Ontario, S.R.: Charles Calder.
Ottawa : { Alexander Lumsden. / Chas. Berkley Powell
Oxford, N.R.: Andrew Pattullo
Oxford, S.R.: Angus McKay.
Parry Sound: William Rabb Beatty.
Peel: John Smith.
Perth, N.R.: John Brown.
Perth, S. R.: William Caven Moscrip.
Peterborough, E. R.: Thomas Blezard.
Peterborough, W.R.: James B. Stratton.
Prescott: Alfred Francis Eugene Evanturel.
Prince Edward: William Ryerson Dempsey.
Renfrew, S.R.: Robert A. Campbell.
Renfrew, N.R.: Andrew Thomas White.
Russell: Oneisme Guibord.
Simcoe, E. R.; Andrew Miscampbell.
Simcoe, W.R.: James Stoddart Duff.
Simcoe, C.R.: A. B. Thompson.
Stormont: John McLaughlin.
Toronto, West: Thomas Crawford.
Toronto, East: Robert Allan Pyne.
Toronto, North: George Frederick Marter.
Toronto, South: James Joseph Foy.
Victoria, E.R.: John H. Carnegie.
Victoria, W.R.: Samuel J. Fox.
Waterloo, N.R.: Henry George Lackner.
Waterloo, S. R.: William A. Kribs.
Welland: William Manley German.
Wellington, S.R.: John Mutrie.
Wellington, E.R.: John Craig.
Wellington W. R.: James Tucker.
Wentworth, N.R.: Thomas Atkins Wardell.
Wentworth, S.R.: John Dickenson.
York, E.R.: John Richardson.
York, W.R.: William James Hill.
York, N.R.: Hon. Elihu James Davis.

THE LEGISLATIVE ASSEMBLY OF ONTARIO.

Table shewing the duration of each Session of the Legislature, etc., since Confederation, with Movers of the Address in reply to the Speech from the Throne.

First Legislature.

House met.	Address moved.	Mover of Address.	Seconder of Address.	Address Carried.	Legislature Prorogued.
1867, Dec. 27	Dec. 30 ..	John Ceyne	A. Greeley	Dec. 30 ..	Mar. 4, 1868.
1868, Nov. 3	Nov. 4 ..	William Lount ...	D. Dexter Calvin.	Nov. 6 ..	Jan. 23, 1869.
1869, Nov. 3.	Nov. 4 ..	F. W. Cumberland	Henry D. Smith ..	Nov. 4 ..	Dec. 24, 1869.
1870, Dec. 7.	Dec. 8 ..	John Carnegie	Thomas Murray ..	Dec. 12 ..	Feb. 15, 1871.

Second Legislature.

1871-2, Dec. 7	Dec 11 ..	H. W. Deroche...	H. S. Macdonald.	Dec. 16 ..	Mar. 2, 1872
1873, Jan. 8.	Jan. 9 ..	W. Caldwell	Rupert N. Wells..	Jan. 10 ..	Mar. 29, 1873.
1874, Jan. 7.	Jan 9 ..	A. S. Hardy	Peter Patterson ..	Jan. 12 ..	Mar. 24, 1874.
*1874, Nov. 12	Nov. 13 ..	D. Sinclair	Gideon Striker ...	Nov. 13 ..	Dec. 21, 1874

Third Legislature.

1875-6 Nov. 21	Nov. 26 ..	J. W. Widdifield.	James M. Ferris ..	Nov. 29 ..	Feb. 10, 1876.
1877, Jan. 3	Jan. 4 ..	John C. Miller ..	James Massie	Jan. 5 ..	Mar. 2, 1877.
1878, Jan. 9.	Jan. 10 ..	A. McLagan Ross.	John Lane	Jan. 14 ..	Mar. 7, 1878.
1879, Jan. 9.	Jan. 10 ..	Richard Harcourt.	David McLaws ...	Jan. 22 ..	Mar. 11, 1879.

Fourth Legislature.

1880, Jan. 7.	Jan. 7 ..	J. W. McLaughlin	John Waters	Jan. 9 ..	Mar. 5, 1880.
1881, Jan. 13.	Jan. 14 ..	John M. Gibson ..	John Dryden	Jan. 18 ..	Mar. 4, 1881.
1882, Jan. 12.	Jan. 13 ..	David D. Hay ...	C. Robinson	Jan. 27 ..	Mar. 10, 1882.
1882-3, Dec. 13	Dec. 14 ..	W. D. Balfour	Charles Drury	Dec. 20 ..	Feb 1, 1883.

Fifth Legislature.

1884, Jan. 23.	Jan. 25 .	D. J. McIntyre ...	Ephraim G. Sills .	Feb. 6 ..	Mar. 25, 1884.
1885, Jan. 28.	Jan. 29 ..	Nicholas Awrey ..	Albert Hagar......	Jan. 29 ..	Mar. 30, 1885.
1886, Jan. 28.	Jan. 29 ..	G. D. Hawley	James Conmee ...	Feb. 2 ..	Mar. 25, 1886.

Sixth Legislature.

1887, Feb. 10.	Mar. 2 ..	Donald Guthrie ..	A. Evanturel	Mar. 2 ..	Apl. 23, 1887.
1888, Jan. 25	Jan. 26 ..	James R. Stratton	Angus McKay....	Jan. 26 ..	Mar. 23, 1888.
1889, Jan. 24.	Jan. 25 ..	George B. Smith..	Elihu J. Davis...	Jan. 25 ..	Mar. 23, 1889.
1890, Jan. 30.	Jan. 31 ..	C. Mackenzie	John T. Gilmour.	Jan. 31 ..	Apl. 7, 1890.

Seventh Legislature.

1891, Feb. 11.	Mar. 10	Joseph Tait	J. T. Garrow	Mar. 10 ..	May 4, 1891.
1892, Feb. 11.	Feb. 15 ..	W. H. Biggar.....	W. T. Lockhart ..	Feb. 15 ..	Apl 14, 1892.
1893, Apl. 4.	Apl. 5 ..	Absalom S. Allen.	G. McKechnie....	Apl. 5 ..	May 27, 1893.
1894, Feb. 14.	Feb. 15 ..	W. B. Wood	James Conmee ..	Feb. 15 ..	May 5, 1894.

Eighth egislature.

1895, Feb. 21.	Feb. 22 ..	John Craig	D. Macnish	Feb. 22	Apl. 16, 1895.
1896, Feb. 11.	Feb. 12 ..	M. Y. McLean ...	T. W. Chapple...	Feb. 12 ..	Apl. 7, 1896.
1897, Feb. 10.	Feb. 11 ..	A. Pattullo.......	John A. Auld	Feb. 11 ..	Apl. 13, 1897.
1897-8 Nov. 30	Dec. 1 ..	W. M. German ..	C. F. Farwell	Dec. 1 ..	Jan. 17, 1898

Ninth Legislature.

1898, Aug. 3.	Aug. 4 ..	H. J. Pettypiece..	Samuel Clarke....	Aug. 12 ..	Oct. 12, 1898.

GENERAL ELECTIONS IN ONTARIO TO LEGISLATIVE ASSEMBLY SINCE CONFEDERATION.

1. 1867. September. Legislature dissolved, 25th February, 1871.
2. 1871. Nominations, 14th March. Poll, 21st March. Legislature dissolved, 23rd December, 1874.
3. 1875. Nominations, 11th January. Poll, 18th January. Legislature dissolved, 25th April, 1879.
4. 1879. Nominations, 29th May. Poll, 5th June. Legislature dissolved, 1st February, 1883.
5. 1883. Nominations, 20th February. Poll, 27th February. Legislature dissolved, 15th November, 1886.
6. 1886. Nominations, 21st December. Poll, 28th December. Legislature dissolved, 26th April, 1890.
7. 1890. Nomination, 29th May. Poll, 5th June. Legislature dissolved, 29th May, 1894.
8. 1894. Nomination, 19th June. Poll, 26th June. Legislature dissolved, 28th January, 1898.
9. 1898. Nomination, 22nd February. Poll, 1st March, 1898.

MEMBERS OF ONTARIO CABINETS.

The following list gives the office held by each Cabinet Minister since Confederation, and the date of his appointment and resignation.

First Cabinet Formed 16th July, 1867.

Hon. J. S. Macdonald : Premier and Attorney-General from 16th July, 1867, to 19th December, 1871.

Hon. M. C. Cameron : Provincial Secretary from 20th July, 1867, to 25th July, 1871 ; Commissioner of Crown Lands from 25th July, 1871, to 19th December, 1871.

Hon. E. B. Wood : Provincial Treasurer from 16th July, 1867, to 19th December, 1871.

Hon. S. Richards : Commissioner of Crown Lands from 16th July, 1867, to 25th July, 1871 ; Provincial Secretary from 25th July, 1871, to 19th December, 1871.

Hon. J. Carling : Commissioner of Agriculture and Public Works from 16th July, 1867, to 19th December, 1871.

Cabinet resigned 19th December, 1871.

Second Cabinet Formed 20th December, 1871.

Hon. E. Blake : Premier and President of Council from 20th December, 1871, to 25th October, 1872.

Hon. A. Mackenzie : Provincial Secretary from 20th December, 1871, to 21st December, 1871 ; Provincial Treasurer from 21st December, 1871, to 25th October, 1872.

Hon. A. Crooks : Attorney-General from 20th December, 1871, to 25th October, 1872.

Hon. A. McKellar : Commissioner of Agriculture and Public Works from 20th December, 1871, to 25th October, 1872.

Hon. R. W. Scott : Commissioner of Crown Lands from 21st December, 1871, to 25th October, 1872.

Hon. P. Gow, Provincial Secretary from 21st December, 1871, to 25th October, 1872.

Cabinet resigned 25th October, 1872.

Third Cabinet Formed 25th October, 1872.

Hon. Sir O. Mowat : Premier and Attorney-General from 25th October, 1872, to July, 1896.

Hon. T. B. Pardee : Provincial Secretary from 25th October, 1872, to 1873 ; Commissioner of Crown Lands from 4th December, 1873, to December, 1888.

Hon. A. Crooks : Provincial Treasurer from 25th October, 1872, to 24th March, 1877 ; Minister of Education from 14th February, 1876, to 23rd November, 1883.

Hon. A. McKellar: Commissioner of Agriculture and Public Works from 25th October, 1872, to 4th April, 1874 ; Commissioner of Agriculture and Provincial Secretary from 4th April, 1874, to 24th July, 1875.

Hon. C. F. Fraser: Provincial Secretary from 25th November. 1873, to 4th April, 1874 ; Commissioner of Public Works from 4th April, 1874, to 30th May, 1894.

Hon. S. C. Wood: Provincial Secretary and Registrar from 25th July, 1875, to March, 1877 ; Provincial Treasurer from 19th March, 1877, to 2nd June, 1883.

Hon. A. S. Hardy : Provincial Secretary and Registrar from 19th March, 1877 to 18th January, 1889 ; Commissioner of Crown Lands from 18th January, 1889, to 14th July, 1896.

Hon. J. Young : Provincial Treasurer and Commissioner of Agriculture from 2nd June, 1883, to 1st November, 1883.

Hon. G. W. Ross : Minister of Education from 23rd November, 1883, to date.

Hon. A. M. Ross : Provincial Treasurer from 2nd November, 1883, to 14th June, 1890 ; Commissioner of Agriculture from 2nd November, 1883, to May, 1888.

Hon. C. Drury : Minister of Agriculture from 1st May, 1888, to 29th September, 1890.

Hon. J. M. Gibson : Provincial Secretary from 18th January, 1889, to 21st July, 1896.

Hon. J. Dryden : Minister of Agriculture from 30th September, 1890, to date.

Hon. R. Harcourt : Provincial Treasurer from 30th September, 1890, to date.

Hon. E. Bronson : Without Portfolio, from 30th September, 1890, to 1898.

Hon. William Harty : Commissioner of Public Works from 30th August, 1894, to date.

Fourth Cabinet Formed 14th July, 1896.

Hon. Arthur Sturgis Hardy : Premier and Attorney-General from 14th July, 1896.

Hon. G. W. Ross : Minister of Education.

Hon. J. M. M. Gibson : Provincial Secretary to July 21, 1896 ; Commissioner of Crown Lands from July 21st, 1896, to date.

Hon. R. Harcourt : Provincial Treasurer.
Hon. J. Dryden : Minister of Agriculture.
Hon. W. Harty : Commissioner of Public Works
Hon. W. D. Balfour : Provincial Secretary from 21st July, 1896, to death, 19th August, 1896.
Hon. E. J. Davis : Without Portfolio, from 21st July, 1896 ; Provincial Secretary, 28th August, 1896.
Hon. E. H. Bronson : Without Portfolio, to 1898.

HEADS OF DEPARTMENTS OF GOVERNMENT SINCE CONFEDERATION.

Attorney-General.

Hon. J. S. MACDONALD, from 16th July, 1867, to 19th December, 1871.
Hon. A. CROOKS, from 20th December, 1871, to 25th October, 1872.
Hon. Sir O. MOWAT, from 25th October, 1872, to 14th July, 1896.
Hon. A. S. HARDY, from 14th July, 1896, to date.

Commissioner of Crown Lands.

Hon. S. RICHARDS, from 16th July, 1867, to 25th July, 1871.
Hon. M. C. CAMERON, from 25th July, 1871, to 19th December, 1871.
Hon. N. W. SCOTT, from 21st December, 1871, to 25th October, 1872.
Hon. T. D. PARDEE, from 4th December, 1873, to December, 1888.
Hon. A. S. HARDY, from 18th January, 1889, to 14th July, 1896.
Hon. J. M. GIBSON, from 21st July, 1896, to date.

Treasurer of Ontario.

Hon. E. B. WOOD, from 16th July, 1867, to 19th December, 1871.
Hon. A. MACKENZIE, from 21st December, 1871, to 25th October, 1872.
Hon. A. CROOKS, from 25th October, 1872, to 19th March, 1877.
Hon. J. C. WOOD, from 19th March, 1877, to 2nd June, 1883.
Hon. JAMES YOUNG, from 2nd June, 1883, to 1st November, 1883.
Hon. A. M. ROSS, from 2nd November, 1883, to 14th June, 1890.
Hon. R. HARCOURT, from 30th September, 1890, to date.

Minister of Education.

Hon. A. CROOKS, from 14th January, 1876, to 23rd November, 1883.
Hon. GEO. WILLIAM ROSS, from 23rd November, 1883, to date.

Commissioner of Public Works.

Hon. JOHN CARLING, from 16th July, 1867, to 19th December, 1871.
Hon. A. MCKELLAR, from 20th December, 1871, to 4th April, 1874.
Hon. C. F. FRASER, from 4th April, 1874, to 30th May, 1894.
Hon. WILLIAM HARTY, from 30th August, 1894, to date.

Commissioner of Agriculture.

Hon. J. CARLING, from 16th July, 1867, to 19th December, 1871.
Hon. A. MCKELLAR, from 20th December, 1871, to 24th July, 1871.
Hon. A. M. ROSS, from 2nd November, 1883, to May, 1888.

Minister of Agriculture.

Hon. CHARLES DRURY, from 1st May, 1888, to 29th September, 1890.
Hon. JOHN DRYDEN, from 30th September, 1890, to date.

Provincial Secretary.

Hon. M. C. CAMERON, from 20th July, 1867, to 25th July, 1871.
Hon. S. RICHARDS, from 25th July, 1871, to 19th December, 1871.
Hon. PETER GOW, from 20th December, 1871, to 25th October, 1872.
Hon. T. D. PARDEE, from 25th October, 1872, to 25th November, 1873.
Hon. C. F. FRASER, from 25th November, 1873, to 4th April, 1874.
Hon. A. MCKELLAR, from 4th April, 1874, to 24th July, 1875.
Hon. S. C. WOOD, from 25th July, 1875, to 19th March, 1877.
Hon. A. S. HARDY, from 19th March, 1877, to 18th January, 1889.
Hon. J. M. GIBSON, from 18th January, 1889, to 21st July, 1896.
Hon. W. D. BALFOUR, from 21st July, 1896, to 19th August, 1896.
Hon. ELIHU J. DAVIS, from 28th August, 1896, to date.

LIEUTENANT-GOVERNORS OF ONTARIO.

Lieut.-General HENRY WILLIAM STISTED, C.B., from July 1, 1867, until July 14, 1868; died December 10, 1875.

Hon. WILLIAM PEARCE HOWLAND, C.B., Priv. Coun., from July 14, 1868, until November 5, 1872.

Hon. JOHN WILLOUGHBY CRAWFORD, Q.C., from November 5, 1872, until his death, May 13, 1875.

Hon. DONALD ALEXANDER MACDONALD, Priv. Coun., from May 18, 1875, until June 29, 1880.

Hon. JOHN BEVERLEY ROBINSON, Q.C., from June 30, 1880, to February, 1887.

Hon. Sir ALEXANDER CAMPBELL, Q.C., Priv. Coun., from June 1, 1887, until his death, May 24, 1892.

Hon. Lieut.-Col. GEORGE AIREY KIRKPATRICK, Q.C., LL.D., appointed May 30, 1892.

Hon. Sir OLIVER MOWAT, G.C.M.G., Priv. Coun., Q.C., November 18, 1897, to date.

PREMIERS OF ONTARIO.

Name.	Constituency.	When Appointed.	Legislature.
Hon. John Sandfield Macdonald	Cornwall	July 16, 1867.	First.
Hon. Edward Blake	West Durham.	Dec. 20, 1871.	Second.
Hon. Sir Oliver Mowat	North Oxford.	Oct. 31, 1872	Part of Second up to Seventh inclusive.
Hon. A. S. Hardy	South Brant	July 14, 1896.	Eighth.

SPEAKERS.
Of the Legislative Assembly of Ontario.

Name of Speaker.	Constituency.	When Elected.	Legislature.
Hon. John Stevenson	Lennox	Dec. 27, 1867	First.
" Richard William Scott.	Ottawa	" 7, 1871	Part of Second.
" George James Currie	Welland	" 21, 1871	Part of Second.
" Rupert Mearse Wells	South Bruce	Jan. 7, 1874	Part of Second.
" " "	"	Nov. 24, 1875	Third.
Charles Clarke	Centre Wellington.	Jan. 7, 1880	Fourth.
"	"	" 23, 1884	Fifth.
Jacob Baxter	Haldimand	Feb. 10, 1887	Sixth.
" Thomas Ballantyne	South Perth	" 11, 1891	Seventh.
" William Douglas Balfour	South Essex	" 21, 1895	Part of Eighth.
" A. F. E. Evanturel	Prescott	" 10, 1897	Part of Eighth.
" " "	"	Aug. 3, 1898	Ninth.

PAYMENT OF WITNESSES.

Payment of witnesses. The Clerk of the House, by Rule 86, is authorized to pay out of the Contingent Fund to Witnesses summoned to attend before any Select Committee of the House, except in the case of Private Bills, a reasonable sum *per diem*, to be determined by the Speaker, during their attendance, and a reasonable allowance for travelling expenses, upon a certificate or order of the Chairman of the Committee before which such witnesses have been summoned; but no witnesses shall be so paid unless a certificate shall first have been filed with the Chairman of such Committee, **Certificate that evidence is material and important.** by some member thereof, stating that the evidence to be obtained from such witness is, in his opinion, material and important; and no such payment shall be made in any case without the authority of the Speaker, which shall be signified by the endorsement of the Speaker upon the **Certificate to be renewed.** aforesaid certificate; and when any witness shall have been in attendance during three days, if his presence is still further required, recourse shall again be had to the Chairman of the Committee, and so on, every three **Certain witnesses not to be paid.** days; and no witness residing at the Seat of Government shall be paid for his attendance.

THE FOLLOWING FORMS ARE NECESSARY IN THE PAYMENT OF WITNESS FEES.

WITNESS FEES.

Certificate.

LEGISLATIVE ASSEMBLY,

TORONTO,............ ....189 .

I hereby certify that the evidence to be obtained from.........

................Esq., by the.....................Committee

.......................is, in my opinion material and important.

                    Member of................*Committee*

                            on.....................

Account.

TORONTO, ...189 .

LEGISLATIVE ASSEMBLY OF ONTARIO.

To......days' attendance as a witness before..............

    Committee on....................at $....per diem......

Travelling expenses - - - - - -

                                                          $

   Received payment.

.........................189 .

I certify that the above bill of charges for attendance of witness

....before ....

......Committee on. .... is correct.

                                               Chairman.

I hereby approve of above bill of charges.

                                               Speaker.

TORONTO,...............189 .

FORMS OF MOTIONS, Etc.

FORM "A."

Notice of intention to introduce a Bill.*

Mr.   gives notice that he will, on   next, move to introduce a Bill to amend the   Act.

FORM "B."

Motion upon introduction of a Bill.

Mr.   moves, seconded by Mr.   , that leave be given to introduce a Bill intituled " An Act to amend the   Act," or, " An Act to incorporate the   Company (*as the case may be*) and that the same be now read the first time.

---

*No notice is necessary for the introduction of a Private Bill, as it is done when Petition is reported to the House by Standing Orders Committee.

FORM "C."

Motion for three months' hoist.

Mr.   moves, in amendment, seconded by Mr.   , That all the words of the Motion after the word "That" be struck out and the following substituted therefor, (or, inserted in lieu thereof), "the Bill be not now read the second time, but be read the second time on this day three months."

FORM "D."

Notice of amendment to Private Bill in full House.*

Mr.   gives notice that he will, when the House is in Committee of the Whole, or, upon the motion for the third reading of Bill (No.   ), to incorporate, etc., (*short title*), move to amend the same by inserting, or striking out, the following (*as the case may be.*)

FORM "E."

Notice of Motion for an Address for Return of Papers.

Mr.   gives notice that he will, on   next, move that an humble Address be presented to His Honour the Lieutenant-Governor, praying that he will cause to be laid before this House a Return of copies of all Orders in Council, correspondence, etc., *re* attending to, or in the matter of, etc.

FORM "F."

Notice of Motion for an Order of the House for a Return of Papers, etc.

Mr.   gives notice that he will, on   next, move for an Order of the House for a Return of Copies of all correspondence, papers, etc., relating to, or, in the matter of, etc.

FORM "G."

Notice of intention to ask a Question of Ministry or Member.

Mr.   gives notice that he will, on   next, enquire of the Ministry. Has, is, or if, etc.

---

*No notice necessary in case of a Public Bill. If it is the wish to amend a Private Bill before Standing Committee, then file a copy, with the proposed amendments inserted, with the Clerk of Committee.

FORM "H."

Motion in Amendment.

Mr.   moves, in amendment, seconded by Mr.   , That all the words of the proposed amendment (or *of the Amendment to the Amendment*) after the word "That" be struck out and that instead thereof there be inserted the following, or, that the following be substituted therefor, or, inserted in lieu thereof, in the opinion of this House, etc.

FORM "I."

Notice of Resolution.

Mr.   gives notice that he will, on   next, move the following Resolution : That in the opinion of this House, etc.

BRITISH NORTH AMERICA ACT.

BRITISH NORTH AMERICA ACT.

IMPERIAL ACT 30-31 VICT. Cap. 3.

An Act for the Union of Canada, Nova Scotia, and New Brunswick, and the Government thereof; and for purposes connected therewith.

[*29th March, 1867.*]

[*The Statute Law Revision Act, 56-57 V. c. 14 (Imp.) repealed, as spent, sections 2, 25, 42, 43, 81, 89, 127 and 145 and also portions of sections 4, 51 and 88.*]

WHEREAS the Provinces of Canada, Nova Scotia, and New Brunswick, have expressed their desire to be federally united into one Dominion under the Crown of the United Kingdom of Great Britain and Ireland, with a constitution similar in principle to that of the United Kingdom:

And whereas such a Union would conduce to the welfare of the Provinces and promote the interests of the British Empire:

And whereas on the establishment of the Union by authority of Parliament it is expedient, not only that the Constitution of the Legislative Authority in the Dominion be provided for, but also that the nature of the Executive Government therein be declared:

And whereas it is expedient that provision be made for the eventual admission into the Union of other parts of British North America:

Be it therefore enacted and declared by the Queen's most Excellent Majesty, by and with the advice and consent of the Lords Spiritual and Temporal, and Commons, in this present Parliament assembled, and by the authority of the same, as follows:

I. PRELIMINARY.

1. This Act may be cited as *The British North America Act, 1867*.   Short title

Application of provisions referring to the Queen.

2. The provisions of this Act referring to Her Majesty the Queen extend also to the heirs and successors of Her Majesty, Kings and Queens of the United Kingdom of Great Britain and Ireland.

II.—UNION.

Declaration by proclamation of Union of Canada, Nova Scotia and New Brunswick, into one Dominion under name of Canada.

3. It shall be lawful for the Queen, by and with the advice of Her Majesty's Most Honourable Privy Council, to declare by Proclamation that on and after a day therein appointed, not being more than six months after the passing of this Act, the Provinces of Canada, Nova Scotia, and New Brunswick shall form and be one Dominion under the name of Canada; and on and after that day those three Provinces shall form and be one Dominion under that name accordingly.

Commencement of subsequent provisions of Act.

Meaning of Canada in such provisions.

4. The subsequent provisions of this Act shall, unless it is otherwise expressed or implied, commence and have effect on and after the Union, that is to say, on and after the day appointed for the Union taking effect in the Queen's Proclamation; and in the same provisions, unless it is otherwise expressed or implied, the name Canada shall be taken to mean Canada as constituted under this Act.

Four Provinces.

5. Canada shall be divided into four Provinces, named Ontario, Quebec, Nova Scotia, and New Brunswick.

[*Canada now also includes the Provinces of Manitoba, British Columbia and Prince Edward Island and the North West Territories.*]

Provinces of Ontario and Quebec.

6. The parts of the Province of Canada (as it exists at the passing of this Act) which formerly constituted respectively the Provinces of Upper Canada and Lower Canada shall be deemed to be severed, and shall form two separate Provinces. The part which formerly constituted the Province of Upper Canada shall constitute the Province of Ontario; and the part which formerly constituted the Province of Lower Canada shall constitute the Province of Quebec.

Provinces of Nova Scotia and New Brunswick.

7. The Provinces of Nova Scotia and New Brunswick shall have the same limits as at the passing of this Act.

Population of Provinces to be distinguished in decennial census.

8. In the general census of the population of Canada which is hereby required to be taken in the year one thousand eight hundred and seventy-one, and in every tenth year thereafter, the respective populations of the four Provinces shall be distinguished.

III. EXECUTIVE POWER.

9. The Executive Government and authority of and over Canada is hereby declared to continue and be vested in the Queen.

Executive Power to continue vested in the Queen.

10. The provisions of this Act referring to the Governor-General extend and apply to the Governor-General for the time being of Canada, or other the Chief Executive Officer or Administrator, for the time being carrying on the Government of Canada on behalf and in the name of the Queen, by whatever title he is designated.

Application of provisions referring to Governor General.

11. There shall be a Council to aid and advise in the Government of Canada, to be styled the Queen's Privy Council for Canada; and the persons who are to be members of that Council shall be from time to time chosen and summoned by the Governor General and sworn in as Privy Councillors, and members thereof may be from time to time removed by the Governor General.

Constitution of Privy Council for Canada.

12. All powers, authorities, and functions which under any Act of the Parliament of Great Britain, or of the Parliament of the United Kingdom of Great Britain and Ireland, or of the Legislature of Upper Canada, Lower Canada, Canada, Nova Scotia, or New Brunswick, are at the Union vested in or exercisable by the respective Governors or Lieutenant Governors of those Provinces, with the advice, or with the advice and consent, of the respective Executive Councils thereof, or in conjunction with those Councils, or with any number of members thereof, or by those Governors or Lieutenant Governors individually, shall, as far as the same continue in existence and capable of being exercised after the Union in relation to the Government of Canada, be vested in and exercisable by the Governor General, with the advice, or with the advice and consent of, or in conjunction with the Queen's Privy Council for Canada, or any members thereof, or by the Governor General individually, as the case requires, subject nevertheless (except with respect to such as exist under Acts of the Parliament of Great Britain or of the Parliament of the United Kingdom of Great Britain and Ireland) to be abolished or altered by the Parliament of Canada.

All powers under Acts to be exercised by Governor General with advice of Privy Council or alone.

13. The provisions of this Act referring to the Governor General in Council shall be construed as referring to the Governor General acting by and with the advice of the Queen's Privy Council for Canada.

Application of provisions referring to Governor General in Council.

Power to Her Majesty to authorize Governor General to appoint Deputies.

14. It shall be lawful for the Queen, if Her Majesty thinks fit, to authorize the Governor General from time to time to appoint any person or any persons jointly or severally to be his Deputy or Deputies within any part or parts of Canada, and in that capacity to exercise during the pleasure of the Governor General such of the powers, authorities, and functions of the Governor General as the Governor General deems it necessary or expedient to assign to him or them, subject to any limitations or directions expressed or given by the Queen ; but the appointment of such a Deputy or Deputies shall not affect the exercise by the Governor General himself of any power, authority or function.

Command of armed forces to continue to be vested in the Queen.

15. The Commander-in-Chief of the Land and Naval Militia, and of all Naval and Military Forces, of and in Canada, is hereby declared to continue and be vested in the Queen.

Seat of Government of Canada.

16. Until the Queen otherwise directs the seat of Government of Canada shall be Ottawa.

IV.—LEGISLATIVE POWER.

Constitution of Parliament of Canada.

17. There shall be one Parliament for Canada, consisting of the Queen, an Upper House styled the Senate, and the House of Commons.

[*Section 18 was repealed by Imperial Act 38 and 39 Vict. c. 38, and the following section substituted therefor.*

Privileges, etc., of Houses.

18. The privileges, immunities, and powers to be held, enjoyed and exercised by the Senate and by the House of Commons and by the members thereof respectively shall be such as are from time to time defined by Act of the Parliament of Canada, but so that any Act of the Parliament of Canada defining such privileges, immunities and powers shall not confer any privileges, immunities or powers exceeding those at the passing of such Act held, enjoyed, and exercised by the Commons House of Parliament of the United Kingdom of Great Britain and Ireland and by the members thereof.]

First Session of the Parliament of Canada.

19. The Parliament of Canada shall be called together not later than six months after the Union.

Yearly Session of the Parliament of Canada.

20. There shall be a Session of the Parliament of Canada once at least in every year, so that twelve months shall not intervene between the last sitting of the Parliament in one Session and its first sitting in the next Session.

The Senate.

21. The Senate shall, subject to the provisions of this Act, consist of seventy-two members, who shall be styled Senators. *Number of Senators.*

[*The Senate now consists of 81 members and includes representatives of the Provinces of Ontario, Quebec, Nova Scotia, New Brunswick, Manitoba, British Columbia, and Prince Edward Island and of the North West Territories.*]

22. In relation to the constitution of the Senate, Canada shall be deemed to consist of three divisions— *Representation of Provinces in Senate.*

1. Ontario;
2. Quebec;
3. The Maritime Provinces, Nova Scotia and New Brunswick; which three divisions shall (subject to the provisions of this Act) be equally represented in the Senate as follows: Ontario by twenty-four Senators; Quebec by twenty-four Senators; and the Maritime Provinces by twenty-four Senators, twelve thereof representing Nova Scotia, and twelve thereof representing New Brunswick.

In the case of Quebec each of the twenty-four Senators representing that Province shall be appointed for one of the twenty-four Electoral Divisions of Lower Canada specified in Schedule A. to chapter one of the Consolidated Statutes of Canada.

23. The qualification of a Senator shall be as follows:— *Qualifications of Senator.*

1. He shall be of the full age of thirty years:
2. He shall be either a natural-born subject of the Queen, or a subject of the Queen naturalized by an Act of the Parliament of Great Britain, or of the Parliament of the United Kingdom of Great Britain and Ireland, or of the Legislature of one of the Provinces of Upper Canada, Lower Canada, Canada, Nova Scotia, or New Brunswick, before the Union, or of the Parliament of Canada after the Union:
3. He shall be legally or equitably seised as of freehold for his own use and benefit of lands or tenements held in free and common socage, or seised or possessed for his own use and benefit of lands or tenements held in franc-aleu or in roture, within the Province for which he is appointed, of the value of $4,000, over and above all rents, dues, debts, charges, mortgages, and incumbrances due or payable out of or charged on or affecting the same:

4. His real and personal property shall be together worth $4,000 over and above his debts and liabilities:

5. He shall be resident in the Province for which he is appointed:

6. In the case of Quebec he shall have his real property qualification in the Electoral Division for which he is appointed, or shall be resident in that Division.

Summoning of Senators. 24. The Governor General shall from time to time, in the Queen's name, by instrument under the Great Seal of Canada, summon qualified persons to the Senate; and, subject to the provisions of this Act, every person so summoned shall become and be a member of the Senate and a Senator.

Summons of first body of Senators. 25. Such persons shall be first summoned to the Senate as the Queen by warrant under Her Majesty's Royal Sign Manual thinks fit to approve, and their names shall be inserted in the Queen's Proclamation of Union.

Addition of Senators in certain cases. 26. If at any time on the recommendation of the Governor General the Queen thinks fit to direct that three or six members be added to the Senate, the Governor General may by summons to three or six qualified persons (as the case may be), representing equally the three divisions of Canada, add to the Senate accordingly.

Reduction of Senate to normal number. 27. In case of such addition being at any time made the Governor General shall not summon any person to the Senate, except on a further like direction by the Queen on the like recommendation, until each of the three divisions of Canada is represented by twenty-four Senators and no more.

Maximum number of Senators. 28. The number of Senators shall not at any time exceed seventy-eight.

[*See note appended to section 21.*]

Tenure of place in Senate. 29. A Senator shall, subject to the provisions of this Act, hold his place in the Senate for life.

Resignation of place in Senate. 30. A Senator may by writing under his hand addressed to the Governor General resign his place in the Senate, and thereupon the same shall be vacant.

Disqualification of Senators. 31. The place of a Senator shall become vacant in any of the following cases:

1. If for two consecutive Sessions of the Parliament he fails to give his attendance in the Senate:
2. If he takes an oath or makes a declaration or acknowledgment of allegiance, obedience, or adherence to a foreign power, or does an act whereby he becomes a subject or citizen, or entitled to the rights or privileges of a subject or citizen, of a foreign power:
3. If he is adjudged bankrupt or insolvent, or applies for the benefit of any law relating to insolvent debtors, or becomes a public defaulter:
4. If he is attainted of treason or convicted of felony or of any infamous crime:
5. If he ceases to be qualified in respect of property or of residence; provided, that a Senator shall not be deemed to have ceased to be qualified in respect of residence by reason only of his residing at the seat of the Government of Canada while holding an office under that Government requiring his presence there.

32. When a vacancy happens in the Senate by resignation, death, or otherwise, the Governor General shall by summons to a fit and qualified person fill the vacancy. *Summons on vacancy in Senate.*

33. If any question arises respecting the qualification of a Senator or a vacancy in the Senate the same shall be heard and determined by the Senate. *Questions as to qualifications and vacancies in Senate.*

34. The Governor General may from time to time, by instrument under the Great Seal of Canada, appoint a Senator to be Speaker of the Senate, and may remove him and appoint another in his stead. *Appointment of Speaker of Senate.*

35. Until the Parliament of Canada otherwise provides, the presence of at least fifteen Senators, including the Speaker, shall be necessary to constitute a meeting of the Senate for the exercise of its powers. *Quorum of Senate.*

36. Questions arising in the Senate shall be decided by a majority of voices, and the Speaker shall in all cases have a vote, and when the voices are equal the decision shall be deemed to be in the negative. *Voting in Senate.*

The House of Commons.

37. The House of Commons shall, subject to the provisions of this Act, consist of one hundred and eighty-one member, of whom eighty-two shall be elected for Ontario, sixty-five for *Constitution of House of Commons in Canada.*

Quebec, nineteen for Nova Scotia, and fifteen for New Brunswick.

[*The number of members is now 213, the Province of Ontario having 92, Quebec 65, Nova Scotia 20, New Brunswick 14, Prince Edward Island 5, British Columbia 6, Manitoba 7, and the North West Territories 4. See Rev. Stats. C., 1886, Chaps. 6 and 7; 55-56 V. Chap. 11.*]

Summoning of House of Commons.

38. The Governor-General shall from time to time, in the Queen's name, by instrument under the Great Seal of Canada, summon and call together the House of Commons.

Senators not to sit in House of Commons.

39. A Senator shall not be capable of being elected or of sitting or voting as a member of the House of Commons.

Electoral districts of the four Provinces.

40. Until the Parliament of Canada otherwise provides, Ontario, Quebec, Nova Scotia, and New Brunswick shall, for the purposes of the election of members to serve in the House of Commons, be divided into Electoral Districts as follows:—

1.—ONTARIO.

Ontario shall be divided into the Counties, Ridings of Counties, Cities, parts of Cities, and Towns enumerated in the first Schedule to this Act, each whereof shall be an Electoral District, each such district as enumerated in that Schedule being entitled to return one member.

2.—QUEBEC.

Quebec shall be divided into sixty-five Electoral Districts, composed of the sixty-five Electoral Divisions into which Lower Canada is at the passing of this Act divided under chapter two of the Consolidated Statutes of Canada, chapter seventy-five of the Consolidated Statutes of Lower Canada, and the Act of the Province of Canada of the twenty-third year of the Queen, chapter one, or any other Act amending the same in force at the Union, so that each such Electoral Division shall be for the purposes of this Act an Electoral District entitled to return one member.

3.—NOVA SCOTIA.

Each of the eighteen Counties of Nova Scotia shall be an Electoral District. The County of Halifax shall be entitled to return two members, and each of the other Counties one member.

4. NEW BRUNSWICK.

Each of the fourteen Counties into which New Brunswick is divided, including the City and County of St. John, shall be an Electoral District; the City of St. John shall also be a separate Electoral District. Each of those fifteen Electoral Districts shall be entitled to return one member.

[*The above provisions as to the electoral districts of the Provinces above named have been varied by subsequent Statutes of the Parliament of Canada.*]

41. Until the Parliament of Canada otherwise provides, all laws in force in the several Provinces at the Union relative to the following matters or any of them, namely,—the qualifications and disqualifications of persons to be elected or to sit or vote as members of the House of Assembly or Legislative Assembly in the several Provinces, the voters at elections of such members, the oaths to be taken by voters, the Returning Officers, their powers and duties, the proceedings at elections, the periods during which elections may be continued, the trial of controverted elections, and proceedings incident thereto, the vacating of seats of members, and the execution of new writs in case of seats vacated otherwise than by dissolution,—shall respectively apply to elections of members to serve in the House of Commons for the same several Provinces. Continuance of existing election laws until Parliament of Canada otherwise provides.

Provided that, until the Parliament of Canada otherwise provides, at any election for a Member of the House of Commons for the District of Algoma, in addition to persons qualified by the law of the Province of Canada to vote, every male British subject aged twenty-one years or upwards, being a householder, shall have a vote.

[*See Rev. Stat. C., 1886, Chaps. 5, 8 and 9 and subsequent Acts amending these Statutes.*]

42. For the first election of members to serve in the House of Commons the Governor-General shall cause writs to be issued by such person, in such form, and addressed to such Returning Officers as he thinks fit. Writs for first election.

The person issuing writs under this section shall have the like powers as are possessed at the Union by the officers charged with the issuing of writs for the election of members to serve in the Province of Canada, Nova Scotia, or New Brunswick; and the Returning Officers to whom writs are directed under this section shall have the like powers as are possessed at the Union by the officers charged with the returning of writs for the election of members to serve in the same respective House of Assembly or Legislative Assembly.

As to vacancies before meeting of Parliament or before provision is made by Parliament in this behalf.
43. In case a vacancy in the representation in the House of Commons of any Electoral District happens before the meeting of the Parliament, or after the meeting of the Parliament before provision is made by the Parliament in this behalf, the provisions of the last foregoing section of this Act shall extend and apply to the issuing and returning of a writ in respect of such vacant District.

As to election of Speaker of House of Commons.
44. The House of Commons on its first assembling after a general election shall proceed with all practicable speed to elect one of its members to be Speaker.

As to filling up vacancy in office of Speaker.
45. In case of a vacancy happening in the office of Speaker by death, resignation or otherwise, the House of Commons shall with all practicable speed proceed to elect another of its members to be Speaker.

Speaker to preside.
46. The Speaker shall preside at all meetings of the House of Commons.

[*See 48-49 V. c. 1 (Dom.) which creates the office of Deputy Speaker.*]

Provision in case of absence of Speaker.
47. Until the Parliament of Canada otherwise provides, in case of the absence of any reason of the Speaker from the chair of the House of Commons for a period of forty-eight consecutive hours, the House may elect another of its members to act as Speaker, and the member so elected shall during the continuance of such absence of the Speaker have and execute all the powers, privileges, and duties of Speaker.

Quorum of House of Commons.
48. The presence of at least twenty members of the House of Commons shall be necessary to constitute a meeting of the House for the exercise of its powers, and for that purpose the Speaker shall be reckoned as a member.

Voting in House of Commons.
49. Questions arising in the House of Commons shall be decided by a majority of voices other than that of the Speaker and when the voices are equal, but not otherwise, the Speaker shall have a vote.

Duration of House of Commons.
50. Every House of Commons shall continue for five years from the day of the return of the writs for choosing the House (subject to be sooner dissolved by the Governor-General), and no longer.

51. On the completion of the census in the year one thousand eight hundred and seventy-one, and of each subsequent decennial census, the representation of the four Provinces shall be re-adjusted by such authority, in such manner and from such time as the Parliament of Canada from time to time provides, subject and according to the following rules:— Decennial Readjustment of Representation.

1. Quebec shall have the fixed number of sixty-five members:
2. There shall be assigned to each of the other Provinces such a number of members as will bear the same proportion to the number of its population (ascertained at such census) as the number sixty-five bears to the number of the population of Quebec (so ascertained):
3. In the computation of the number of members for a Province a fractional part not exceeding one-half of the whole number requisite for entitling the Province to a member shall be disregarded: but a fractional part exceeding one-half of that number shall be equivalent to the whole number:
4. On any such re-adjustment the number of members for a Province shall not be reduced unless the proportion which the number of the population of the Province bore to the number of the aggregate population of Canada at the then last preceding re-adjustment of the number of members for the Province is ascertained at the then latest census to be diminished by one-twentieth part or upwards:
5. Such re-adjustment shall not take effect until the termination of the then existing Parliament.

[*See now* Rev. Stat. C., 1886, Cap. 6.]

52. The number of members of the House of Commons may be from time to time increased by the Parliament of Canada, provided the proportionate representation of the Provinces prescribed by this Act is not thereby disturbed. Increase of number of House of Commons.

Money Votes: Royal Assent.

53. Bills for appropriating any part of the public revenue, or for imposing any tax or impost, shall originate in the House of Commons. Appropriation and tax bills.

54. It shall not lawful for the House of Commons to adopt or pass any vote, resolution, address, or bill for the appropriation of any part of the public revenue, or of any tax or impost, to any purpose that has not been first recommended to that House Recommendation of money votes.

by message of the Governor-General in the Session in which such vote, resolution, address, or bill is proposed.

Royal assent to bills, etc.

55. Where a bill passed by the Houses of the Parliament is presented to the Governor General for the Queen's assent, he shall declare according to his discretion, but subject to the provisions of this Act and to Her Majesty's instructions, either that he assents thereto in the Queen's name, or that he withholds the Queen's assent, or that he reserves the bill for the signification of the Queen's pleasure.

Disallowance by order in Council of Act assented to by Governor General.

56. Where the Governor General assents to a bill in the Queen's name, he shall by the first convenient opportunity send an authentic copy of the Act to one of Her Majesty's Principal Secretaries of State; and if the Queen in Council within two years after the receipt thereof by the Secretary of State thinks fit to disallow the Act, such disallowance (with a certificate of the Secretary of State of the day on which the Act was received by him) being signified by the Governor General, by speech or message to each of the Houses of the Parliament, or by proclamation, shall annul the Act from and after the day of such signification.

Signification of Queen's pleasure on bill reserved.

57. A bill reserved for the signification of the Queen's pleasure shall not have any force unless and until within two years from the day on which it was presented to the Governor General for the Queen's assent, the Governor General signifies, by speech or message to each of the Houses of the Parliament or by proclamation, that it has received the assent of the Queen in Council.

An entry of every such speech, message, or proclamation shall be made in the Journal of each House, and a duplicate thereof duly attested shall be delivered to the proper officer to be kept among the Records of Canada.

V.—PROVINCIAL CONSTITUTIONS.

Executive Power.

Appointment of Lieutenant Governors of Provinces.

58. For each Province there shall be an officer, styled the Lieutenant Governor, appointed by the Governor General in Council by instrument under the Great Seal of Canada.

Tenure of office of Lieutenant Governor.

59. A Lieutenant Governor shall hold office during the pleasure of the Governor General; but any Lieutenant Governor appointed after the commencement of the first Session of the Parliament of Canada shall not be removable within five years from his appointment, except for cause assigned, which shall be communicated to him in writing within one month after the order for his removal is made, and shall be communicated by message to the Senate and to the House of Commons within one week thereafter if the Parliament is then sitting, and if not then within one week after the commencement of the next Session of the Parliament.

60. The salaries of the Lieutenant Governors shall be fixed and provided by the Parliament of Canada. Salaries of Lieutenant Governors

61. Every Lieutenant Governor shall, before assuming the duties of his office, make and subscribe before the Governor General or some person authorized by him, oaths of allegiance and office similar to those taken by the Governor General. Oaths, etc., of Lieutenant Governor.

62. The provisions of this Act referring to the Lieutenant Governor extend and apply to the Lieutenant Governor for the time being of each Province or other the chief executive officer or administrator for the time being carrying on the government of the Province, by whatever title he is designated. Application of provisions referring to Lieutenant Governor.

63. The Executive Council of Ontario and of Quebec shall be composed of such persons as the Lieutenant Governor from time to time thinks fit, and in the first instance of the following officers, namely: The Attorney General, the Secretary and Registrar of the Province, the Treasurer of the Province, the Commissioner of Crown Lands, and the Commissioner of Agriculture and Public Works, and within Quebec, the Speaker of the Legislative Council and the Solicitor General. Appointment of executive officers for Ontario and Quebec.

[*See now as to Ontario, Rev. Stat. Ont., 1897, Cap. 14.*]

64. The Constitution of the Executive Authority in each of the Provinces of Nova Scotia and New Brunswick shall, subject to the provisions of this Act continue as it exists at the Union until altered under the authority of this Act. Executive Government of Nova Scotia and New Brunswick.

65. All powers, authorities, and functions which under any Act of the Parliament of Great Britain, or of the Parliament of the United Kingdom of Great Britain and Ireland, or of the Legislature of Upper Canada, Lower Canada, or Canada, were or are before or at the Union vested in or exercisable by the respective Governors or Lieutenant Governors of those Provinces, with the advice, or with the advice and consent, of the respective Executive Councils thereof, or in conjunction with those Councils, or with any number of members thereof, or by those Governors or Lieutenant Governors individually, shall, as far as the same are capable of being exercised after the Union in relation to the Government of Ontario and Quebec respectively, be vested in and shall or may be exercised by the Lieu- All powers under Acts to be exercised by Lieutenant Governor of Ontario or Quebec with advice of Executive Council or alone.

tenant Governor of Ontario and Quebec respectively, with the advice or with the advice and consent of or in conjunction with the respective Executive Councils, or any members thereof or by the Lieutenant Governor individually, as the case requires, subject nevertheless (except with respect to such as exist under Acts of the Parliament of Great Britain, or of the Parliament of the United Kingdom of Great Britain and Ireland,) to be abolished or altered by the respective Legislatures of Ontario and Quebec.

<small>Application of provisions referring to Lieutenant Governor in Council.</small>

66. The provisions of this Act referring to the Lieutenant Governor in Council shall be construed as referring to the Lieutenant Governor of the Province acting by and with the advice of the Executive Council thereof.

<small>Administration in absence, etc., of Lieutenant Governor.</small>

67. The Governor General in Council may from time to time appoint an administrator to execute the office and functions of Lieutenant Governor during his absence, illness, or other inability.

<small>Seats of Provincial Governments.</small>

68. Unless and until the Executive Government of any Province otherwise directs with respect to that Province, the seats of Government of the Provinces shall be as follows, namely,— of Ontario, the City of Toronto ; of Quebec, the City of Quebec ; of Nova Scotia, the City of Halifax ; and of New Brunswick, the City of Fredericton.

Legislative Power.

1.—ONTARIO.

<small>Legislature for Ontario.</small>

69. There shall be a Legislature for Ontario consisting of the Lieutenant Governor and of one house, styled the Legislative Assembly of Ontario.

<small>Electoral districts.</small>

70. The Legislative Assembly of Ontario shall be composed of eighty-two members, to be elected to represent the eighty-two Electoral Districts set forth in the first Schedule to this Act.

(*The number of members is now 94, representing 93 Electoral Districts. See Rev. Stat. Ont., 1897, Cap. 6.*)

2.—QUEBEC.

<small>Legislature for Quebec.</small>

71. There shall be a Legislature for Quebec consisting of the Lieutenant Governor and two Houses, styled the Legislative Council of Quebec and the Legislative Assembly of Quebec.

72. The Legislative Council of Quebec shall be composed of twenty-four members, to be appointed by the Lieutenant Governor in the Queen's name, by instrument under the Great Seal of Quebec, one being appointed to represent each of the twenty-four electoral divisions of Lower Canada in this Act referred to, and each holding office for the term of his life, unless the Legislature of Quebec otherwise provides under the provisions of this Act.
Constitution of Legislative Council.

73. The Qualifications of the Legislative Councillors of Quebec shall be the same as those of the Senators of Quebec.
Qualification of Legislative Councillors.

74. The place of a Legislative Councillor of Quebec shall become vacant in the cases *mutatis mutandis*, in which the place of Senator becomes vacant.
Resignation, disqualification, etc.

75. When a vacancy happens in the Legislative Council of Quebec, by resignation, death, or otherwise, the Lieutenant Governor, in the Queen's name by instrument under the Great Seal of Quebec, shall appoint a fit and qualified person to fill the vacancy.
Vacancies.

76. If any question arises respecting the qualification of a Legislative Councillor of Quebec, or a vacancy in the Legislative Council of Quebec, the same shall be heard and determined by the Legislative Council.
Questions as to vacancies, etc.

77. The Lieutenant Governor may from time to time, by instrument under the Great Seal of Quebec, appoint a member of the Legislative Council of Quebec to be Speaker thereof, and may remove him and appoint another in his stead.
Speaker of Legislative Council.

78. Until the Legislature of Quebec otherwise provides, the presence of at least ten members of the Legislative Council, including the Speaker, shall be necessary to constitute a meeting for the exercise of its powers.
Quorum of Legislative Council.

79. Questions arising in the Legislative Council of Quebec shall be decided by a majority of voices, and the Speaker shall in all cases have a vote, and when the voices are equal the decision shall be deemed to be in the negative.
Voting in Legislative Council.

80. The Legislative Assembly of Quebec shall be composed of sixty-five members, to be elected to represent the sixty-five electoral divisions or districts of Lower Canada in this Act referred to, subject to alteration thereof by the Legislature of Quebec: Provided that it shall not be lawful to present to the Lieutenant Governor of Quebec for assent any bill for altering the limits of any of the Electoral Divisions or Districts men-
Constitution of Legislative Assembly of Quebec.

tioned in the second Schedule to this Act, unless the second and third readings of such bill have been passed in the Legislative Assembly with the concurrence of the majority of the members representing all those Electoral Divisions or Districts and the assent shall not be given to such bills unless an address has been presented by the Legislative Assembly to the Lieutenant Governor stating that it has been so passed.

3.—ONTARIO AND QUEBEC.

First Session of Legislatures.

81. The Legislatures of Ontario and Quebec respectively shall be called together not later than six months after the Union.

Summoning of Legislative Assemblies.

82. The Lieutenant Governor of Ontario and of Quebec shall from time to time, in the Queen's name, by instrument under the great seal of the Province, summon and call together the Legislative Assembly of the Province.

Restriction on election of holders of offices.

83. Until the Legislature of Ontario or of Quebec otherwise provides, a person accepting or holding in Ontario or in Quebec any office, commission or employment permanent or temporary, at the nomination of the Lieutenant Governor, to which an annual salary, or any fee, allowance, emolument, or profit of any kind or amount whatever from the Province is attached, shall not be eligible as a member of the Legislative Assembly of the respective Province, nor shall he sit or vote as such ; but nothing in this section shall make ineligible any person being a member of the Executive Council of the respective Province, or holding any of the following offices, that is to say, the offices of Attorney-General, Secretary and Registrar of the Province, Treasurer of the Province, Commissioner of Crown Lands, and Commissioner of Agriculture and Public Works, and, in Quebec, Solicitor-General, or shall disqualify him to sit or vote in the House for which he is elected, provided he is elected while holding such office.

[*Acts have since been passed with the view of further securing the independence of the Legislative Assembly of Ontario. See Rev. Stat. Ont., 1897, Cap. 11, ss. 6 to 17.*]

Continuance of existing election laws.

84. Until the Legislatures of Ontario and Quebec respectively otherwise provide, all laws which at the Union are in force in those Provinces respectively, relative to the following matters, or any of them, namely,— the qualifications and disqualifications of persons to be elected or to sit or vote as members of the Assembly of Canada, the qualifications or disqualifications of voters, the oaths to be taken by voters, the Returning Officers,

heir powers and duties, the proceedings at elections, the periods during which such elections may be continued, and the trial of controverted elections and the proceedings incident thereto, the vacating of the seats of members and the issuing and execution of new writs in cases of seats vacated otherwise than by dissolution, shall respectively apply to elections of members to serve in the respective Legislative Assemblies of Ontario and Quebec.

[See note as to Ontario Rev. Stat. Ont., 1897, Chaps. 9 and 11.]

Provided that until the Legislature of Ontario otherwise providess, at any election for a member of the Legislative Assembly of Ontario for the District of Algoma, in addition to persons qualified by the law of the Province of Canada to vote, every male British subject aged twenty-one years or upwards, being a householder, shall have a vote.

[See now Rev. Stat. Ont., 1897, Cap. 9, ss. 9-15.]

5. Every Legislative Assembly of Ontario and every Legislative Assembly of Quebec shall continue for four years from the day of the return of the writs for choosing the same (subject nevertheless to either the Legislative Assembly of Ontario or the Legislative Assembly of Quebec being sooner dissolved by the Lieutenant Governor of the Province), and no longer. *Duration of Legislative Assemblies.*

[See now as to Ontario, Rev. Stat. Ont., 1897, Cap. 12, s. 3.]

6. There shall be a session of the Legislature of Ontario and of that of Quebec once at least in every year, so that twelve months shall not intervene between the last sitting of the Legislature in each Province in one session and its first sitting in the next session. *Yearly Sessions of Legislature.*

[See now as to Ontario, Rev. Stat. Ont., 1897, Cap. 12, s. 4.]

7. The following provisions of this Act respecting the House of Commons of Canada, shall extend and apply to the Legislative Assemblies of Ontario and Quebec, that is to say, the provisions relating to the election of a Speaker originally and on vacancies, the duties of the Speaker, the absence of the Speaker, the quorum, and the mode of voting, as if those provisions were here re-enacted and made applicable in terms to each such Legislative Assembly. *Speaker, Quorum, et*

[See sections 44, 45, 46, 47, 48 and 49 of this Act, and as to Ontario, Rev. Stat. Ont., 1897, Cap. 11, ss. 38-43, 65 and 66.]

4.—NOVA SCOTIA AND NEW BRUNSWICK.

Constitutions of Legislatures of Nova Scotia and New Brunswick.

88. The constitution of the Legislature of each of the Provinces of Nova Scotia and New Brunswick shall, subject to the provisions of this Act, continue as it exists at the Union until altered by the authority of this Act; and the House of Assembly of New Brunswick existing at the passing of this Act shall, unless sooner dissolved, continue for the period for which it was elected.

5.—ONTARIO, QUEBEC AND NOVA SCOTIA.

First elections.

89. Each of the Lieutenant Governors of Ontario, Quebec and Nova Scotia shall cause writs to be issued for the first election of members of the Legislative Assembly thereof in such form and by such person as he thinks fit, and at such time and addressed to such Returning Officer as the Governor General directs, and so that the first election of member of Assembly for any Electoral District or any subdivision thereof shall be held at the same time and at the same places as the election for a member to serve in the House of Commons of Canada for that Electoral District.

6.—THE FOUR PROVINCES.

Application to Legislatures of provisions respecting money votes, etc.

90. The following provisions of this Act respecting the Parliament of Canada, namely,—the provisions relating to appropriation and tax bills, the recommendation of money votes, the assent to bills, the disallowance of Acts, and the signification of pleasure on bills reserved,—shall extend and apply to the Legislatures of the several Provinces as if those provisions were here re-enacted and made applicable in terms to the respective Provinces and the Legislatures thereof, with the substitution of the Lieutenant Governor of the Province for the Governor General, of the Governor General for the Queen and for a Secretary of State, of one year for two years, and of the Province for Canada.

VI.—DISTRIBUTION OF LEGISLATIVE POWERS.

Powers of the Parliament.

Legislative authority of Parliament Canada.

91. It shall be lawful for the Queen, by and with the advice and consent of the Senate and the House of Commons, to make laws for the peace, order and good government of Canada, in relation to all matters not coming within the classes of subjects by this Act assigned exclusively to the Legislatures of the Provinces; and for greater certainty, but not so as to restrict the generality of the foregoing terms of this section, it is hereby declared that (notwithstanding anything in this Act) the exclusive legislative authority of the Parliament of Canada extends to all matters coming within the classes of subjects next hereinafter enumerated ; that is to say :—

1. The Public Debt and Property.
2. The regulation of Trade and Commerce.
3. The raising of money by any mode or system of Taxation.
4. The borrowing of money on the public credit.
5. Postal service.
6. The Census and Statistics.
7. Militia, Military and Naval Service and Defence.
8. The fixing of and providing for the salaries and allowances of civil and other officers of the Government of Canada.
9. Beacons, Buoys, Lighthouses and Sable Island.
10. Navigation and Shipping.
11. Quarantine and the establishment and maintenance of Marine Hospitals.
12. Sea coast and inland Fisheries.
13. Ferries between a Province and any British or Foreign country or between two Provinces.
14. Currency and Coinage.
15. Banking, incorporation of banks, and the issue of paper money.
16. Savings' Banks.
17. Weights and Measures.
18. Bills of Exchange and Promissory Notes.
19. Interest.
20. Legal tender.
21. Bankruptcy and Insolvency.
22. Patents of invention and discovery.
23. Copyrights.
24. Indians and lands reserved for the Indians.
25. Naturalization and Aliens.
26. Marriage and Divorce.

27. The Criminal Law, except the Constitution of Courts of Criminal Jurisdiction, but including the Procedure in Criminal Matters.
28. The Establishment, Maintenance, and Management of Penetentiaries.
29. Such classes of subjects as are expressly excepted in the enumeration of the classes of subjects by this Act assigned exclusively to the Legislatures of the Provinces.

And any matter coming within any of the classes of subjects enumerated in this section shall not be deemed to come within the class of matters of a local or private nature comprised in the enumeration of the classes of subjects by this Act assigned exclusively to the Legislatures of the Provinces.

Exclusive Powers of Provincial Legislature.

Subjects of exclusive Provincial Legislation.

92. In each Province the Legislature may exclusively make laws in relation to matters coming within the classes of subjects next hereinafter enumerated, that is to say,—

1. The Amendment from time to time, notwithstanding anything in this Act, of the Constitution of the Province, except as regards the office of Lieutenant-Governor.
2. Direct Taxation within the Province in order to the raising of a revenue for Provincial purposes.
3. The borrowing of money on the sole credit of the Province.
4. The establishment and tenure of Provincial offices and the appointment and payment of Provincial officers.
5. The management and sale of the Public Lands belonging to the Province and of the timber and wood thereon.
6. The establishment, maintenance and management of public and reformatory prisons in and for the Province.
7. The establishment, maintenance and management of hospitals, asylums, charities and eleemosynary institutions in and for the Province, other than marine hospitals.
8. Municipal institutions for the Province.
9. Shop, saloon, tavern, auctioneer and other licenses, in order to the raising of a revenue for Provincial, local or municipal purposes.

10. Local works and undertakings other than such as are of the following classes,—

    a. Lines of steam or other ships, railways, canals. telegraphs and other works and undertakings connecting the Province with any other or others of the Provinces, or extending beyond the limits of the Province ;

    b. Lines of steam ships between the Province and any British or foreign country ;

    c. Such works as, although wholly situate within the Province, are before or after their execution declared by the Parliament of Canada to be for the general advantage of Canada or for the advantage of two or more of the Provinces.

11. The incorporation of companies with Provincial objects.

12. The solemnization of marriage in the Province.

13. Property and civil rights in the Province.

14. The administration of justice in the Province, including the constitution, maintenance and organization of Provincial Courts, both of civil and of criminal jurisdiction, and including procedure in civil matters in those Courts.

15. The imposition of punishment by fine, penalty or imprisonment for enforcing any law of the Province made in relation to any matter coming within any of the classes of subjects enumerated in this section.

16. Generally all matters of a merely local or private nature in the Province.

Education.

93. In and for each Province the Legislature may exclusively make laws in relation to education, subject and according to the following provisions :— *Legislation respecting education.*

1. Nothing in any such law shall prejudicially affect any right or privilege with respect to denominational schools which any class of persons have by law in the Province at the Union.

2. All the powers, privileges and duties at the union by law conferred and imposed in Upper Canada on the separate schools and school trustees of the Queen's Roman Catholic subjects shall be and the same are hereby

extended to the dissentient schools of the Queen's Protestant and Roman Catholic subjects in Quebec.

3. Where in any Province a system of separate or dissentient schools exists by law at the Union or is thereafter established by the Legislature of the Province, an appeal shall lie to the Governor-General in Council from any Act or decision of any Provincial authority affecting any right or privilege of the Protestant or Roman Catholic minority of the Queen's subjects in relation to education.

4. In case any such Provincial law as from time to time seems to the Governor-General in Council requisite for the due execution of the provisions of this section is not made, or in case any decision of the Governor-General in Council on any appeal under this section is not duly executed by the proper Provincial authority in that behalf, then and in every such case, and as far only as the circumstances of each case require, the Parliament of Canada may make remedial laws for the due execution of the provisions of this section and of any decision of the Governor-General in Council under this section.

Uniformity of Laws in Ontario, Nova Scotia and New Brunswick.

Legislation for uniformity of laws in the three Provinces as to property and civil rights and uniformity of procedure in Courts.

94. Notwithstanding anything in this Act, the Parliament of Canada may make provision for the uniformity of all or any of the laws relative to property and civil rights in Ontario, Nova Scotia and New Brunswick, and of the procedure of all or any of the Courts in those three Provinces; and from and after the passing of any Act in that behalf the power of the Parliament of Canada to make laws in relation to any matter comprised in any such Act shall, notwithstanding anything in this Act, be unrestricted; but any Act of the Parliament of Canada making provision for such uniformity shall not have effect in any Province unless and until it is adopted and enacted as law by the Legislature thereof.

Agriculture and Immigration.

Concurrent powers of Legislation respecting Agriculture and Immigration.

95. In each Province the Legislature may make laws in relation to Agriculture in the Province, and to Immigration into the Province; and it is hereby declared that the Parliament of Canada may from time to time make laws in relation to Agriculture in all or any of the Provinces, and to Immigration into all or any of the Provinces; and any law of the Legislature of a Province relative to Agriculture or to Immigration shall have

effect in and for the Province as long and as far only as it is not repugnant to any Act of the Parliament of Canada.

VII.—JUDICATURE.

96. The Governor-General shall appoint the Judges of the Superior, District and County Courts in each Province, except those of the Courts of Probate in Nova Scotia and New Brunswick. <small>Appointment of Judges.</small>

97. Until the laws relative to property and civil rights in Ontario, Nova Scotia and New Brunswick, and the procedure of the Courts in those Provinces are made uniform, the Judges of the Courts of those Provinces appointed by the Governor-General shall be selected from the respective Bars of those Provinces. <small>Selection of Judges in Ontario, etc.</small>

98. The Judges of the Courts of Quebec shall be selected from the Bar of that Province. <small>Selection of Judges in Quebec.</small>

99. The Judges of the Superior Courts shall hold office during good behavior, but shall be removable by the Governor-General on address of the Senate and House of Commons. <small>Tenure of office of Judges of Superior Courts.</small>

100. The salaries, allowances and pensions of the Judges of the Superior, District and County Courts (except the Courts of Probate in Nova Scotia and New Brunswick), and of the Admiralty Courts in cases where the Judges thereof are for the time being paid by salary, shall be fixed and provided by the Parliament of Canada. <small>Salaries etc. of Judges.</small>

101. The Parliament of Canada may, notwithstanding anything in this Act, from time to time, provide for the constitution, maintenance and organization of a general Court of Appeal for Canada, and for the establishment of any additional Courts for the better administration of the Laws of Canada. <small>General Court of Appeal, etc.</small>

VIII.—REVENUES; DEBTS; ASSETS; TAXATION.

102. All duties and revenues over which the respective Legislatures of Canada, Nova Scotia and New Brunswick before and at the Union had and have power of appropriation, except such portions thereof as are by this Act reserved to the respective Legislatures of the Provinces, or are raised by them in accordance with the special powers conferred on them by this Act, shall form one Consolidated Revenue Fund, to be appropriated for the public service of Canada in the manner and subject to the charges in this Act provided. <small>Creation of Consolidated Revenue Fund.</small>

Expenses of collection, etc.	**103.** The Consolidated Revenue Fund of Canada shall be permanently charged with the costs, charges and expenses incident to the collection, management and receipt thereof, and the same shall form the first charge thereon, subject to be reviewed and audited in such manner as shall be ordered by the Governor-General in Council until the Parliament otherwise provides.
Interest of Provincial public debts.	**104.** The annual interest of the public debts of the several Provinces of Canada, Nova Scotia and New Brunswick at the Union shall form the second charge on the Consolidated Revenue Fund of Canada.
Salary of Governor-General.	**105.** Unless altered by the Parliament of Canada, the salary of the Governor-General shall be ten thousand pounds sterling money of the United Kingdom of Great Britain and Ireland, payable out of the Consolidated Revenue Fund of Canada, and the same shall form the third charge thereon.
Appropriation of fund subject to charges.	**106.** Subject to the several payments by this Act charged on the Consolidated Revenue Fund of Canada, the same shall be appropriated by the Parliament of Canada for the public service.
Transfer to Canada of stocks, etc., belonging to two Provinces.	**107.** All stocks, cash, banker's balances and securities for money belonging to each Province at the time of the Union, except as in this Act mentioned, shall be the property of Canada, and shall be taken in reduction of the amount of the respective debts of the Provinces at the Union.
Transfer of property in schedule.	**108.** The public works and property of each Province, enumerated in the third schedule to this Act, shall be the property of Canada.
Lands, mines, etc., belonging to Provinces, to belong to them.	**109.** All lands, mines, minerals, and royalties belonging to the several Provinces of Canada, Nova Scotia and New Brunswick at the Union, and all sums then due or payable for such lands, mines, minerals, or royalties, shall belong to the several Provinces of Ontario, Quebec, Nova Scotia and New Brunswick in which the same are situate or arise, subject to any trusts existing in respect thereof, and to any interest other than that of the Province in the same.
Assets connected with Provincial debts.	**110.** All assets connected with such portions of the public debt of each Province as are assumed by that Province shall belong to that Province.
Canada to be liable for Provincial debts.	**111.** Canada shall be liable for the debts and liabilities of each Province existing at the Union.

112. Ontario and Quebec conjointly shall be liable to Canada for the amount (if any) by which the debt of the Province of Canada exceeds at the Union $62,500,000, and shall be charged with interest at the rate of five per centum per annum thereon. *Liability of Ontario and Quebec to Canada.*

113. The assets enumerated in the fourth schedule to this Act belonging at the Union to the Province of Canada shall be the property of Ontario and Quebec conjointly. *Assets of Ontario and Quebec.*

114. Nova Scotia shall be liable to Canada for the amount (if any) by which its public debt exceeds at the Union $8,000,000, and shall be charged with interest at the rate of five per centum per annum thereon. *Liability of Nova Scotia to Canada.*

115. New Brunswick shall be liable to Canada for the amount (if any) by which its public debt exceeds at the Union $7,000,000, and shall be charged with interest at the rate of five per centum per annum thereon. *Liability of New Brunswick to Canada.*

116. In case the public debt of Nova Scotia and New Brunswick do not at the Union amount to $8,000,000 and $7,000,000 respectively, they shall respectively receive by half-yearly payments in advance from the Government of Canada interest at five per centum per annum on the difference between the actual amounts of their respective debts and such stipulated amounts. *Payment of interest to Nova Scotia and New Brunswick if their public debts are less than the stipulated amounts.*

117. The several Provinces shall retain all their respective public property not otherwise disposed of in this Act, subject to the right of Canada to assume any lands or public property required for fortifications or for the defence of the country. *Provincial public property.*

118. The following sums shall be paid yearly by Canada to the several Provinces for the support of their Governments and Legislatures: *Grants to Provinces.*

		Dollars.
Ontario		Eighty thousand.
Quebec	-	Seventy thousand.
Nova Scotia	-	Sixty thousand.
New Brunswick	- -	Fifty thousand.
		Two hundred and sixty thousand.

and an annual grant in aid of each Province shall be made, equal to eighty cents per head of the population as ascertained by the Census of 1861, and in the case of Nova Scotia and New Brunswick, by each subsequent decennial census until the population of each of those two Provinces amounts to four hundred thousand souls, at which rate such grant shall thereafter remain. Such grants shall be in full settlement of all future demands on

Canada, and shall be paid half-yearly in advance to each Province ; but the Government of Canada shall deduct from such grants, as against any Province, all sums chargeable as interest on the Public Debt of that Province in excess of the several amounts stipulated in this Act.

Further grant to New Brunswick for ten years.
119. New Brunswick shall receive by half-yearly payments in advance from Canada, for the period of ten years from the Union an additional allowance of $63,000 per annum : but as long as the Public Debt of that Province remains under $7,000,000, a deduction equal to the interest at five per centum per annum on such deficiency shall be made from that allowance of $63,000.

Form of payments.
120. All payments to be made under this Act, or in discharge of liabilities created under any Act of the Provinces of Canada, Nova Scotia and New Brunswick respectively, and assumed by Canada, shall, until the Parliament of Canada otherwise directs, be made in such form and manner as may from time to time be ordered by the Governor General in Council.

Manufactures, etc., of one Province to be admitted free into the others.
121. All articles of the growth, produce, or manufacture of any one of the Provinces shall, from and after the Union, be admitted free into each of the other Provinces.

Continuance of Customs and Excise Laws.
122. The Customs and Excise Laws of each Province shall, subject to the provisions of this Act, continue in force until altered by the Parliament of Canada.

Exportation and importation as between two Provinces.
123. Where Customs duties are, at the Union, leviable on any goods, wares, or merchandises in any two Provinces those goods, wares and merchandises may, from and after the Union, be imported from one of those Provinces into the other of them on proof of payment of the Customs duty leviable thereon in the Province of exportation and on payment of such further amount (if any) of Customs duty as is leviable thereon in the Province of importation.

Lumber dues in New Brunswick.
124. Nothing in this Act shall affect the right of New Brunswick to levy the lumber dues provided in chapter fifteen, of title three, of the Revised Statutes of New Brunswick, or in any Act amending that Act before or after the Union, and not increasing the amount of such dues ; but the lumber of any of the Provinces other than New Brunswick shall not be subject to such dues.

Exemption of public lands, etc., from taxation.
125. No lands or property belonging to Canada or any Province shall be liable to taxation.

126. Such portions of the duties and revenues over which the respective Legislatures of Canada, Nova Scotia and New Brunswick had before the Union power of appropriation as are by this Act reserved to the respective Governments or Legislatures of the Provinces, and all duties and revenues raised by them in accordance with the special powers conferred upon them by this Act, shall in each Province form one Consolidated Revenue Fund to be appropriated for the public service of the Province. *Provincial Consolidated Revenue Fund.*

IX.—MISCELLANEOUS PROVISIONS.

General.

127. If any person being at the passing of this Act a Member of the Legislative Council of Canada, Nova Scotia or New Brunswick, to whom a place in the Senate is offered, does not within thirty days thereafter, by writing under his hand, addressed to the Governor General of the Province of Canada, or to the Lieutenant Governor of Nova Scotia or New Brunswick (as the case may be), accept the same, he shall be deemed to have declined the same ; and any person who, being at the passing of this Act a member of the Legislative Council of Nova Scotia or New Brunswick, accepts a place in the Senate, shall thereby vacate his seat in such Legislative Council. *As to Legislative Councillors of Provinces becoming Senators.*

128. Every member of the Senate or House of Commons of Canada shall before taking his seat therein, take and subscribe before the Governor General or some person authorized by him, and every member of a Legislative Council or Legislative Assembly of any Province shall before taking his seat therein, take and subscribe before the Lieutenant Governor of the Province or some person authorized by him, the oath of allegiance contained in the fifth schedule to this Act ; and every member of the Senate of Canada and every member of the Legislative Council of Quebec shall also, before taking his seat therein, take and subscribe before the Governor General or some person authorized by him, the declaration of qualification contained in the same Schedule. *Oath of allegiance, etc.*

129. Except as otherwise provided by this Act, all laws in force in Canada, Nova Scotia or New Brunswick at the Union, and all Courts of civil and criminal jurisdiction, and all legal commissions, powers and authorities, and all officers, judicial, administrative and ministerial, existing therein at the Union, shall continue in Ontario, Quebec, Nova Scotia and New Brunswick respectively, as if the Union had not been made ; subject nevertheless (except with respect to such as are enacted by or exist under Acts of the Parliament of Great Britain or of the *Continuance of existing laws, courts, officers, etc.*

Parliament of the United Kingdom of Great Britain and Ireland,) to be repealed, abolished or altered by the Parliament of Canada, or by the Legislature of the respective Province, according to the authority of the Parliament or of that Legislature under this Act.

Transfer of officers to Canada.

130. Until the Parliament of Canada otherwise provides, all officers of the several Provinces having duties to discharge in relation to matters other than those coming within the classes of subjects by this Act assigned exclusively to the Legislatures of the Provinces shall be officers of Canada, and shall continue to discharge the duties of their respective offices under the same liabilities, responsibilities and penalties as if the Union had not been made.

Appointment of new officers.

131. Until the Parliament of Canada otherwise provides, the Governor General in Council may from time to time appoint such officers as the Governor General in Council deems necessary or proper for the effectual execution of this Act.

Power for performance of treaty obligations by Canada as part of British Empire.

132. The Parliament and Government of Canada shall have all powers necessary or proper for performing the obligations of Canada or of any Province thereof, as part of the British Empire, towards foreign countries, arising under treaties between the Empire and such foreign countries.

Use of English and French languages.

133. Either the English or the French language may be used by any person in the debates of the Houses of the Parliament of Canada and of the Houses of the Legislature of Quebec ; and both those languages shall be used in the respective records and journals of those Houses ; and either of those languages may be used by any person or in any pleading or process in or issuing from any Court of Canada established under this Act, and in or from all or any of the Courts of Quebec.

The Acts of the Parliament of Canada and of the Legislature of Quebec shall be printed and published in both those languages.

Ontario and Quebec.

Appointment of executive officers for Ontario and Quebec.

134. Until the Legislature of Ontario or of Quebec otherwise provides, the Lieutenant Governors of Ontario and Quebec may each appoint under the great seal of the Province the following officers, to hold office during pleasure, that is to say :—the Attorney General, the Secretary and Registrar of the Province, the Treasurer of the Province, the Commissioner of Crown Lands, and the Commissioner of Agriculture and Public Works, and in the case of Quebec the Solicitor General ; and may, by order of the Lieutenant Governor in Council, from time to time prescribe the duties of those officers and of the several departments over which they shall preside or to which they shall belong, and of the officers and clerks thereof, and may also appoint other and additional officers to hold the office during pleasure, and may from time to time prescribe the duties of those officers, and of the several departments over which they shall preside or to which they shall belong, and of the officers and clerks thereof.

135. Until the Legislature of Ontario or Quebec otherwise provides, all rights, powers, duties, functions, responsibilities, or authorities at the passing of this Act vested in or imposed on the Attorney General, Solicitor General, Secretary and Registrar of the Province of Canada, Minister of Finance, Commissioner of Crown Lands, Commissioner of Public Works, and Minister of Agriculture and Receiver General, by any law, statute or ordinance of Upper Canada, Lower Canada, or Canada, and not repugnant to this Act, shall be vested in or imposed on any officer to be appointed by the Lieutenant Governor for the discharge of the same or any of them ; and the Commissioner of Agriculture and Public Works shall perform the duties and functions of the office of Minister of Agriculture at the passing of this Act imposed by the law of the Province of Canada, as well as those of the Commissioner of Public Works. *Powers, duties, etc. of executive officers.*

136. Until altered by the Lieutenant Governor in Council, the Great Seals of Ontario and Quebec respectively shall be the same, or of the same design, as those used in the Provinces of Upper Canada and Lower Canada respectively before their Union as the Province of Canada. *Great Seal.*

137. The words "and from thence to the end of the then next ensuing Session of the Legislature," or words to the same effect, used in any temporary Act of the Province of Canada not expired before the Union, shall be construed to extend and apply to the next Session of the Parliament of Canada, if the subject matter of the Act is within the powers of the same, as defined by this Act, or to the next Session of the Legislatures of Ontario and Quebec respectively, if the subject matter of the Act is within the powers of the same as defined by this Act. *Construction of temporary Acts.*

138. From and after the Union, the use of the words "Upper Canada" instead of "Ontario," or "Lower Canada" instead of "Quebec," in any deed, writ, process, pleading, document, matter or thing, shall not invalidate the same. *As to errors in names.*

139. Any Proclamation under the Great Seal of the Province of Canada issued before the Union to take effect at a time which *As to issue of proclamations before*

Union, to commence after Union.	is subsequent to the Union, whether relating to that Province, or to Upper Canada or to Lower Canada, and the several matters and things therein proclaimed shall be and continue of like force and effect as if the Union had not been made.
As to issue of Proclamations after Union under authority of Acts before Union.	**140.** Any Proclamation which is authorized by any Act of the Legislature of the Province of Canada to be issued under the Great Seal of the Province of Canada, whether relating to that Province, or to Upper Canada, or to Lower Canada, and which is not issued before the Union, may be issued by the Lieutenant Governor of Ontario or of Quebec, as its subject matter requires, under the Great Seal thereof: and from and after the issue of such proclamation the same and the several matters and things therein proclaimed shall be and continue of the like force and effect in Ontario and Quebec as if the Union had not been made.
Penitentiary.	**141.** The Penitentiary of the Province of Canada shall, until the Parliament of Canada otherwise provides, be and continue the Penetentiary of Ontario and of Quebec.
Arbitration respecting debts, etc.	**142.** The division and adjustment of the debts, credits, liabilities, properties and assets of Upper Canada and Lower Canada shall be referred to the arbitrament of three arbitrators, one chosen by the Government of Ontario, one by the Government of Quebec, and one by the Government of Canada; and the selection of the arbitrators shall not be made until the Parliament of Canada and the Legislatures of Ontario and Quebec have met; and the arbitrator chosen by the Government of Canada shall not be a resident either in Ontario or in Quebec.
Division of records.	**143.** The Governor General in Council may from time to time order that such and so many of the records, books and documents of the Province of Canada as he thinks fit shall be appropriated and delivered either to Ontario or to Quebec, and the same shall thenceforth be the property of that Province; and any copy thereof or extract therefrom, duly certified by the officer having charge of the original thereof, shall be admitted as evidence.
Constitution of townships in Quebec.	**144.** The Lieutenant Governor of Quebec may from time to time, by Proclamation under the Great Seal of the Province, to take effect from a day to be appointed therein, constitute townships in those parts of the Province of Quebec in which townships are not then already constituted, and fix the metes and bounds thereof.

X.—INTERCOLONIAL RAILWAY.

115. Inasmuch as the Provinces of Canada, Nova Scotia and New Brunswick have joined in a declaration that the construction of the Intercolonial Railway is essential to the consolidation of the Union of British North America, and to the assent thereto of Nova Scotia and New Brunswick, and have consequently agreed that provision should be made for its immediate construction by the Government of Canada : Therefore, in order to give effect to that agreement, it shall be the duty of the Government and Parliament of Canada to provide for the commencement within six months after the Union of a railway connecting the River St. Lawrence with the City of Halifax in Nova Scotia, and for the construction thereof without intermission, and the completion thereof with all practicable speed. *Duty of Government and Parliament of Canada to make railway herein described.*

XI.—ADMISSION OF OTHER COLONIES.

116. It shall be lawful for the Queen, by and with the advice of Her Majesty's Most Honourable Privy Council, on Addresses from the Houses of Parliament of Canada, and from the Houses of the respective Legislatures of the Colonies or Provinces of Newfoundland, Prince Edward Island, and British Columbia, to admit those Colonies or Provinces, or any of them, into the Union, and on Address from the House of Parliament of Canada to admit Rupert's Land and the North-western Territory, or either of them, into the Union, on such terms and conditions in each case as are in the Addresses expressed and as the Queen thinks fit to approve, subject to the provisions of this Act ; and the provisions of any Order in Council in that behalf shall have effect as if they had been enacted by the Parliament of the United Kingdom of Great Britain and Ireland. *Power to admit Newfoundland, Prince Edward Island British Columbia, Rupert's Land, and North Western Territory into the Union by Order in Council.*

117. In case of the admission of Newfoundland and Prince Edward Island, or either of them, each shall be entitled to a representation in the Senate of Canada of four members, and (notwithstanding anything in this Act) in case of the admission of Newfoundland the normal number of Senators shall be seventy-six and their maximum number shall be eighty two ; but Prince Edward Island, when admitted, shall be deemed to be comprised in the third of the three divisions into which Canada is, in relation to the constitution of the Senate, divided by this Act, and accordingly, after the admission of Prince Edward Island, whether Newfoundland is admitted or not, the representation of Nova Scotia and New Brunswick in the Senate shall as vacancies occur, be reduced from twelve to ten members respectively, and the representation of each of those Provinces shall not be increased at any time beyond ten, except under the provisions of this Act for the appointment of three or six additional Senators under the direction of the Queen. *As to representation of Newfound land and Prince Edward Island in Senate.*

SCHEDULE.

The FIRST SCHEDULE.

Electoral Districts of Ontario.

[*This Schedule is omitted, as the Division of Ontario into Electoral Districts has been altered by subsequent Dominion and Provincial legislation.*]

The SECOND SCHEDULE.

Electoral Districts of Quebec specially fixed.

[*See Section 80.*]

COUNTIES OF—

Pontiac.	Missisquoi.	Compton.
Ottawa.	Brome.	Wolfe and Rich
Argenteuil.	Shefford.	mond
Huntingdon.	Stanstead.	Megantic.
	Town of Sherbrooke.	

The THIRD SCHEDULE.

Provincial Public Works and Property to be the Property of Canada.

1. Canals, with Lands and Water Power connected therewith.
2. Public Harbours.
3. Lighthouses and Piers, and Sable Island.
4. Steamboats, Dredges and public Vessels.
5. Rivers and Lake improvements.
6. Railways and Railway Stocks, Mortgages, and other debts due by Railway Companies.

7. Military Roads.
8. Custom Houses, Post Offices, and all other Public Buildings, except such as the Government of Canada appropriate for the use of the Provincial Legislatures and Governments.
9. Property transferred by Imperial Government and known as Ordnance Property.
10. Armouries, Drill Sheds, Military Clothing, and Munitions of War, and Lands set apart for general public purposes.

The FOURTH SCHEDULE.

Assets to be the Property of Ontario and Quebec conjointly.

Upper Canada Building Fund.
Lunatic Asylums.
Normal School.
Court Houses, in Aylmer, Montreal, Kamouraska. } Lower Canada.
Law Society, Upper Canada.
Montreal Turnpike Trust.
University Permanent Fund.
Royal Institution
Consolidated Municipal Loan Fund, Upper Canada.
Consolidated Municipal Loan Fund, Lower Canada.
Agricultural Society, Upper Canada.
Lower Canada Legislative Grant.
Quebec Fire Loan.
Tamiscouata Advance Account.
Quebec Turnpike Trust.
Education East.
Building and Jury Fund, Lower Canada.
Municipalities Fund.
Lower Canada Superior Education Income Fund.

The FIFTH SCHEDULE.

OATH OF ALLEGIANCE.

I, *A. B.* do swear, That I will be faithful and bear true Allegiance to Her Majesty Queen Victoria.

Note.—The name of the King or Queen of the United Kingdom of Great Britain and Ireland for the time being is to be substituted from time to time, with proper terms of reference thereto.

DECLARATION OF QUALIFICATION.

I, *A. B.* do declare and testify, that I am by law duly qualified to be appointed a Member of the Senate of Canada [*or as the case may be*], and that I am legally or equitably seised as of freehold for my own use and benefit of lands or tenements held in free and common socage [*or seised or possessed for my own use and benefit of lands or tenements held in franc-alleu or in roture (as the case may be)*,] in the Province of Nova Scotia [*or as the case may be*] of the value of four thousand dollars over and above all rents, dues, debts, mortgages, charges, and incumbrances due or payable out of or charged on or affecting the same, and that I have not collusively or colourably obtained a title to or become possessed of the said lands and tenements or any part thereof for the purpose of enabling me to become a Member of the Senate of Canada [*or as the case may be*], and that my real and personal property are together worth four thousand dollars over and above my debts and liabilities.

BOUNDARIES OF ONTARIO.

IMPERIAL ACT, 52-53 VICT. Cap. 28.

An Act to declare the Boundaries of the Province of Ontario in the Dominion of Canada.

[*12th August, 1889.*]

WHEREAS the Senate and Commons of Canada in Parliament assembled, have presented to Her Majesty the Queen, the address set forth in the Schedule to this Act respecting the boundaries of the Province of Ontario.

And whereas the Government of the Province of Ontario have assented to the boundaries mentioned in that address;

And whereas such boundaries so far as the Province of Ontario adjoins the Province of Quebec are identical with those fixed by the proclamation of the Governor-General, issued in November, 1791, which has ever since existed;

And whereas such boundaries so far as the Province of Ontario adjoins the Province of Manitoba are identical with those found to be the correct boundaries by a report of the Judicial Committee of the Privy Council, which Her Majesty, the Queen in Council, on the eleventh day of August, one thousand eight hundred and eighty-four, ordered to be carried into execution:

And whereas it is expedient that the boundaries of the Province of Ontario should be declared by authority of Parliament in accordance with the said address;

Be it therefore enacted by the Queen's most excellent Majesty by and with the advice and consent of the Lords Spiritual and Temporal and Commons in this present Parliament assembled, and by the authority of the same as follows:

1. This Act may be cited as the Canada (Ontario Boundary) Act, 1889. *Short title*

2. It is hereby declared that the westerly, northerly and easterly boundaries of the Province of Ontario are those described in the address set forth in the Schedule to this Act. *Declaration of boundaries of Ontario.*

SCHEDULE.

ADDRESS TO THE QUEEN FROM THE SENATE AND HOUSE OF COMMONS OF CANADA.

We, your Majesty's most dutiful and loyal subjects the Senate and Commons of Canada in Parliament Assembled, humbly approach Your Majesty with the request that Your Majesty may be graciously pleased to cause a measure to be submitted to the Parliament of the United Kingdom, declaring and providing the following to be the westerly, northerly and easterly boundaries of the Province of Ontario, that is to say :—

Commencing at the point where the international boundary between the United States of America and Canada strikes the western shores of Lake Superior, thence westerly along the said boundary to the north-west angle of the Lake of the Woods, thence along a line drawn due north until it strikes the middle line of the course of the river discharging the waters of the lake called Lake Seul or the Lonely Lake, whether above or below its confluence with the stream flowing from the Lake of the Woods towards Lake Winnipeg, and thence proceeding eastward from the point at which the before mentioned line strikes the middle line of the course of the river last aforesaid, along the middle line of the course of the same river (whether called by the name of the English River, or, as to the part below the confluence, by the name of the River Winnipeg), up to Lake Seul or the Lonely Lake, and thence along the middle line of Lake Seul or Lonely Lake to the head of that lake, and thence by a straight line to the nearest point of the middle line of the waters of Lake St. Joseph, and thence along that middle line until it reaches the foot or outlet of that lake, and thence along the middle line of the river by which the waters of Lake St. Joseph discharge themselves, to the shore of the part of Hudson's Bay commonly known as James' Bay, and thence south-easterly following upon the said shore to a point where a line drawn due north from the head of Lake Temiscamingue would strike it, and thence due south along the said line to the head of the said lake, and thence through the middle channel of the said lake into the Ottawa River, and thence descending along the middle of the main channel of the said river to the intersection by the prolongation of the western limits of the Seigneurie of Rigaud, such mid-channel being as indicated on a map of the Ottawa Ship Canal Survey, made by Walter Shanley, C.E., and approved by order of the Governor-General in Council dated the twenty-first July, one thousand eight hundred and eighty-six; and thence southerly following the said westerly boundary of the Seigneurie of Rigaud to the south-west angle of the said Seigneurie, and then southerly along the western boundary of the augmentation of the Township of Newton to the north-west angle of the Seigneurie of Longueuil, and thence south-easterly along the south-western boundary of the said Seigneurie of New Longueuil to a stone boundary on the north bank of the Lake St. Francis, at the cove west of Point au Baudet, such line from the Ottawa River to Lake St. Francis being as indicated on a plan of the line of boundary between Upper and Lower Canada made in accordance with the Act, 23 Victoria, chapter 21, and approved by order of the Governor-General in Council, dated the 16th March, 1861.

INDEX

TO

DECISION OF MR. SPEAKER.

ADDRESS :
   An address for information relative to certain matters beyond the control of the Provincial Government ruled in order, 103.

AMENDMENTS :
   An amendment differing in form, but identical in purport with an amendment already rejected, cannot be entertained, 102.
   An amendment to a substantive motion, striking out all but the word "That," and on a cognate subject, is in order, 92.
   An amendment on third reading, identical with one rejected on reception of Report of Committee of the Whole, is declared out of order, 93.
   An indefinite amendment, and one not conveying accurate instructions to a committee, cannot be entertained, 95.
   An amendment, similar in wording, but differing in fact from a previously rejected amendment, is in order, 95.
   An amendment involving the expenditure of public money cannot be entertained, 100.
   An amendment which diverts public money from purposes recommended by the Crown, cannot be passed, 100.
   An amendment, substantially the same as one already debated upon and disposed of, cannot be submitted, 92, 112.
   It is not in order to move an amendment to an amendment to the motion to go into a Committee of Supply, 105.
   An amendment seeking to divert Public Revenue is out of order, 108.
   An amendment to an amendment concluding with the words, "That the said resolution be now concurred in," is out of order, as partaking of the character of the "Previous Question," 109.
   An amendment which declares some principle adverse to the measure, or is otherwise opposed to its progress, may be moved to the Third Reading of a Bill, 110.
   An amendment of which no notice has been given, cannot be made in a Private Bill on its Third Reading, 112.

An amendment identical with one already disposed of is out of order, 116.

Upon the Second or Third Reading of a Bill, amendments may be moved declaratory of any principle adverse to the Bill or opposed to its further progress. But an amendment, to be in order, must relate to some provision of the Bill, 110.

An amendment, in substance, but not in precise form, the same as one already passed upon by the House during the same session, is out of order, 116.

An amendment to an amendment, adding words to the amendment, having been put and carried, a motion to strike out the first part of the amendment as amended, is out of order, 119.

A proposed amendment to a Private Bill, if no notice has been given, is out of order, 120.

The House having amended an amendment, and passed the original motion as amended, no further amendment, involving non-concurrence, can be put, 121.

An amendment of similar character to, and yet going further than the original motion, is in order, 121.

An amendment to the amendment to the motion, "That Mr. Speaker do now leave the chair," is in order, except when going into Supply, 125.

No amendment can be moved on the Second Reading or other stage of a Bill, by way of mere addition to the question, 126.

An amendment of the same purport as one already rejected cannot be put, 98.

An amendment should be so framed as to leave out certain words ; to leave out certain words in order to insert or add others ; or to insert or add certain words, 127.

BILLS :

The House decides that when in Committee of the Whole on a Bill, the first section must be first considered, 93.

A change of names, by the Private Bills' Committee, in the preamble of a Private Bill, is in order, 91.

The Chairman decides that a section of a Bill, giving power to expend public moneys, may be considered, if applying to charges hereafter to be provided for by vote in Committee of Supply, 93.

A Bill to amend the Ontario Medical Act declared to be a Public Bill, 95.

A Bill to make the Benchers of the Law Society elective by the Bar thereof, declared to be a Private Bill, 96.

Notice must be given of proposed amendments to a Private Bill, 96, 108.

A Bill to unite the County of Perth for Registration purposes declared to be a Private Bill, 99.

A Bill authorizing expenditure of Public Moneys refused introduction because approval thereof, by the Lieutenant-Governor, had not been communicated to the House, 100.

A Bill is in order which leaves the amount of a proposed salary in blank and does not impose a burden, 101.

A Bill amended in Railway Committee objected to, as containing provisions not prayed for in petition, is sent back to Committee on Standing Orders, and it is recommended by that Committee that, with regard to such amendment, the Rules of the House be suspended, 101.

Notice must be given of amendments to a Private Bill, 96.

Amendments may be moved to Third Reading of a Bill, 112.

It is in order for the House to refer to the Committee on Standing Orders, a Bill amended in Committee on Private Bills, 110.

Notice must be given of amendment to a Private Bill on its Third Reading, 112.

Amendments may be moved on Third Reading of Public Bill, 112.

On Second Reading or other stage of a Bill, no amendment can be moved by way of mere addition to the Question, 127.

CHARGES ON REVENUE :

A Bill may furnish machinery for expenditure of Public Money, without direct recommendation of Crown, if charges thereunder are to be provided for by vote in Committee of Supply, 114.

A proposal for the free distribution of statutes to magistrates regarded as a charge on the revenue, 94.

As timber yields revenue, no question as to the disposal of it can be entertained without the recommendation of the Lieutenant-Governor, 92.

A motion seeking to interfere with the collection of revenue from Crown Lands objected to, but decision reserved and not afterwards given, 94.

No important variation can be made in the purposes for which a grant of money, recommended by the Crown for a specific purpose, can be put, without a fresh recommendation, 104.

Where there is no variation of the destination of a fund, and no change in the purpose for which it was originally intended, there is no necessity for a new recommendation, 106.

A motion seeking to commit the House to a future expenditure of money, without a recommendation from the Crown, is out of order, 107.

An amendment seeking to divert Public Revenue is out of order, 108.

A debate upon a motion involving a charge upon the people, cannot be presently entered upon, 111.

A proposed interference with an expenditure of Public Money recommended by the Crown, not in order, 113.

A Bill making no definite appropriation of, or charges upon any part of the Public Revenue, may be read a second time, without a recommendation from the Crown ; but if, in its passage through the House, it is sought to make a specific charge upon the people, such charge must be recommended in the usual way, 115.

Abstract resolutions upon matters affecting the revenue are of doubtful propriety, 105, 111.

COMMITTEES :

Concurrence in the report of a Special or Standing Committee must be moved, if it makes recommendations. If no special recommendations are made, and no member objects to the report when presented, it is regarded as concurred in, 123.

Concurrence is not necessary upon a report containing no recommendation, 123.

The fact of a Committee of the Whole having risen without reporting a Bill or other matter, does not prevent a motion for replacing the measure upon the Orders of the Day, 97.

Several instances of Committee having risen without report, 97.

DEBATE :

An arrangement made by the House for permission to speak tantamount to an order, 95.

DECISION BY THE CLERK :

House not properly constituted for the reception of documents, until election of Speaker, 128.

LETTERS :

A letter may be read in the House without disclosure of the signature thereto, if the member reading it assumes responsibility for its contents, 113.

MOTIONS :

A Motion must correspond with its Notice, 99.

A question which has passed in the negative cannot be again proposed in the same session, 103, 118.

Motions of an abstract character, in regard to particular branches of taxation, are inadvisable, 105.

A case in point, 105.

A question already decided cannot be again put, 118.

The House having declared that a considerable extension of the Franchise is especially a subject upon which the people ought to be consulted in a coming election, any proposition to now admit large numbers of persons to the Franchise cannot be entertained, 116, 118.

MENTAL INCAPACITY :
In case of permanent incapacity of a member, through incurable mental malady, reported by Committee on Privileges and Elections, no notice of a motion for the issue of a Writ is necessary, 118.

PAPERS :
A proposal to lay a paper upon the table, and that it be now read, declared irregular, 119.

PECUNIARY INTEREST :
Votes of certain members on an Assessment Bill objected to, because supposed to have pecuniary interest therein, but admitted because Bill was of public character, 96.

No objection can be taken on the ground of pecuniary interest without a substantive motion, 127.

PETITIONS :
No Petition can be received praying for a grant not previously recommended by the Crown, 95.

A Petition may be received which asks for legislation prohibiting sale and use of intoxicating liquors, 100.

A Petition praying for a grant from the Public Treasury cannot be received, 103.

A Petition cannot be read on presentation, unless by common consent ; but it is read at length by the Clerk at the table, two days after presentation, if desired, 122, 123.

POWERS OF LEGISLATURE :
The regulation of the Sale of Poisons is within the powers of the Provincial Legislature, 96.

A Bill to prohibit the Sale of Intoxicating Liquors as a beverage is not within the powers of the Provincial Legislature, 101.

PREROGATIVE OF THE CROWN :
A Bill seeking to fix the date for meeting of the Legislature declared to be an interference with the Prerogative of the Crown, 108.

PREVIOUS QUESTION .
Mr. Speaker decided that "The Previous Question" cannot be put when an amendment is under consideration, 104.

The Previous Question put, 105.

SUPPLY :
The advisers of His Honour, the Lieutenant-Governor, are responsible for communications from him respecting the matter of Supply, 114.

WRIT :
No notice is required for issue of Writ, 119.

INDEX

TO

MEMBERS' MANUAL.

ABSENCE OF SPEAKER:
Provision in case of, 57.

ABSENCE OF MEMBERS: 72.

ACCOUNTANT OF HOUSE: 69.

ACCOUNTS AND PAPERS: 56.
Notice of Order of House for, 56—Order of House for, 56—Address to Crown for Papers, 56

ADDRESS: 13.
Moved and seconded, and passage of since Confederation, 170.

ADJOURNMENT: 54.
Rule respecting, 54—A member cannot move Adjournment of Debate and of House, 54—On Motion to Adjourn cannot discuss an Order of Day, 54—Irregular to use Motion of Adjournment to prolong Debate, 54—Amendment relating to some other matter cannot be proposed, 54—Member who has spoke in Debate cannot move Adjournment, 54—Adjournment may supersede a stage of Bill, 55—Cannot be Moved while another is speaking, 55—No names recorded on Motion to Adjourn, 55—Right of reply, 55—May Adjourn when no Quorum, 55—Counting out, 55—Adjournments on death of members, 55.

ADMITTANCE TO FLOOR AND GALLERIES: 16.

AMENDMENTS: 29.
What is an Amendment, 29—Sir R. Palgrave's definition of, 29—American practice, 32—Time of Moving, 29—Must be seconded, excepting in Committee of Whole, 29—Words added cannot be struck out, 29—Words may be added to after part of Amendment, 29—Repetition of question inadmissible, 30—Substitution of Motion cannot be moved until Amendment is withdrawn, 30—Amendments in order when omitting matter of recital in original Motion, 30—No priority because of notice, 30—Further Amendment permissible, 30
Must be relevant to Motion, 30—Cannot leave out all the words of Amendment, 30—When Amendment to Amendment not in order, 31—When notice of unnecessary, 31—Notice of to Public Bill unnecessary, 31—Resolutions reported may be Amended, 31—Can-

[227]

not increase proposed burden, 31— Proposing different appropriation of funds out of order, 31—May leave out all but the first word "That," 31—Member may speak to, 31—Order of, 31—Withdrawn, 31—Cannot speak to Motion and afterwards move, 32—Cannot speak to Motion after proposing, 32—Mover of has no right to reply, 32—Six months "hoist," 32—Form of, 32.

ANNUAL SESSION :

Twelve months shall not intervene between Sessions, 11, 73.

APPENDIX : 155.

ASSEMBLY, LEGISLATIVE : 11.

AYES AND NOES : 34.

BILLS : 40.

What is a Public Bill ? 39, 40—What is an Estate Bill ? 50—What is a Private Bill ? 47 Illegal promotion of, 52—No member or his partner shall receive remuneration for promoting a Bill, 52—Drafting a Bill, 40—Offer of money to a member for influence a high crime, 52—Offer of bribe punishable as breach of privilege, 53.

BILLS, PRIVATE :

What are they ? 40, 47—Power of Provincial Legislatures as to, 47—And railway, 48—Petitions for, 48—Six weeks' notice of, 49—In duplicate, 48—Against, 48—Received within first ten days of Session 48—Sent to Committee on Standing Orders, 49—Copy and one hundred dollars to be sent to Clerk, 49 Presented within first seventeen days of Session, 48—Reported within thirty days, 48—Relating to Railways, 48, 49—Notice respecting, 49—Information as to tolls, 49—Maps and plans relating to, 49 First reading, 50—Promoters and opponents heard by Committee, 51—Casting vote of Chairman, 51 Second reading, 51—Reprinted when Amended, 51 Two days' notice of Amendment, 51—Fees on in some cases remitted, 51—On Orders of Day, 52 Preamble first considered, 52—Royal assent, 52—Procedure in House as with Public Bills, 52—Estate Bills, 50—Report of Commissioners thereon, 50—Five days' notice before consideration of Committee, 51.

BILLS, PUBLIC :

What is a Bill, 39—Introduced *pro forma*, 12—Public and Private, 40 First reading, 41—Unusual to oppose, 41—When refused, "now," 41—Cannot revive when rejected, 41—Name of mover and date endorsed on Bill, 41—Reading title, 41—Second reading, 41 Reference to Committee, 41—After report, 42—Recommittal, 42 Importance of preamble, 42—Third reading, 42—Amendments, 44—Passing and title, 43—Forwarded to Law Clerk, 43 Royal assent, 43 Procedure in Committee, 43—If no Amendment, proposed clause put, 43—Notice of Amendment unnecessary, 31, 45 When Amendment should be offered, 43—Putting amended clause, 44 New clauses 44—Clause postponed,

45—May be recommitted, 45—Signature of Chairman, 45   Rejected cannot be revived same Session, 41—No addition to Motion for second reading, 45—Schedules, 44—Additions to Motion for third reading doubtful, 45   Clauses initiated in Committee of Whole, 45—Amendments to any part admissible, 45—Open to Amendment at different stages, 44—Amendments must be consistent and relevant, 45 ; Rejected Amendment cannot be again offered, 44—Amendments at third reading, 45—Reinstated in Orders of the Day, 46—Passed at unusual speed, 46—Royal assent refused, 47.

BILLS DISALLOWED : 53.

By Lieutenant-Governor, 46.

BILLS RESERVED BY LIEUTENANT-GOVERNOR : 47.

BOUNDARIES OF ONTARIO : Act respecting, 219.

BRITISH NORTH AMERICA ACT, 185

CABINET, THE ONTARIO : 64.

Responsible Government in Ontario, 64—Appeal to electors, 64   Without portfolio, 64—Ministers combining departments, 65—Four since Confederation, 65—Ineligibility of members of H. of C. to seat in 65—First 66, 172 Second, 66, 172—Third, 66, 172—Fourth, 66, 173.

CALLING OF LEGISLATURE : 70.

CHAIRMAN, Mr. : 157.

CLERK, The : 68.

Clerk Assistant, 68—Law, 69.

CLOSING OF MAILS : 81.

CLOTURE OR CLOSURE : 82

COMMITTEES : 35.

Definition of, 35   Power to call witnesses, 35   Oaths to, 35 - Form of Oath, 35—Power of Assembly to punish, 36 Tampering with, 36—False evidence before, 36—Disobedience to subpoena, 36 Presenting false documents to, 36—Falsifying records, 36—Affidavits, 35—Payment of witnesses, 178.

COMMITTEES, SELECT ; 36.

Standing Sessional, 36—Titles of, 37   Reference to proceedings before, 36—Report out of order, 37   When Committee of Whole necessary, 37- Rules of Debate in, 37—Questions of Order, 37—Seconder unnecessary, 38—Cannot adjourn in Committee of Whole, 38—Previous question inadmissible in, 38—Motion to leave Chair supersedes business, 38   Votes in, 38 - Reception of Report, 38   Quorum, 38   Disposition of existing charges need not originate in, 38—Member may be excused from attendance, 38—Permission to sit, 39 Ordered to report evidence, 39   Sessional order respecting Municipal Committee, 59—Chairman has second vote, 39.

DEBATE :

Interruption of, 28—Must address presiding officer, 25—Personal explanation, 25—Explanation permitted when misunderstood, 26—Moving adjournment, 27—None after members are called in for division, 28—Allusion to previous, 26—Out of order, if without Motion, 25—When reply allowed, 26—Permission to speak a second time, 26—Motion to adjourn equivalent to speaking, 27—Words taken down, 27—Objectionable words, 27—"Naming a Member," 27—When reply allowed, 26—Reply to charges made elsewhere, 26—Speaking to point of order or privilege, 27—When member must withdraw, 27—When relevancy not insisted on, 28—Reference to Proceedings of Committee out of order, 36—On Second Readings discussion of clauses inadvisable, 28—Question to be read during, if required, 28—Speaker does not take part in, 26.

DECISIONS OF MR. SPEAKER : 91.

See "Index" thereof, 221.

DECISION OF THE CLERK : 128.

DISTRIBUTIONS OF PUBLIC DOCUMENTS : 74.

Number of reports, etc., 75.

DIVISIONS : 33.

Putting the question, 33—Ayes and Noes, 34—Yeas and Nays, 34—Excused from voting, if "paired," 34—Announcement of result, 34—Pecuniary interest, 34—Must hear question, 35—No record of votes on an Adjournment, 35—Members seated after, 35.

DURATION OF EACH SESSION SINCE CONFEDERATION : 170.

ELECTIONS, GENERAL, SINCE CONFEDERATION : 171.

ESTATE BILLS : 50.

ETIQUETTE OF HOUSE : 14.

Obeisance to Chair, 14—Message from Lieutenant-Governor, 14—Entrance of Lieutenant-Governor, 14—Adjournment, 14—Order after a division, 14—Ought not to pass between member speaking and the Chair, 14—Not to pass between Speaker and Mace, 14—Position of Mace, 14—Removal of strangers, 14—Who shall speak, 14—Use of proper names, 15—"Mr. Chairman," 15—Selection of seats, 15—First business of Session, 15—Disrespectful allusions forbidden, 15—Reading Speeches, 15—Conversation, 16—"Hear, hear," 16—Introduction of a Member, 16—Admittance to the Chamber, 16—When Mr. Speaker rises, 17—Members called to order, 17.

EXPENDITURE DURING ELECTIONS :

Declaration respecting, 71.

FIRST READINGS : 41.

FORM OF SPEAKER'S WARRANT : 60.

FORMS, VARIOUS : 179.

GENERAL ELECTIONS SINCE CONFEDERATION : 171.
"HONORABLE," TITLE OF : 83.
HOUSEKEEPER, THE : 69.
ILLEGAL PROMOTION OF BILLS : 52.
INELIGIBLE FOR MEMBERSHIP : 10.
INTERRUPTION OF DEBATE : 28.
INTRODUCTION OF A MEMBER : 16.
IRREGULAR QUESTIONS : 24.
INDEMNITY TO MEMBERS : 72.
   Sessional indemnity, 72—Deduction for non-attendance, 72—Partial payment, 72—Mileage, 72—Declaration as to attendance, 72—Form of, 73.
LEGISLATIVE ASSEMBLY :
   Opening of, 11 How Meeting is called, 10—Duration of each Session of, 170.
LETTERS :
   Subject to postage, 81.
LIBRARY, RULES OF :
   Rules of, 84.
LIBRARIAN : 69.
LIEUTENANT-GOVERNORS :
   List of, 176.
LIEUTENANT-GOVERNOR, SALUTE OF : 79.
   When acting in behalf of Queen, 79—Governor-General entitled to general salute, 80—Lieutenant-Governor at opening and closing of House, 80—15 guns, 80—Cavalry escort, 80.
LIST OF SPEAKERS OF ONTARIO : 177.
LIST OF PREMIERS OF ONTARIO : 177.
MACE, THE : 77.
   Position of, 14.
MAILS, CLOSING OF : 81.
MEMBERS :
   Of first Legislative Assembly, Ontario, 157 Second, 158—Third, 159 Fourth, 161—Fifth, 162 Sixth, 164—Seventh, 165 Eighth, 166 Ninth, 168—Payment of, 72—Introduction, 16 Declaration to obtain Sessional allowance, 73 Ineligible as, 10 Resignation of, 66—Called to Order, 17—Naming, 28—Indemnity, 72.
MESSENGERS : 69, 74.
MILEAGE : 72.
MOTIONS :
   Must be written and seconded, with certain exceptions, 21 Conform to notice, 21 Speaker will check when contrary to rule,

21—May "Stand," 22 Cannot be withdrawn without permission, 22—Judgment of House modified, 22—For appropriation of public revenue, 22—When renewable, 22—Not renewable after judgment expressed, 22—Of adjournment, 22—That Orders of the Day be now read, 23—Must be made by its promoter, 23—For Accounts and Papers, 56— For Order of the House, 56 When formal Notice may be dispensed with, 23 For Address to the Crown, 56—For a Bill, 23—Must not anticipate. 23—Notices of, 20 How to evade, 22—Charges pending judicial proceedings, 23—" Naming " a Member, 27—Withdrawal of, 27—Motion and Amendment, form of, 32—For Bill, form of, 23.

NOTICE OF MOTION :
Two days necessary, 20—Formal sometimes dispensed with, 21—By unanimous consent, 20 Resuming discussion on after 6 p.m., 21- Resuming discussion after adjournment, 21—None required for certain Motions, 21—Modification of permissible, 21—May be withheld, 21.

OATHS : 71.
As to payments other than through agents, 71—Of Allegiance, 71.

OFFICERS AND SERVANTS : 68.
Clerk, 68—Clerk Assistant, 68—Sergeant-at-Arms, 68—Law Clerk, 69—Librarian, 69—House-Keeper and Chief Messenger, 69.

OPENING OF LEGISLATIVE ASSEMBLY : 11.

ORDER OF THE HOUSE : 56.

ORDER OF PROCEDURE : 17.
Daily routine, 17—First readings, 17 Orders of Day, 17—Third readings, 17 Consideration of Amendments to Bills, 17—Private Members' days, 17—Government days, 17—Dropped orders, 18 Order of business after daily routine, 18.

PAGES : 74.

" PAIRS," 63—Announcement of, 63—New rule, 63.

PAYMENT OF MEMBERS : 60, 72.

PAYMENT OF MESSENGERS : 74.

PAYMENT OF WITNESSES : 178.

PECUNIARY INTEREST : 27, 127.

PETITIONS :
Signatures to, 18—Presentation of, 19—Endorsement of, 19 (See Decisions of Speaker), 122—Form of, 20— Must not ask money aid, 19—Postage free, 81—Prayer necessary, 19—Signatures must be original, 19 - Interlineations inadmissible, 19—Chairman of public meeting, 19.

POSTAGE : 81.
All letters subject to, 81—Printed matter mailed free, 81 Petitions, Addresses, etc., free, 81—Statutes and library books subject to, 81—Departmental reports delivered free of in U. S.,

81 Letters must have names or initials of sender on envelope, 81—
Envelopes covering Bills must not be sealed, 81—Closing the mails,
81—When post office open, 81.

POSTMASTER : 69.

POWERS AND PRIVILEGES OF PROVINCIAL LEGISLATURE : 57.
  As to Private Bills, 47—To call for witnesses and papers, 57—
Speakers warrant, 58—Form of, 60—Privilege of speech, 58—
Freedom from arrest, 58—Exempt from service as jurors, 58—
Members not to receive fees for drafting Bills, 58—A corrupt practice, 58—Partners of members not to receive fees, 58—Penalty, 58
—Assembly a Court of Record for punishment of certain offences,
59—Term of punishment of offenders, 59—Votes of appropriation
of consolidated revenue, 60.

PRAYERS : 70.

PRECEDENCE in CANADA : 87.

PREMIERS :
  List of, 177.

PREVIOUS QUESTION : 63.
  Precludes further amendments, 63—Cannot be put when Amendment before the House, 64—No Amendment to be moved in nature
of, 64 (See Decisions of Speaker, 104, 105).

PRINTED MATTER :
  Mailed free, 81.

PRIVATE BILLS : 47.

PRIVILEGE : 58.

PROCEDURE :
  Order of, 17.

PROPERTY QUALIFICATION :
  Unnecessary for members, 10.

PROROGATION : 12.

PUBLIC BILLS : 39.

PUTTING THE QUESTION : 33.

QUESTIONS :
  Notice of, 24 Putting, 25—Character of, 24 —Answer to, 24—
What may be put, 24 No argument or opinion to be offered, 24—
Personal, 25—Irregular, 24 - Speaker may object to, 24.

QUESTION, THE PREVIOUS :
  Precludes further amendment, but cannot be put when amendment is before the House, 63—No amendment can be moved to it,
64—No amendment to be moved in nature of, 64.

REPRESENTATION IN 1867 AND 1893 : 10.

RESIGNATION OF MEMBER : 66.
  Double election, 66—After election of Speaker, 66 When cannot resign, 66 Acceptance of office, 67—Form of resignation, 67.

Royal Assent : 12.
Rules of Legislative Assembly : 131.
  Index to, 149.
Rules, Suspension of : 70.
  Regarding extension of time, etc., under report of Committee, 70.
Salute to Lieutenant Governor : 79.
Seat :
  Preliminaries to taking, 11, 16.
Seats, Selection of : 15.
Second Reading : 41.
  Private Bills, 47.
Sergeant-at-Arms : 68.
Sessional Indemnity : 72.
Sessions, Time Between : 11, 73.
Single Chamber : 5.
"Speaker, Mr." : 57.
  Selection of, 57—Returns thanks, 11—Accepted by Lieutenant-Governor, 12—Absence of, 57—May call Member to Chair, 57—Assembly may elect for day, 57—Acts valid under certain circumstances, 57—Salary, 57 – Will check Motions contrary to Rule, 21—List of Speakers, 177—Decisions of, 91.
Six Months "Hoist" : 32.
Speech from the Throne : 12.
Speeches, Reading of : 15.
Stationery for Members : 82.
Statutes Subject to Postage : 81.
Strangers : 14.
Supply Bill : 13.
Sureties :
  Ineligible, 10.
Suspension of Rules : 70.
  For extension of time, 70—On report of two Committees, 70—Of reception of Petition, must be recommended by Committee on Standing Orders, 70—For printing, etc., upon report of Standing Committee, 70—After due notice, 70.
Third Readings : 42.
Warrants of "Mr. Speaker" : 60.
Witnesses :
  Payment of, 178—Tampering with, 36.
"Whips" :
  Duties of, 62.
Yeas and Nays : 34.

www.ingramcontent.com/pod-product-compliance
Lightning Source LLC
Chambersburg PA
CBHW020812230426
43666CB00007B/978